DECISIONS AT PERRYVILLE

OTHER BOOKS IN THE COMMAND DECISIONS IN AMERICA'S CIVIL WAR SERIES

Decisions at Gettysburg:
The Twenty Critical Decisions That Defined the Battle
Matt Spruill

Decisions at Stones River:
The Sixteen Critical Decisions That Defined the Battle
Matt Spruill and Lee Spruill

Decisions at Second Manassas:
The Fourteen Critical Decisions That Defined the Battle
Matt Spruill III and Matt Spruill IV

Decisions at Chickamauga:
The Twenty-Four Critical Decisions That Defined the Battle
Dave Powell

Decisions at Chattanooga:
The Nineteen Critical Decisions That Defined the Battle
Larry Peterson

Decisions of the Atlanta Campaign:
The Twenty-One Critical Decisions That Defined the Operation
Larry Peterson

Decisions of the 1862 Kentucky Campaign:
The Twenty-Seven Critical Decisions That Defined the Operation
Larry Peterson

Decisions at The Wilderness and Spotsylvania Court House:
The Eighteen Critical Decisions That Defined the Battles
Dave Townsend

Decisions of the Tullahoma Campaign:
The Twenty-Two Critical Decisions That Defined the Operation
Michael R. Bradley

Decisions at Antietam:
The Fourteen Critical Decisions That Defined the Battle
Michael S. Lang

Decisions of the Seven Days:
The Sixteen Critical Decisions That Defined the Battles
Matt Spruill

Decisions at Fredericksburg:
The Fourteen Critical Decisions That Defined the Battle
Chris Mackowski

DECISIONS
AT
PERRYVILLE

The Twenty-Two Critical Decisions
That Defined the Battle

Larry Peterson
Maps by Tim Kissel

COMMAND DECISIONS
IN AMERICA'S CIVIL WAR
Matt Spruill and Larry Peterson,
Series Editors

The University of Tennessee Press / Knoxville

Copyright © 2022 by The University of Tennessee Press / Knoxville.
All Rights Reserved. Manufactured in the United States of America.
First Edition.

Library of Congress Cataloging-in-Publication Data

Names: Peterson, Larry, author. | Kissel, Tim, cartographer.
Title: Decisions at Perryville : the twenty-two critical decisions that defined the battle / Larry Peterson ; maps by Tim Kissel.
Description: First edition. | Knoxville : The University of Tennessee Press, [2022] | Series: Command decisions in America's Civil War | Includes bibliographical references and index. | Summary: "The Battle of Perryville was the culmination of the Confederate Heartland Offensive as General Braxton Bragg's army won a strategic victory over Major General Don Carlos Buell's corps from the Union Army of the Ohio. However, as Bragg retreated into Tennessee shortly after the battle, he effectively granted control of Kentucky to the Union, and the North would hold this critical border state for the remainder of the American Civil War. In *Decisions at Perryville*, Larry Peterson examines the critical decisions that shaped the way the battle unfolded. Rather than offering a history of the battle, Peterson focuses on the critical decisions confronting Federal and Confederate leaders and ultimately shaping the battle as we know it today"—Provided by publisher.
Identifiers: LCCN 2021053094 (print) | LCCN 2021053095 (ebook) | ISBN 9781621906797 (paperback) | ISBN 9781621906803 (kindle edition) | ISBN 9781621906810 (pdf)
Subjects: LCSH: Perryville, Battle of, Perryville, Ky., 1862. | Command of troops—Case studies. | Kentucky—History—Civil War, 1861–1865—Campaigns. | United States—History—Civil War, 1861–1865—Campaigns.
Classification: LCC E474.39 .P48 2022 (print) | LCC E474.39 (ebook) | DDC 973.7/33—dc23/eng/20211029
LC record available at https://lccn.loc.gov/2021053094
LC ebook record available at https://lccn.loc.gov/2021053095

To the soldiers and their families and descendants, Union and Confederate, who fought at the Battle of Perryville—"this grand havoc of battle," according to Pvt. Samuel Watkins, Company H, First Tennessee Infantry, CSA.

CONTENTS

Preface	xiii
Acknowledgments	xix
Introduction	1
Chapter 1. The Confederate High Tide, June–December 1862	9
Chapter 2. Before the Battle, September 29–October 7, 1862	15
Chapter 3. Initiating the Battle of Perryville, October 8, 1862	41
Chapter 4. The Battle of Perryville, October 8, 1862	55
Chapter 5. After the Battle, October 8–24, 1862	91
Chapter 6. Aftermath and Conclusions	97
Appendix I. Driving Tour of the Critical Decisions of the Battle of Perryville	103
Appendix II. Union Order of Battle	163
Appendix III. Confederate Order of Battle	171
Notes	177
Bibliography	203
Index	209

ILLUSTRATIONS

Figures

Maj. Gen. Don Carlos Buell, USA	16
Maj. Gen. William "Bull" Nelson, USA	17
"Acting Maj. Gen." Charles C. Gilbert, USA	18
Brig. Gen. Joshua W. Sill, USA	23
Gen. Braxton Bragg, CSA	26
Maj. Gen. Leonidas Polk, CSA	27
Old Kentucky Capitol Building, Frankfort	31
Maj. Gen. William J. Hardee, CSA	34
Maj. Gen. Edmund Kirby Smith, CSA	37
Brig. Gen. Philip H. Sheridan, USA	45
John Crawford House, Bragg's Headquarters, near Perryville, Kentucky	49
Maj. Gen. Alexander McD. McCook, USA	56
Col. John H. Warton, CSA	59
Maj. Gen. Benjamin F. Cheatham, CSA	62
Brig. Gen. Daniel S. Donelson, CSA	62
Open Knob Today, Perryville Battlefield State Historic Site	63
Brig. Gen. Alexander P. Stewart, CSA	66

Henry P. Bottom House, Perryville Battlefield State Historic Site	71
Maj. Gen. Simon B. Buckner, CSA	72
Col. John C. Starkweather, USA	78
Brig. Gen. Robert D. Mitchell, USA	82
Brig. Gen. St. John R. Liddell, CSA	86
Visitor Center, Perryville Battlefield State Historic Site	105
Confederate Cemetery, Perryville Battlefield State Historic Site	106
View along the Old Lebanon Pike, near Perryville	117
View along the Old Springfield Pike, near Perryville	142
View of Western Perryville	146
Starkweather's Hill, Perryville Battlefield State Historic Site	149
Starkweather's Final Position, Perryville Battlefield State Historic Site	152
Russell House, Perryville Battlefield State Historic Site, circa 1927	154

Maps

The Western Theater in 1862	2
Route of Kirby Smith's Invasion of Kentucky, August 13–October 8, 1862	5
Route of Bragg's Invasion of Kentucky and Buell's Retreat, August 26–October 8, 1862	6
Union and Confederate Advance to Perryville, October 1–7, 1862	22
Battle of Perryville, Initial Battle Lines, October 8, 1862, 7:00 a.m.	44
Battle of Perryville, Cheatham's Assault, October 8, 1862, 2:00 p.m.	65
Battle of Perryville, Maney's Assault, October 8, 1862, 3:00 p.m.	67
Battle of Perryville, Fighting at the Henry P. Bottom House, October 8, 1862, 3:45 p.m.	74
Battle of Perryville, Powel's Reconnaissance in Force, October 8, 1862, 4:15 p.m.	77
Battle of Perryville, Starkweather's Final Position, October 8, 1862, 4:30 p.m.	80
Battle of Perryville, Mitchell's Advance, October 8, 1862, 5:00 p.m.	83
Battle of Perryville, Liddell's Final Advance, October 8, 1862, 6:00 p.m.	87
Battle of Perryville, Final Battle Lines, October 8, 1862, 8:00 p.m.	89

Bragg's and Buell's Retreat Out of Kentucky, October 9–24, 1862	94
Driving Tour of the Critical Decisions of the Battle of Perryville	104
Driving Tour Stop 1: Perryville Battlefield Visitor Center and Cemetery	107
Driving Tour Stop 2: The Dorsey House—Buell's Headquarters	113
Driving Tour Stop 3: The Lebanon Pike	118
Driving Tour Stop 4: The Crawford House—Bragg's Headquarters	121
Driving Tour Stop 5: The Open Knob	125
Driving Tour Stop 6: The Henry P. Bottom House	131
Driving Tour Stop 7: Powel's Reconnaissance in Force	143
Driving Tour Stop 8: Mitchell's Advance	145
Driving Tour Stop 9: Starkweather's Hill	150
Driving Tour Stop 10: The Russell House	155

PREFACE

This book is the result of some rethinking on how the Command Decisions in America's Civil War series should be titled. Let me explain: The original standard title for each book was to concern the critical decisions of a particular battle. For instance, my first contribution to the series was *Decisions at Chattanooga: The Nineteen Critical Decisions That Defined the Battle*. I had a problem with that title, as the Chattanooga Campaign actually stretched over several months, but it was not a major concern to me at the time. However, when I undertook writing about the Atlanta Campaign, it quickly became obvious that the work's title could not be designated "Decisions at Atlanta." The Battle of Atlanta was actually only one of ten battles during that campaign. Therefore, editor Thomas Wells, coeditor Matt Spruill, and I decided we needed to specify a new standard title for campaigns, which we did. This led us to a new concept for the series.[1]

Our concept is to create a book covering the critical decisions of a campaign in general, and then one or more books presenting the critical decisions of battles within that campaign. This started with a University of Tennessee reader of my manuscript that became *Decisions of the 1862 Kentucky Campaign: The Twenty-Seven Critical Decisions That Defined the Operation* (note the slightly different title style). While the reader indicated that the Battle of Perryville deserved more focus due to its importance, he realized that it was only a part of the overall campaign. *Decisions at Perryville* addresses that battle in more detail not otherwise possible, reviews the critical decisions specific to the battle, and places the engagement where it belongs in terms of its importance to the Civil War.²

Readers of this work do not necessarily need to read the Kentucky Campaign book first, but that earlier volume would certainly provide a better overview of the campaign and where the Battle of Perryville fits into it. However, I set the scene here as the authors do in all books in the series.

The Command Decisions in America's Civil War series is founded on the concept of why a particular battle or campaign was fought at a given location and why it evolved as it did: i.e., why events happened and not just what happened. Originally, we believed that once our audience understood what had taken place during an engagement, they would then be able to grasp why the fighting occurred as it did. Receiving feedback from readers of this series indicating that they actually understood a battle or campaign for the first time, I now believe that it is in the readers' best interest to turn that concept around and begin with the why, then indulge in the what.

After studying the critical decisions that caused the fighting and gaining a firm grasp of why events evolved as they did, readers then can dive into more of the many incidents and minutiae the typical "battle books" provide. For instance, the numerous documented instances of soldiers predicting their own demise in an upcoming battle makes for poignant reading, but their tragic premonitions and deaths typically had no overall influence on the outcome. Likewise, many actions occurred that, while important and maybe extremely well known and interesting, had no overarching impact on an engagement's result. These may be omitted or only casually mentioned in our series, but they can be explored in the battle books. The guiding feature of the critical-decisions books is providing the big picture of events while not getting lost in the minutiae. As opposed to an in-depth scrutiny of the battle, consider this work, and all others in the series, as more of a guide to understanding it.

We constantly deal with two objections to the critical-decisions concept. The first is that these decisions are already designated in the many battle and campaign books already available. However, these choices are often comingled with other ones that are important but not critical, or they simply aren't emphasized. In this series we endeavor to prominently delineate critical choices for the convenience of our readers, who will not have to diligently search for this information.

The second objection we deal with is that critical decisions are obvious, and, of course, many are. But the question of what critical decision Gen. Robert E. Lee made on the third day of the Battle of Gettysburg indicates that this is not always true. The standard response is Pickett's Charge, but that

Preface

is incorrect. Lee had three (technically four) choices that day: he could attack, defend, or retreat (also—and he undoubtedly never considered this choice—he could surrender). He made the critical decision to attack, which resulted in the famous or infamous Pickett-Pettigrew-Trimble Charge. How might the course of Lee's campaign have changed had he chosen differently on July 3?

For the purpose of this and all critical-decisions books, I define a critical decision as one that shaped not only the events following it but also the conduct of the battle or campaign from that point on. Realize that armies make thousands of decisions daily. Many of these are important decisions, but only a handful are deemed critical decisions. A decisions hierarchy might look like this:

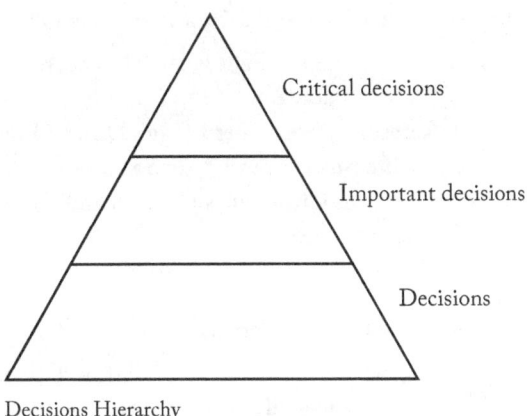

Decisions Hierarchy

Be careful to recognize that a natural and required response to a critical decision is typically not a critical decision, as that decision-maker usually has no choice but to respond.

The six types of critical decisions concern strategy, tactics, organization, operations, personnel, and logistics. Typically, certain critical decisions made prior to the actual campaign or battle tend to heavily influence the outcome. This was true with the Battle of Perryville.

While the reader may disagree with one or more of the critical decisions, or believe some have been left out, a major goal is to induce the reader to reflect on the battle. Also realize that the concept of critical decisions can and should be applied to other battles and campaigns in this or any other war or major event.

The list of the time frames and critical decisions addressed in each chapter follows:

Preface

Chapter 2. Before the Battle: September 29–October 7, 1862
    Buell Replaces Nelson with Gilbert (September 29)
    Buell Orders an Advance Supplemented with a Diversionary Movement (October 1)
    Polk Disobeys Bragg's Orders to Advance Toward Frankfort (October 4)
    Bragg Installs a Confederate Governor at Frankfort (October 4)
    Polk Orders Hardee to Halt Buckner's Division at Perryville (October 7)
    Bragg Orders Polk to March to Perryville and Attack the Approaching Union Force (October 7)

Chapter 3. Initiating the Battle of Perryville: October 8, 1862
    McCook's Brigade Is Sent Forward to Search for Water (October 8, 3:00 a.m.)
    Polk Refuses to Attack per Bragg's Direct Order and Assumes the "Offensive-Defensive" (7:00 a.m.)
    Bragg Realigns Cheatham's Division and Orders the Assault (10:00 a.m.–2:00 p.m.)
    Buell Postpones His Planned Attack (11:00 a.m.)

Chapter 4. The Battle of Perryville: October 8, 1862
    McCook Strengthens the Union Left (1:00 p.m.–2:00 p.m.)
    Wharton Fails to Fully Discover the Union Left (2:00 p.m.)
    Cheatham Orders Maney's and Stewart's Brigades to Assist Donelson (2:30 p.m.–4:00 p.m.)
    Buell Orders Reinforcements to McCook (4:00 p.m.)
    Buckner Orders Adams to Break the Deadlock at the Bottom House (4:00 p.m.)
    Powel Ordered to Make a Reconnaissance in Force (4:15 p.m.)
    Starkweather Holds the Union Left (4:30 p.m.)
    Gilbert Refuses to Let Mitchell Advance into Perryville. (5:00 p.m.)
    Hardee Orders Liddell to Make a Final Assault (5:45 p.m.)
    Polk Orders All Fighting to Cease (7:15 p.m.)

Chapter 5. After the Battle: October 8–24, 1862
    Bragg Decides to Retreat (October 8, 9:00 p.m.)
    Buell Initially Fails to Aggressively Pursue Bragg (October 9)

Because the Battle of Perryville was a major part of the Confederate high tide, I have added a chapter at the beginning of the book to briefly discuss why the fighting helped to mark that point. I then show where the Battle of Perryville interacted with the high tide and why it is important.

For ease in understanding, each critical decision is presented in an identical format. Discussion begins with the description of a decision-maker's situation or circumstances. The narrative then presents and examines the logical options available and identifies the critical decision chosen. Finally, readers learn about the results of the critical decision and its impact on the rest of the battle. In a unique feature of this series, and one that causes consternation for some, authors occasionally pose an alternative scenario and discuss what the outcome might have been had the decision-maker chosen another option. This allows readers to speculate independently about how different decisions might have changed future events.

The driving tours included in this series have received many compliments. As anyone who has visited a battlefield knows, there is nothing like seeing what the commander on scene may have visualized, especially concerning the terrain. This driving tour of the critical decisions of the Battle of Perryville brings the reader to many of the actual locations where choices were made. Due to time and distance constraints, not all critical-decision sites are included, but all are addressed. Please understand that this is not specifically a tour of the battle and battlefield. Of course, readers may visit at their discretion any and all battlefield stops and locations in conjunction with the tour.

Appendix II and appendix III contain the Union and Confederate orders of battle as a handy reference aid identifying the participating commanders and their place within the chain of command.

Three important reminders: first, the system of identifying Union (and occasionally) Confederate corps by Roman numerals did not begin until long after the Civil War. While this series does not utilize Roman numerals within the works' text, our cartographers may use Roman numerals in the accompanying maps for convenience and spacing. Also, authors use the Civil War–era abbreviations appropriate for each military rank, not the current abbreviations. Finally, the times indicated in this work are approximate. Standard time and time zones had not yet been designated during the Civil War, so chroniclers often differed as to the hour of the day. I believe that former longtime battlefield park manager Kurt Holman's *Battle of Perryville: Movement Maps* currently identifies the most realistic timetable of the fighting, so I generally rely on his times for specific events.[3]

ACKNOWLEDGMENTS

I would like to express my sincere thanks to some of the many people that have helped me with this project. First I want to thank Kenneth Noe, Kenneth Hafendorfer, Chris Kolakowski, James McDonough, Thomas Connelly, Earl Hess, Stuart Sanders, and the many other historians who have so faithfully researched and described the Battle of Perryville. Thanks also to former Perryville Battlefield State Historic Site managers Kurt Holman and Joni House for their many thoughts and suggestions, as well as the rest of the site staff that does such a wonderful job interpreting and maintaining it. Special thanks to site guide, historian, and photographer Chuck Lott for all of his efforts to educate me about the battle and his battlefield photos. Current site manager Bryan Bush has been especially helpful to me in understanding Leonidas Polk's behavior. Thanks to my good friend and battlefield guru Wayne Basconi, who spent countless hours driving me around and describing the battlefield to me.

Many years ago, I began researching my great-great-grandfather Brig. Gen. Alfred J. Vaughan Jr., CSA, who as Colonel Vaughan led the Thirteenth Tennessee in Brig. Gen. Preston Smith's brigade, the only brigade not committed to the fighting. Ever since then, I have been astounded at the preservation efforts by the former Civil War Trust, now the American Battlefield Trust. Hats off to past president Jim Lighthizer, president David Duncan, and the staff for completing acquisition of virtually the entire battlefield. Again, thanks to my editor Thomas Wells, and to director Scot

Acknowledgments

Danforth, Jon Boggs, Linsey Perry, Stephanie Thompson, Tom Post, and the staff of the University of Tennessee Press for publishing this book. Also especial thanks to copyeditor Elizabeth Crowder for her excellent skill in making this work more readable. I also extend gratitude to my series co-editor and close friend Matt Spruill, without whom this series would never have evolved. I appreciate my cats Lucy and Charlotte for graciously sharing their chair with me at my writing desk. Finally, special thanks to my wife, Kathleen, who has supported my writing efforts for so many years.

Larry Peterson
Evergreen, Colorado

DECISIONS AT PERRYVILLE

INTRODUCTION

The American Civil War effectively began with the Confederate forces at Charleston, South Carolina, shelling the Union-held Fort Sumter on April 12, 1861. Both sides of the conflict initially assumed that the war would be very short. In the Eastern Theater Pres. Abraham Lincoln forced army field commander Maj. Gen. Irvin McDowell to confront the Rebel army. McDowell did so at the First Battle of Bull Run near Manassas, Virginia, about twenty-five miles west-southwest of Washington, DC, on July 21 with his largely untrained and unprepared army. After initial success, the Union troops were defeated by a similarly inexperienced Confederate force, and the soldiers fled back to Washington, DC. Both sides regrouped, designated standard uniforms and flags, and began to raise large armies and conduct extensive training.[1]

Lincoln selected Maj. Gen. George B. McClellan to administer to the needs of the new Army of the Potomac and train it to competently fight in the field. McClellan performed that task in an excellent manner, and by spring his army was highly skilled and outfitted for combat. He convinced Lincoln that the best means of winning the war was for his Army of the Potomac to sail to Fort Monroe in southeast Virginia, then advance on land directly to the Confederate capital at Richmond, Virginia. McClellan eventually arrived within sight of that city.[2]

After the wounding of Gen. Joseph E. Johnston, new commander Gen. Robert E. Lee initiated the Seven Days, a series of battles at the end of June 1862 that resulted in McClellan's army retiring back to Washington, DC.

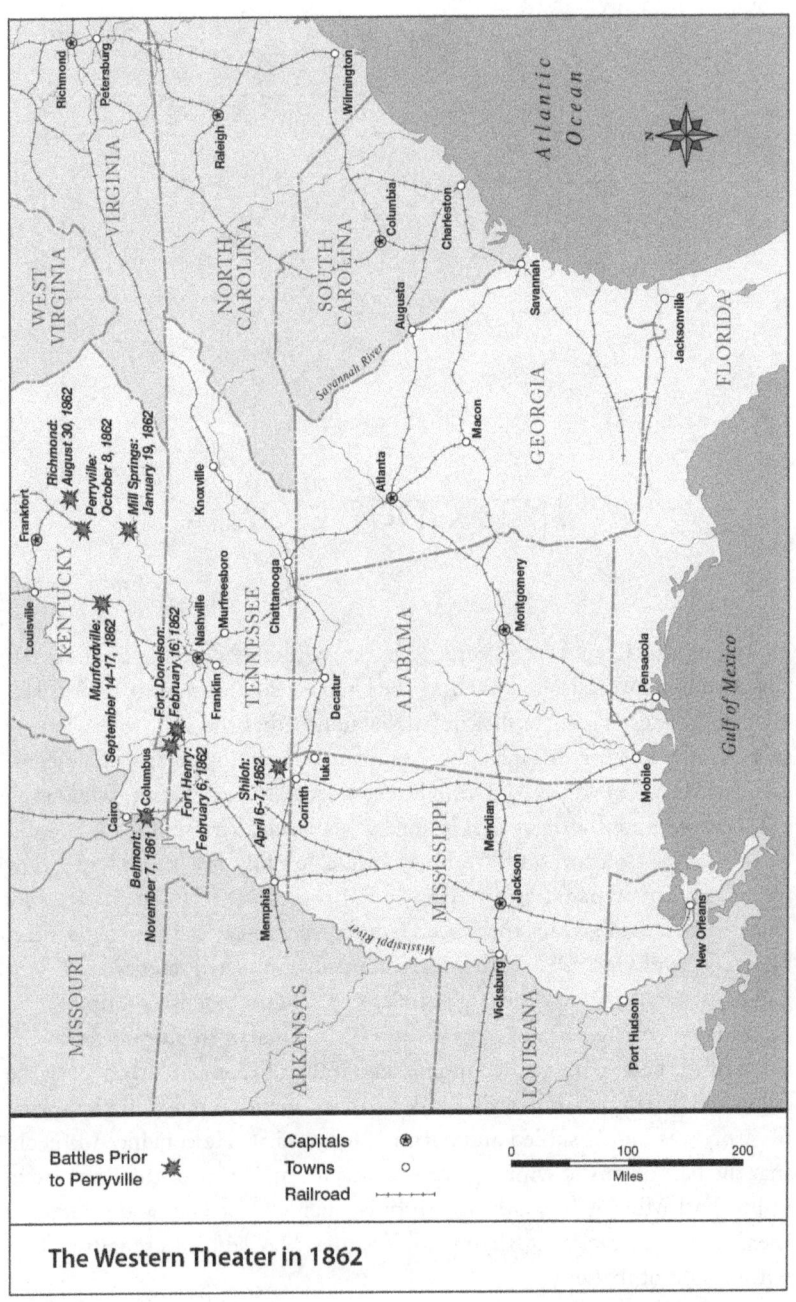

Emboldened, Lee attacked a new army under Maj. Gen. Ambrose Burnside once again near Manassas and whipped the Federals. Lee then felt it best to carry the fighting into the North. His invasion of Maryland ultimately resulted in the bloodiest day in American history, the Battle of Antietam or Sharpsburg on September 17, 1862. Facing overwhelming odds, Lee successfully retreated into Virginia.[3]

Meanwhile, in the Western Theater, the Commonwealth of Kentucky adopted a position of strict neutrality. The state had the ability to supply considerable foodstuffs as well as horses. Although Kentucky was a slave state, a majority of its citizens turned out to be pro-Union. Its northern boundary, the Ohio River, provided a main supply corridor for the Union. For the Confederacy, the Ohio River provided a natural defensive boundary. Kentucky thus was a key state—Lincoln reputedly stated, "I think to lose Kentucky is nearly the same as to lose the whole game."[4]

However, Maj. Gen. Leonidas Polk, who had been a cadet at the United States Military Academy with current Confederate president Jefferson Davis, and who was now a Davis appointee, decided that the excellent defensive position at Columbus, Kentucky, must be captured in order to guard the Mississippi River from Union gunboats. Polk seized the position on September 4, 1861. His action violated the neutrality the Commonwealth of Kentucky had previously ordered, and Brig. Gen. Ulysses S. Grant immediately captured Paducah for the Union.[5]

Polk was Davis's temporary commander for essentially the entire Western Theater until the long-awaited arrival of Gen. Albert S. Johnston. Upon his arrival in mid-September, based on Polk's seizure of Columbus, Johnston established a 400-mile-long Confederate line stretching from Cumberland Gap in the east through Bowling Green to Columbus in the west. Johnston had some 57,500 troops defending this line, an inadequate force. Polk had 22,000 men at Columbus and another 5,000 under his command at Forts Henry and Donelson guarding the Tennessee and Cumberland Rivers, which provided easy access into Tennessee and beyond. Maj. Gen. William J. Hardee led 24,500 Rebels at Bowling Green, and Maj. Gen. George Crittenden oversaw 6,000 more in East Tennessee. Hardee alone faced 75,000 Union troops commanded by Maj. Gen. Don Carlos Buell. Although responsible for defending the gap between Bowling Green and Columbus, Polk fixated only on Columbus, leaving the rivers vulnerable to Union advance.[6]

On January 19, 1862, Maj. Gen. George H. Thomas broke the Confederate line in East Tennessee at the Battle of Mill Springs near Somerset, Kentucky. This action forced Johnston to begin a retreat along most of his lengthy line. However, Polk remained firmly established at Columbus.[7]

Introduction

After an initial foray to Belmont, Missouri, across the Mississippi River from Columbus, Kentucky, in November 1861, Grant captured Forts Henry and Donelson in February 1862. The Cumberland and Tennessee Rivers were then open to Union invasion. Grant next established an encampment at Pittsburg Landing, south of Savannah on the Tennessee River. He did so in preparation for an advance to capture the very important railroad junction at Corinth, Mississippi, some twenty-plus miles south. However, Grant was ordered to wait for reinforcements from Maj. Gen. Don Carlos Buell's Army of the Ohio, en route from Nashville.[8]

Determined to attack Grant before he was reinforced, Gen. Albert S. Johnston attacked on April 6, 1862, with a conglomeration of Confederate units from several areas of the South. Grant barely held his troops together on day one of the fighting, beginning near the Shiloh Church. On day two, Grant assumed the offensive with Buell's support and defeated the Confederate Army of the Mississippi at the Battle of Shiloh or Pittsburg Landing. Johnston had died from an unrecognized leg wound on the afternoon of the first day of battle, and Gen. P. G. T. Beauregard assumed command. Union victories at Island Number 10 and New Madrid quickly followed. Maj. Gen. Henry Halleck, now in overall command, inched his three combined armies forward and captured Corinth, Mississippi, a most important railroad junction. He then dispersed his various units, ordering Buell to take four divisions and advance to Chattanooga.[9]

The newly assigned commander of the Department of East Tennessee was Maj. Gen. Edmund Kirby Smith, a hero of the First Battle of Bull Run. Discovering Buell's advance, Kirby Smith cried for assistance to protect his department, which covered the area between Cumberland Gap in the east and Chattanooga in the west. After Beauregard took unauthorized leave, Pres. Jefferson Davis appointed Gen. Braxton Bragg as the new commander of the Army of the Mississippi. Bragg viewed Halleck's dividing his armies and divisions as an opportunity to escape from Tupelo, where the Confederates had retreated as Union troops advanced on Corinth. The Rebel general decided to move his soldiers to Chattanooga and assist Kirby Smith. In one of the more remarkable transportation movements the Confederacy conducted during the entire war, Bragg transferred his infantry 776 miles on six separate railroads and a ferry ride across Mobile Bay to Chattanooga. His artillery and wagons moved on a more direct route.[10]

On the evening of July 31, Bragg and Kirby Smith met face to face. Bragg was somewhat horrified to discover that he was now a guest in Kirby Smith's Department of East Tennessee, but the two nonetheless agreed to jointly advance into Tennessee and Kentucky. Bragg initially planned for both Kirby

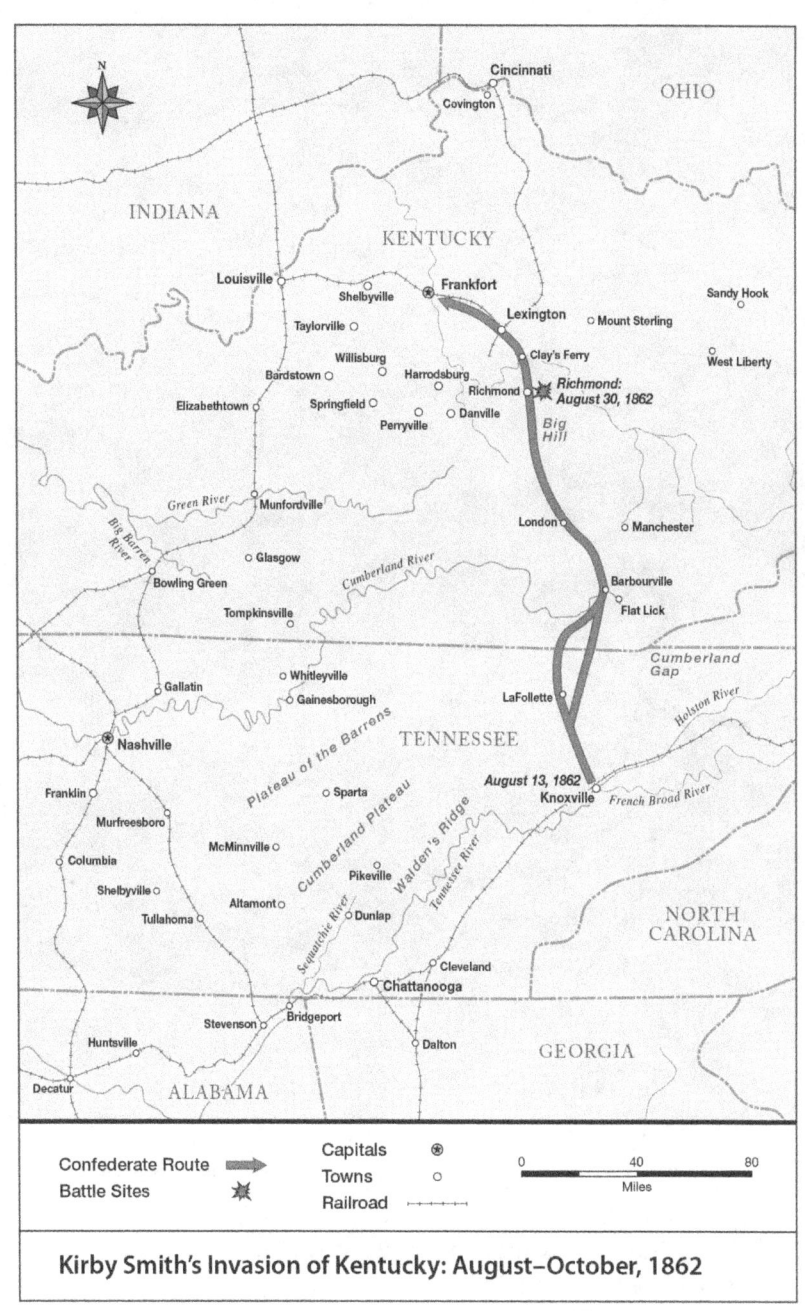
Kirby Smith's Invasion of Kentucky: August–October, 1862

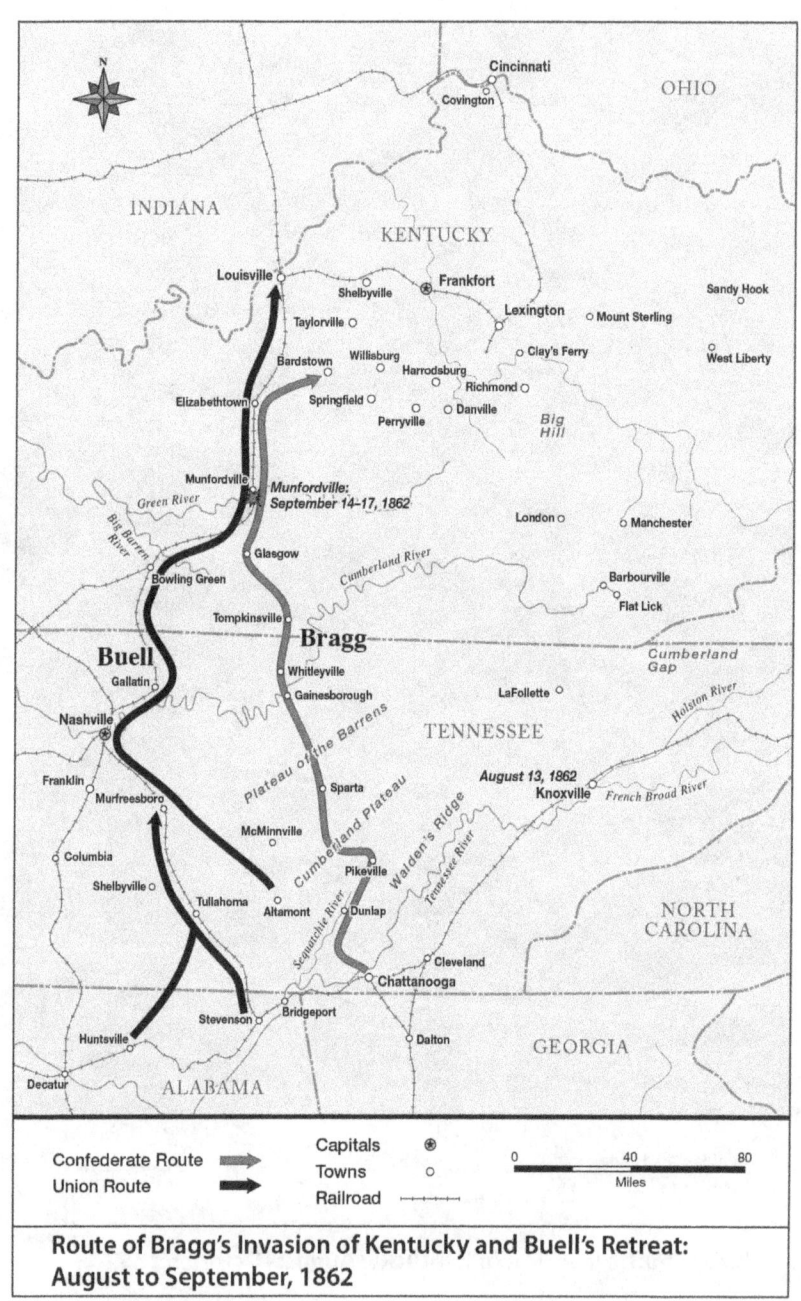

Route of Bragg's Invasion of Kentucky and Buell's Retreat: August to September, 1862

Smith's army and his own to strike Buell's supply base at Nashville. While Bragg awaited the arrival of his wagons and artillery, Kirby Smith would advance to Cumberland Gap and capture it from the Union garrison there. Then the officers' combined force would capture Nashville while concurrently protecting Chattanooga.[11]

However, Kirby Smith received a message from Col. John H. Morgan, his cavalry commander raiding in Kentucky: "The whole country can be secured, and 25,000 or 30,000 men will join you at once." Kirby Smith quickly decided to break his agreement with Bragg, bypass Cumberland Gap while leaving a division to monitor it, and march into and liberate the Commonwealth of Kentucky. This action began the 1862 Kentucky Campaign. Unhappy with Kirby Smith's decision, Bragg was forced to await the arrival of his wagons and artillery before he, too, could advance. President Davis's prior decision to deny Bragg, the senior general, command of both armies by keeping the two departments separate severely hindered the campaign from the outset.[12]

Leaving Knoxville on August 13, Kirby Smith quickly decided on his own to bypass Cumberland Gap. Capturing it might take a siege of a month or more, and he sought immediate glory. Kirby Smith thus marched his small army, now augmented with a division from Bragg's army, toward his objective of Lexington and/or the capital at Frankfort. The Union dispatched its Provisional Army of Kentucky in response. Commanded by Maj. Gen. William "Bull" Nelson but under the direct command of Brig. Gen. Mahlon Manson, this force aimed to confront Kirby Smith's army before it reached Richmond, Kentucky, south of Lexington. At the Battle of Richmond on August 30, Kirby Smith's hardened veterans easily routed Manson's brand-new levees. The Confederates marched on and captured Lexington and Frankfort.[13]

Bragg was displeased with Kirby Smith's disregard of their agreement, but he could do little about it. He left Chattanooga on August 26 and led his Army of the Mississippi into Tennessee, bypassing Nashville. Meanwhile, Buell had retreated to Nashville to defend it from a Rebel attack. Bragg decided to bypass that city and advance into Kentucky, where he would reunite with Kirby Smith. After one of his cavalry subordinates failed to capture the very strategic railroad bridge across the Green River at Munfordville, Kentucky, Bragg advanced his entire army there and laid siege to the small Union command guarding it. When he took time to capture these four thousand Federals, Bragg lost focus, perhaps by choice, on directly confronting Buell's army, and/or he gave Buell the opportunity to march back to his base at Louisville unmolested. Here Bragg lost control of the campaign, effecting a major change in its momentum. After quickly capturing the bridge and the enemy troops, the Confederate general faced a lack of forage and supplies in the area and moved his army northeast to Bardstown. Buell and his army took advantage of Bragg's departure; after a fatiguing march, the soldiers arrived at Louisville to help protect this vital city. In addition, Buell immediately began to refit and resupply his force. On September 28 Bragg left his army at Bardstown, rode to Lexington, and assumed command of Kirby Smith's army. This is where our narrative begins.[14]

Since the Battle of Perryville and the 1862 Kentucky Campaign were part of what historians have labeled the Confederate high tide, we will first discuss this phenomenon in chapter 1.

CHAPTER 1

THE CONFEDERATE HIGH TIDE, JUNE–DECEMBER 1862

Two topics continue to enthrall students of the Civil War: the turning point of the war and the Confederate "high tide." We will leave the turning point issue for debate in another venue. However, the Confederate high tide was a very significant part of the war, and the Battle of Perryville played an important part within the high tide. Therefore, in this chapter we will briefly examine that topic.[1]

Simply defined, the Confederate high tide was that period when the Confederacy had its best chance to achieve recognition as its own nation by either winning the Civil War or otherwise separating from the former Union. It can easily be confused with one or more turning points of the war, such as the Battle of Gettysburg's famous Pickett-Pettigrew-Trimble Charge. Establishing when the Confederate high tide actually occurred requires historians to look back on history, which is normally considered unacceptable. However, in this case, the results of the entire war must be examined in order to pinpoint exactly when the Confederacy had its best opportunity for victory and freedom. Most historians generally consider the second half of 1862 the Confederate high tide. During this time frame, the South benefited from several important factors in its favor that it lost soon thereafter. The Battle of Perryville was a significant part of the high tide, and its outcome had a major impact in ending it.[2]

Interestingly, some Civil War buffs have proposed that the Confederate high tide occurred the day before Fort Sumter was fired on! This argument is somewhat corroborated by Archer Jones in *Civil War Command & Strategy*, and Jones apparently derived it from Bell I. Wiley. According to Jones, expectations of Confederate victory were certainly falling by the end of the Battle of Antietam.[3]

Before briefly examining the factors and campaigns defining the Confederate high tide, consider a few significant numbers that placed the new Confederacy in an awkward and tough situation compared to the Union it was trying to leave. The Confederacy desired to establish its authority over at least 13 of the 15 existing slave states. These 878,000 square miles of territory equated to about one-half of the old Union. Within these 13 states were about 11.5 million inhabitants, about a 1 to 1.7 disadvantage. Factoring in pro-Union regional loyalties within the Confederacy, the number of inhabitants fell to around 10 million, increasing the disparity to 1 to 2.1. The ratio of Confederate Whites to Union Whites was 1 to 3.5, and of those White males 18 to 45 years old and most likely eligible for military service, the ratio climbed to 1 to 3.7. While the Confederacy produced 42 percent of the grain and 50 percent of the livestock, it had only 34 percent of the railroads, 27 percent of the banking capital, and 13 percent of the manufacturing capability of the Union.[4]

In order to overcome these odds, the Confederacy had to react quickly. What circumstances caused the Confederate high tide to occur at this time? Three significant factors and up to ten campaigns/battles saw the high tide arise and falter. One consideration was the hope that foreign nations, particularly Britain and France, would recognize the Confederacy as a legitimate entity. Certainly the Confederacy desired recognition from these and other countries, as well as direct assistance in fighting the war, and it appeared for a time, particularly in the second half of 1862, that the South might achieve foreign acknowledgment. After Gen. Robert E. Lee's victories and success in driving Maj. Gen. George B. McClellan's army away from the new Confederate capital at Richmond, Virginia (the Seven Days Battles), it appeared to both Britain and France that the Confederacy could actually win the war. Napoleon III was also interested in gaining a buffer for his planned conquest of Mexico and the old Union. This was great news for the Confederacy as it headed into the fall and fueled the high tide concept.[5]

Two problems would eventually overcome the desire for recognition by Britain and France. First, the Confederacy was overconfident in the economic leverage of its cotton crop and its apparent dominance within the world market. The South had supplied about two-thirds of the world's supply of cotton. Of this amount, about 79 percent went to Britain, which directly affected some four to five million British citizens who were dependent on cotton for a living. Yet Britain, recognizing the potential for a loss of cotton imported from the new Confederacy, had already stockpiled over one million bales of the product in 1861. The nation had also begun searching the world for alternate sources, which it found. While Britain's cotton inventory was reduced considerably in 1862 to about two hundred thousand bales, in the long term it simply found other sources.[6]

The other significant problem for Confederate recognition was Pres. Abraham Lincoln's issuance of his Preliminary Emancipation Proclamation on September 22, 1862. This directive was officially to go into effect on January 1, 1863, and Lincoln made it public after the Battle of Antietam on September 17, considered a Union victory. Most foreign nations would no longer deal with slaveholding nations, and the proclamation changed the Union's goal to include eliminating slavery in addition to recovering its wayward states. As a result, the Confederacy's potential of foreign recognition shining so brightly in the fall of 1862 had all but disappeared by the end of that year.[7]

Another major factor leading the Confederate high tide in the fall of 1862 was the matter of raising armies. As previously noted, the Confederacy had to face the reality that it simply did not have as large a manpower pool from which to recruit its soldiers as the Union did. However, the South wasted little time in building up its armies, and for a while, especially in the latter half of 1862, it remained fairly competitive with the Union. On April 16, 1862, the Confederate Congress passed the Conscription Act requiring all eligible White males eighteen to thirty-five years old to be conscripted or forced to join the Rebel armies for a term of three years. This act also extended the term of service for those already serving for one year to a three-year term. Pressured to avoid the stigma of being drafted, men voluntarily enlisted instead, a trend their womenfolk strongly favored. Eventually, about 80 percent of men ages eighteen to forty-five served in the Confederate armies! Contrastingly, approximately 30 percent of those eligible eventually served in the Union military.[8]

During the period of the Confederate high tide, the Rebel armies held their best ratios compared to the Union. On January 1, 1862, there were some 351,000 Confederate soldiers compared to 576,000 Union servicemen, for a ratio of 1 to 1.6 or 63 percent. This ratio remained the same in April 1, 1862, with 401,000 Confederates to 637,000 Yankees. By June 1, 1862, roughly the beginning of the high tide, more efficient "recruiting" and conscription had resulted in 477,000 Rebel soldiers compared to 624,000 Yankee soldiers, for a ratio of 1 to 1.3 or 76 percent. This was the best ratio that the Confederacy would enjoy during the war.[9]

While the Confederacy had added soldiers to its armies faster than the

Union, Lincoln did not sit by idly. Rather, he called for 300,000 more enlistees in July and August. The Rebels suffered heavy losses during the high tide, and by December 31, 1862, the tide's generally accepted end, 447,000 Confederate and 918,000 Federal troops were in service, for a ratio of 1 to 2 or 49 percent. During the remaining 28 months of the Civil War the ratios remained from 1 to 1.8 up to 1 to 2.2.[10]

A third factor built on the previous one in making the fall of 1862 the likely Confederate high tide. Particularly within the Western Theater, slaves escaped or were "freed" by Federals as the Union armies advanced farther into the Confederacy. This circumstance became a double-edged sword for the South. First, the region lost valuable workers (slaves) who performed necessary supporting labor, in many cases freeing the Rebel soldiers to concentrate on fighting. Additionally, many formerly enslaved men (as well as some freedmen) were quick to enlist in the Union armies and fight their former masters. This fact resulted in a double negative for Rebeldom and a solid gain for the Union. Some 188,000 Black men eventually served in the Union armies, and approximately 20,000 more served in the Union navy. The Rebel government did not formally address the loss of these former slaves, nor did it consider enlisting male slaves into the Confederate armies until far too late in the war, an action that never resulted in additional troops. In the fall of 1862 this phenomenon had not yet become commonplace.[11]

Based on the above factors, the fall of 1862 definitely provided the Confederacy with its best chance to win the war or at least achieve a stalemate. A series of military campaigns throughout the Eastern and Western Theaters and the trans-Mississippi West gave the South hope for eventual success. As we will see, the Battle of Perryville was among these operations.[12] Unfortunately for the Confederacy, this series of campaigns and battles was not coordinated—the South lacked what we would today designate a grand form of strategy. Nonetheless, these actions in the second half of 1862 had the best potential for Confederate triumph.[13]

Beginning in the Eastern Theater, Gen. Robert E. Lee first successfully protected Richmond via the Seven Days Battles. Building on that achievement, he defeated a new Union army under the command of Maj. Gen. Ambrose Burnside at Second Manassas or Bull Run. Lee subsequently took his army and invaded Maryland, culminating in the Battle of Antietam, the single bloodiest day of the Civil War or any other war involving Americans. The Rebel general managed to hold off the Union army commanded by Maj. Gen. George McClellan, but he was then forced to retreat, ending the possibility of further success.[14]

In southwestern Virginia, Maj. Gen. William W. Loring advanced and captured Charleston. His cavalry commander Brig. Gen. Albert G. Jenkins raided some five hundred miles, even briefly into Ohio, causing havoc along the way.[15] Maj. Gen. Ambrose Burnside's unfortunate series of assaults at Fredericksburg provided a final boost and gave Lee a substantial victory in December.[16] Brig. Gen. Humphrey Marshall took his small command from Virginia into Kentucky and eventually lent assistance to General Bragg and Maj. Gen. Edmund Kirby Smith during their invasion of Kentucky.[17]

In the Western Theater, Bragg and Kirby Smith separately invaded Kentucky, hoping to gain the commonwealth for the Confederacy. Bragg ultimately faced Maj. Gen. Don C. Buell and his army at Perryville, the subject of this book. While Bragg tactically won the Battle of Perryville, the presence of Buell's larger army, the lack of supplies, and the failure of Kentucky men to join his own force in large numbers persuaded Bragg to retreat out of Kentucky.[18]

Sterling Price and Earl Van Dorn, both major generals who commanded small armies in Mississippi, were ordered to march north into western Tennessee. However, they jointly decided to attack a Union force at Corinth, Mississippi, commanded by Maj. Gen. William S. Rosecrans. The Federals eventually halted the Confederate assault, then countercharged and defeated Price's and Van Dorn's troops. This action stopped the Rebel generals from reinforcing Bragg in Kentucky and possibly contributing to a more successful outcome for the Confederacy in that state.[19]

Maj. Gen. John C. Breckinridge's small army was also ordered from Port Hudson, Louisiana, to reinforce Bragg. However, the force remained in Tennessee, also unavailable to support Bragg.[20] Van Dorn's December 20 raid on Holly Springs, Mississippi, provided some consolation, destroying $1 million worth of Grant's supplies and forcing him to retreat from his movement into central Mississippi.[21] In the trans-Mississippi West, Maj. Gen. Thomas C. Hindman conscripted an army and drove Union forces almost out of Arkansas before fighting the Battle of Prairie Grove on December 7. While this battle was a tactical stalemate, it essentially secured northwest Arkansas for the Union.[22]

Two additional factors which would eventually hinder Confederate success were the implementation of the Union blockade of Rebel ports and the Southern infrastructure, particularly the railroads. At this time in 1862 the blockade was not yet effective, and the deterioration of the railroads was just beginning.

In summary, by the beginning of 1863 the Confederacy had lost its chance for foreign recognition, due significantly to the Emancipation Proclamation. The Union had greatly expanded its armies by recruiting and conscription, and Blacks were increasingly escaping to freedom, where many also turned on their former masters. Also the Union Naval blockade had not yet become effective, and the Rebel infrastructure, especially the railroads, was still fairly solid. Although the Confederacy achieved some military victories, they were not enough to bring the Union to any kind of terms. As we will see, the Battle of Perryville played a vital role in keeping Kentucky under Union control for the rest of the war. The Confederate high tide was not high enough![23]

CHAPTER 2

BEFORE THE BATTLE, SEPTEMBER 29–OCTOBER 7, 1862

If you have bypassed the preface, please direct your attention there and read the definition of a critical decision in order to more fully understand the discussions in this book, and what it does and does not provide.

Six critical decisions preceded the Battle of Perryville. Typically, critical decisions reached prior to a battle greatly define its outcome, even if they are not directly connected to the fighting. The critical decisions are presented chronologically in this work, but please realize that they may occasionally overlap.

Buell Replaces Nelson with Gilbert (September 29)

Situation

As previously noted in the introduction, Maj. Gen. Don Carlos Buell arrived in Louisville in late September, along with ragtag groups of his men who were worn out from the recent campaigning. Buell was born in what is now Lowell, Ohio, on March 23, 1818. He graduated from West Point in 1841 and ranked thirty-second out of the fifty-two members of his class. After serving in the Florida Indian wars and on the frontier, Buell fought in the Mexican-American War, was wounded at the Battle of Churubusco, and won the brevets of captain and major. Afterward, he was assigned to the adjutant general's department on the frontier and in Washington, DC. He had achieved the rank of lieutenant colonel by the outbreak of the Civil War, then stationed in San Francisco. Buell was commissioned a brigadier general, and he helped Maj. Gen. George B. McClellan train the newly constituted Army of the Potomac. McClellan subsequently appointed Buell commander of the Army of the Ohio.[1]

Buell was a slow, methodical commander, a micromanager bureaucrat unbeloved by his subordinates. Like many of his peers, he had concluded that the best course of action was to anticipate and prepare for every eventuality in order to outmaneuver the enemy instead of fighting him. Buell regarded the enemy as an inconvenience to his organizational efforts rather than a threat. Once fully supplied and prepared, he expected opponents to conform to his expectations. As a longtime officer in the regular army, he was also a strict disciplinarian who was unimpressed with the volunteer army. In 1843 Buell was court-martialed for striking a private in the regular army to which he belonged with the back of his sword. Though Buell was ultimately acquitted, this incident provides insight into his lack of regard for his men. Unlike many other officers, he neither related to nor inspired his troops, and, in turn, they felt no love or respect for him. In fact, many within Buell's army called for his resignation after giving up much of Tennessee.[2]

Not surprisingly, while his men continued to flow into Louisville, Buell quickly resorted to administrative procedures to prepare his command to

Maj. Gen. Don Carlos Buell, USA.
Library of Congress.

September 29–October 7, 1862

protect Kentucky from the Rebel invasion. He knew that he must quickly assume the offensive or lose his position as commander. Once his troops were back in the city, he proceeded to reequip and resupply them, integrating new recruits into the existing commands. Specifically, he attempted to integrate one new regiment with three veteran regiments per brigade. While this was a great theory, the veterans took advantage of the new recruits' vulnerability by stealing much of their supplies. In addition, Buell reorganized his Army of the Ohio.[3]

Two actions placed Buell under additional pressure. First, on September 29, disappointed by Buell's failure to confront Gen. Braxton Bragg and his Army of the Mississippi (after the campaign it would be relabeled the Army of Tennessee), Pres. Abraham Lincoln, Secretary of War Edward M. Stanton, and General-in-Chief Maj. Gen. Henry W. Halleck issued orders replacing Buell with Maj. Gen. George H. Thomas. Thomas was a highly competent general and the victor of the Battle of Mill Springs, but he believed that this was not the best time for a change of command. He refused the new position, and the order was rescinded later that same day.[4]

Also on the same day, Buell's plans for his corps commanders changed drastically. Buell had reorganized his Army of the Ohio into three corps. He designated Maj. Gen. Alexander McD. McCook as his First Corps commander, Maj. Gen. Thomas L. Crittenden as his Second Corps commander, and Maj. Gen. William "Bull" Nelson as his Third Corps commander. A very

Maj. Gen. William "Bull" Nelson, USA.
Library of Congress.

large man who physically and mentally intimidated his subordinates, Nelson was not particularly well liked. As the Union commander of the Army of Kentucky, he arrived late during the Battle of Richmond, Kentucky, assuming command from the on-scene commander, Brig. Gen. Mahlon Manson. Nelson then failed to rally his troops, losing the one-sided battle to Maj. Gen. Edmund Kirby Smith's invading army. Moreover, Nelson was not impressed with the performance of the troops from Indiana, and he quickly came to despise an Indiana brigadier general with the unlikely name of Jefferson C. Davis. After an altercation on the morning of the twenty-ninth, Davis murdered Nelson. Astonishingly, Davis never went to trial and ultimately commanded the Fourteenth Corps during Maj. Gen. William T. Sherman's March to the Sea. Nelson's death forced Buell to find a replacement.[5]

Options

After recovering from the news of Nelson's murder, Buell had to quickly name a replacement. He apparently distrusted the obvious candidate, the highly experienced and competent Maj. Gen. George H. Thomas. Buell initially offered command of the Third Corps to both Brig. Gens. James S. Jackson and Charles Cruft, but the officers believed themselves unqualified and turned him down. Perhaps Jackson had signed his own death warrant, as he was killed while leading his division at the upcoming Battle of Perryville. Buell's selection process quickly narrowed the field to two other candidates: Brig. Gen. Albin E. Schoepf or "Maj. Gen." Charles C. Gilbert.[6]

"Acting Maj. Gen." Charles C. Gilbert, USA. Photographic History, Vol. X.

September 29–October 7, 1862

Option 1

Buell's more obvious choice was Brig. Gen. Albin E. Schoepf, who had obtained combat experience in the Austrian army and fought at the Battles of Wildcat Mountain and Mill Springs. Unfortunately, from Buell's viewpoint Schoepf was a strong supporter of Thomas and was apparently displeased with Buell's record against Bragg. Politically, Buell needed a corps commander that he could trust.[7]

Option 2

Buell's other choice was "Acting Maj. Gen." Charles C. Gilbert, who ranked twenty-first in the West Point class of 1846. His classmate George B. McClellan was second, and George E. Pickett ranked last among the graduates at fifty-ninth. Gilbert took part in the Mexican-American War and taught at West Point. During the Civil War, he fought at the Battle of Wilson's Creek as captain of a company of regulars, and at the Battle of Shiloh as inspector general of the Army of the Ohio. After Nelson was wounded at the Battle of Richmond, Department of the Ohio commander Maj. Gen. Horatio G. Wright appointed Gilbert "acting major general" to command the Army of Kentucky. President Lincoln appointed Gilbert to the rank of brigadier general on September 4, 1862. However, the Senate never confirmed him, and his commission expired on March 4, 1863, at which time he was not reappointed. Gilbert's status as a potential major general was doubtful, yet Buell knew him as a friend and former staff officer.[8]

Decision

Buell immediately replaced Nelson with Gilbert, apparently overlooking the latter's suspicious advancement in rank. Gilbert had been a captain only a month before, but Buell preferred someone he trusted over an officer with more experience.[9]

Results/Impact

Having selected Gilbert to command his Third Corps, Buell assigned Thomas the somewhat meaningless position as second-in-command. The assignment of Gilbert proved to be unwise. He quickly lost the confidence of his men by becoming a martinet, and his life was actually threatened at least once. The crux of Gilbert's leadership of the Third Corps came at the Battle of Perryville, where he followed without challenge or initiative Buell's orders not to engage the enemy until the following day. (Discussion of another critical decision will cover this action.) Gilbert's failure to support his First Corps comrades under severe assault by parts of Bragg's army resulted in the temporary setback and near severe defeat of McCook's First Corps, positioned to Gilbert's left. A number of historians including longtime Perryville Battlefield State Historic Site manager Kurt Holman posit that had Nelson remained in command of the Third Corps, he would likely have gone to McCook's aid regardless of his orders. This theory will be discussed in more detail with regard to other critical decisions.[10]

Alternate Scenario

While this argument is certainly speculative, "Bull" Nelson had the reputation of a fighter, and many historians believe that, had he remained in command of the Third Corps at the Battle of Perryville, he would have disobeyed orders and assisted McCook's First Corps. Nelson's demeanor was such that he would not likely have simply observed his fellow soldiers in the First Corps face annihilation. Rather, he would have provided at least some assistance even if he did not personally lead it. We will address this issue again.[11]

Buell Orders an Advance Supplemented with a Diversionary Movement (October 1)

Situation

Bragg failed to confront Buell after the capture of the Union garrison at Munfordville, due in large part to the absence of forage and food within the area. Had Bragg focused on seizing Louisville and/or blocking Buell from marching to his supply base there, he might well have been more successful. However, while Bragg and his army marched off to Bardstown, Buell and his soldiers, no longer blocked by the Confederates, force marched back to Louisville to protect their base of operations. Buell knew that he was under intense pressure from the Lincoln administration to pursue the Rebel armies within the Commonwealth of Kentucky and drive them away. In fact, as noted concerning the previous critical decision, Lincoln had already sent orders to Buell in Louisville relieving him of command of the Army of the Ohio. Luckily, Thomas refused to accept the command as ordered, as he did not wish to interfere with Buell's preparations. Buell wasted little time in refitting, resupplying, and integrating new arrivals into his army.[12]

Buell structured his Army of the Ohio into three corps with three divisions in each. In the hope that the veterans would share their experience, he placed one raw regiment of newly enlisted soldiers and three veteran regiments in each brigade. Instead, many veterans took advantage of the new enlistees by stealing their supplies and accoutrements. Buell's First Corps was commanded by Maj. Gen. Alexander McD. McCook. Under McCook were Brig. Gen. Joshua Sill's Second Division, Brig. Gen. Lovell H. Rousseau's Third Division, and Brig. Gen. James S. Jackson's Tenth Division. Buell's Second Corps was led by Maj. Gen. Thomas L. Crittenden. Under Crittenden were Brig. Gen. William S. Smith's Fourth Division, Brig. Gen. Horatio Van Cleve's Fifth Division, and Brig. Gen. Thomas J. Wood's Sixth Division. "Acting Maj. Gen." Charles C. Gilbert now commanded Buell's Third Corps. This corps included Brig. Gen. Albin Schoepf's First Division, Brig. Gen. Robert D. Mitchell's Ninth Division, and Brig. Gen. Philip H. Sheridan's Eleventh Division.[13]

Options

Upon reorganizing his army and seeing to its preparation for action, Buell needed a plan for advancing toward the Confederate forces lurking east of Louisville. He could march out on one major road, or he could split his corps up and have troops advance over more than one road. Alternatively, he could advance his main army and create some kind of a diversion to fool Bragg as to his real intentions.[14]

Option 1

Logically, Buell would want to advance while keeping his army together. In so doing, he would be fully ready to commit his soldiers upon encountering one or more of the Confederate forces within the Commonwealth of Kentucky. This order of march would prevent Rebels from individually assaulting units of Buell's army. However, the concentration of men posed a major problem with keeping Buell's entire force together, as soldiers would quickly devour any foodstuffs along the way. More importantly, the extreme drought often forced individual soldiers to search for miles for a source of water. The quest for water would, in fact, bring on the Battle of Perryville.[15]

Option 2

In order to deal with the drought, a better option would be for Buell to split up his corps in order for them to spread out and cover a greater area in the search for potable water and forage, especially fruit. This plan's potential to confuse the Confederate forces as to Buell's specific objective would be an additional benefit. By confounding Bragg, Buell might catch at least some of the Rebel units vulnerable to attack.[16]

Option 3

Another option would be deploying a small force as a feint to confuse the Rebel command as to where Buell's main line of advance might be. Doing so might force Confederate units to disperse in order to better observe the Union movements, all the while sowing doubt as to the direction in which the primary advance was actually marching. This course of action could also make individual Rebel units vulnerable to attack.[17]

Decision

Buell decided to combine Options 2 and 3. He ordered his three corps to advance initially toward Bardstown via three separate roads, and he also ordered a feint directly at the capital city of Frankfort. This plan proved very adept at confusing Bragg as to the actual location and direction of Buell's army. Of particular interest regarding this decision is the fact that Buell for

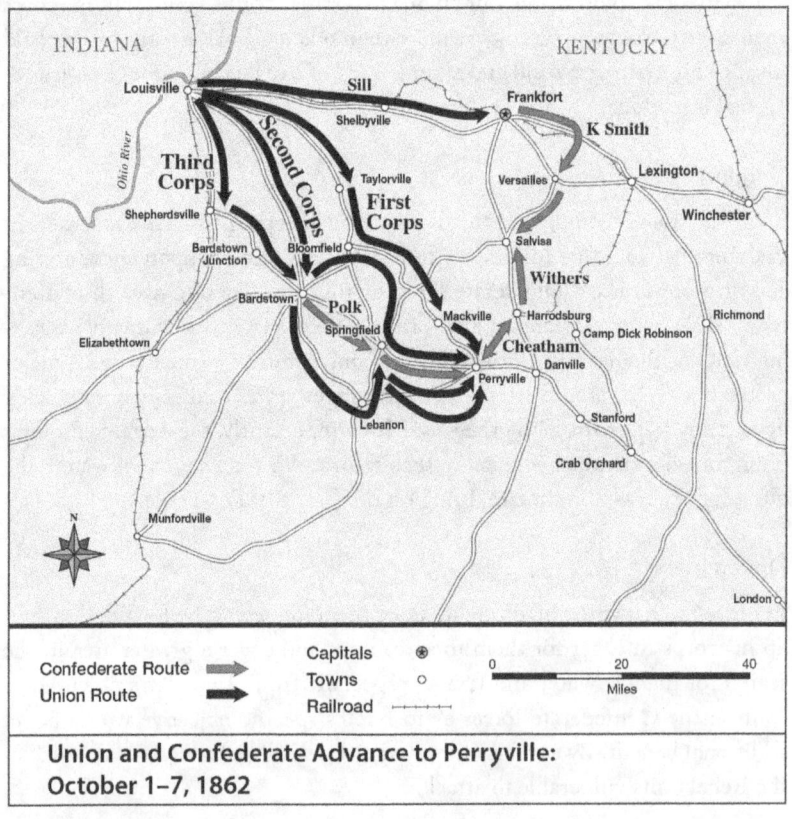

Union and Confederate Advance to Perryville: October 1–7, 1862

September 29–October 7, 1862

Brig. Gen. Joshua W. Sill, USA.
Library of Congress.

the first time moved to confront Bragg and his armies directly instead of marching to a fixed destination.[18]

Results/Impact

Buell's decision to split up his command left Gen. Braxton Bragg and the Confederates immensely confused as to where Buell's army was headed. Buell ordered the First Corps to advance to Bardstown via Taylorsville, Bloomfield, and Mackville. He directed his Second Corps to march directly to Bardstown, while the Third Corps was to advance via Shepherdsville and Bardstown Junction before joining the other corps at Bardstown.[19]

Additionally, Buell ordered Sill's division of McCook's First Corps, augmented by an unattached division of new enlistees under the command of Brig. Gen. Ebenezer Dumont, to conduct a feint from Louisville directly to Frankfort via Shelbyville. These two divisions absolutely fooled Bragg into believing they were Buell's main army and their objective was Frankfort. Compounding this confusion, Bragg had assigned his two cavalry brigades under Col. John H. Wharton and Col. Joseph Wheeler to each of his wing commanders, Maj. Gens. Leonidas Polk and William J. Hardee. While the cavalry provided reconnaissance information to their respective commanders concerning the Union corps' movements toward Bardstown, Bragg had no direct access to any cavalry. Col. John Scott's small cavalry brigade, assigned to Maj. Gen. Edmund Kirby Smith's small army, provided Bragg with some information on Sill's and Dumont's advance toward Frankfort. But the brigade was unable to determine whether the bulk of Buell's army was approaching.[20]

As a result, Bragg concluded that Buell's entire force was, in fact, advancing directly on Frankfort. Subsequently, Bragg attempted to have Hardee and eventually Polk, having halted at Perryville, assault "Buell's army" on its right flank before it reached Frankfort. Bragg expected the battle for Kentucky would occur somewhere around Versailles. Polk was first ordered to assume overall command at Perryville and attack the "small" Union force near the town in preparation for the main battle to follow. Bragg's misidentification of the location of Buell's three corps after they left Bardstown and marched to Perryville directly caused the Battle of Perryville. Sill's (Buell's) deception had worked astonishingly well![21]

Alternate Scenario

A key component to fooling Bragg into committing to fighting at Perryville was the feint toward Frankfort that Sill's and Dumont's divisions conducted. Had Buell not ordered this feint, Bragg probably would have been better prepared to confront Buell's army as it marched toward Perryville, consolidated with Kirby Smith's army, and attempted to defeat Buell somewhere near the site of the actual battle. Perhaps fighting on the defensive, as Buell was under great pressure to rid Kentucky of the Rebel armies, Bragg might have temporarily stopped him, prolonging his stay in Kentucky. Still, in the long run, additional Union forces would likely have forced Bragg to leave the Commonwealth of Kentucky.[22]

Polk Disobeys Bragg's Orders to Advance Toward Frankfort (October 4)

Situation

During the very brief siege at Munfordville, Bragg deployed his entire army to capture the small Union command there guarding the strategic railroad bridge over the Green River. Afterward, Bragg faced an extreme lack of food and forage in the area. He then marched his army northeast to Bardstown, where supplies he ordered from Kirby Smith awaited his army. While this brief siege had no long-term effect on Bragg's campaign, his saving face here distracted him from his original objective of defeating Buell, perhaps marking the beginning of his campaign's doom. As a result, Buell's army could march uncontested to Louisville to regroup and refit, while Bragg's army did the same at Bardstown. Historian Stanley Horn maintains that Bragg showed his timidity here by advancing to Bardstown.[23]

Bragg was born on March 22, 1817, and he graduated from West Point in 1837, ranking fifth in his class of fifty. Serving initially in the Seminole Indian War, Bragg then served gallantly in the Mexican-American War. In the latter conflict he gained fame at the Battle of Buena Vista, during which army commander Zachary Taylor supposedly ordered him, "Give a little more grape Captain Bragg!" Following the war, Bragg married the wealthy Eliza Brooks Ellis in 1847. After his suggestions on improving parts of the army were ignored by Secretary of War Jefferson Davis, and after he served in unhappy assignments on the frontier, Bragg resigned from the army in 1856 and became a Louisiana planter. When the Civil War began, Bragg was known by President Davis and recognized for his outstanding ability to organize troops. He thus brought his well-disciplined twelve-plus regiments from his Gulf Coast garrison at Pensacola to Corinth. In addition to acting as Gen. Albert S. Johnston's chief of staff, Bragg led the Second Corps at the Battle of Shiloh and was promoted to full general, effective April 6, 1862, based on his performance there and Johnston's death. President Davis appointed Bragg second-in-command, and then Davis replaced commander Gen. P. G. T. Beauregard with Bragg when Beauregard took unapproved medical leave from the Army of the Mississippi.[24]

While widely recognized as an excellent organizer and administrator, Bragg failed to lead, eventually becoming one of the more despised Confederate commanding generals. Caused in part by health issues, his dour personality and rigid sense of discipline contributed to many of his subordinates' distrust of and disrespect for him. Beginning with this campaign, Bragg failed to gain and hold the regard of his senior commanders and instill an aura of mutual cooperation among them. Problematic as these factors influencing Bragg during the 1862 Kentucky Campaign were, his relationship with his subordinate commanders would continue to degenerate over time. Maj. Gen. Leonidas Polk led the group of senior commanders dissatisfied with Bragg's performance as leader of the army.[25]

These factors complicated events when Bragg finally decided to obtain control of Kirby Smith and his army. He rode to Lexington to meet with Kirby Smith, leaving Polk in command of the army. Still fooled by Sill's diversionary force, Bragg decided to confront Sill west of Frankfort with Kirby Smith's army as a blocking force. Meanwhile, Bragg's own army under Polk's temporary command would attack the Union force in the right flank and rear. On October 2 Bragg ordered Polk to march via Bloomfield and be prepared to attack. However, Polk was concerned with the apparent concentration of

Gen. Braxton Bragg, CSA.
Library of Congress.

Union forces nearing Bardstown, and he believed Bragg's order was incorrect for the situation. The lack of cavalry under Bragg's direct command to provide reconnaissance further contributed to his confusion; he had only two cavalry brigades, one assigned to each wing commander.[26]

Before we discuss the situation and options Maj. Gen. Leonidas Polk faced, we need to briefly review his military and civilian career to this point, thereby attempting to understand his possible motivation. Polk was born on April 10, 1806, into an influential, wealthy family. Because of his age, he appeared as an elder statesman to his army peers during the Civil War. Polk entered the United States Military Academy and graduated with the class of 1827, one year ahead of his good friend and fellow cadet Jefferson Davis. This friendship was to become influential during the Civil War. During his time at West Point, Polk fell under the influence of the academy chaplain and professor of ethics, the Reverend Charles McIlvaine. Although he graduated eighth in his class, Polk immediately chose to resign his military commission and eventually decided to become an Episcopal minister. In 1838 he was elected missionary bishop of the Southwest, and in 1841 he was elected bishop of Louisiana.[27]

In terms of Polk's personal life, in 1830 he married a wealthy lady from North Carolina, Francis Ann Devereux, and used her money to purchase a plantation in Louisiana. Hundreds of slaves worked the property, and he administered them with mixed results. He later repositioned his family and

September 29–October 7, 1862

Maj. Gen. Leonidas Polk, CSA.
Photographic History, Vol. X.

himself by selling that plantation and purchasing another in Mississippi in 1854. In addition, as bishop of Louisiana, a position of great influence within the Episcopal Church, Polk led the effort to successfully establish the University of the South at Sewanee, Tennessee, a proposed New World rival to England's Oxford and Cambridge.[28]

Upon the outbreak of the Civil War, Polk grew concerned for the protection of his and his neighbor's plantations in Mississippi, and he traveled to the new Confederate capital at Richmond, Virginia, to confer with his old friend Jefferson Davis, now the Confederate president. The outcome of this visit was that Davis appointed Polk, who had never given an order in any military organization after graduation from West Point, a major general! Davis initially named him commander of District 2, which comprised West Tennessee, northern Alabama, western Mississippi, the river parishes of northern Louisiana, and all of Arkansas and Mississippi, or roughly one-third of the Confederacy. Davis selected Polk for this position until the arrival of Albert Sidney Johnston, another long-term friend. Johnston was ultimately destined to take charge.[29]

As an Episcopal bishop for some twenty years, Polk seemed to report to no one within the church. With the advent of the Civil War, the Episcopal Church, like many Protestant churches, suffered a split between North and South. Polk led the separation of Southern Episcopalians by guiding the Louisiana Convention of the Episcopal Church out from the Episcopal

Church of the United States and forming a separate institution within the Confederate States of America. He was a man used to this range of power, a man who perhaps had a natural instinct to take charge of things that many men of the cloth shared. Like other religious leaders, Polk might also have been tempted to believe himself superior to the common people. Thus he tended to view himself above most, including Braxton Bragg, a man he was supposed to obey by virtue of rank. When he observed Bragg's baptism and confirmation at Shelbyville, Tennessee, in June 1863, Polk had been a bishop for more than twenty years. Though pleased with the ceremony, Polk probably viewed Bragg as a neophyte in his church and, as such, his inferior.[30]

While we will leave evaluating Polk's motivation and personality to the many available books attempting to do so, this quote from Dr. William Glenn Robertson perhaps best sums up the major general's attitude: "Gracious and indulgent to underlings who did not challenge his supremacy, he was beloved by his troops even though he wasted their lives through indecision and incompetence." Polk tended to consider orders from his few superiors more as suggestions, and he believed himself to be the better general. Biographer Grady McWhiney opines, "Polk probably had been a bishop too long to be a successful subordinate." Not surprisingly, Polk had quickly come to despise Gen. Braxton Bragg and had continuously worked behind the scenes to engineer his dismissal. Of course, Bragg was long frustrated by Polk and his cohorts, but he was unable to persuade Davis to transfer him out of his command. Bragg later wrote President Davis, "With all of his ability, energy and zeal, General Polk, by education and habit, is unfitted for executing the orders of others. He will convince himself his own views are better, and will follow them without reflecting on the consequences."[31]

I believe that Bryan Bush, present manager of Perryville Battlefield State Historic Site, best summarizes Polk's motivations. Bush maintains that Polk lived his life as a southern gentleman, which required him to conduct his life to the highest ethical standards and adhere to the "rule of honor." To comply with the rule of honor and remain a southern gentleman, Polk, had learned never to admit that he was wrong. Instead, he shifted the blame for any poor outcomes to other individuals and factors. The major general demonstrated this way of acting time after time, and this theory seems to better explain why he often acted contrary to the desires of others, especially his superiors.[32]

I have offered this short explanation of Polk's tendency to challenge orders to provide background for how he often viewed commands from Bragg. Finally, Bragg concluded that he was confident that Hardee and Polk, with most of his army, faced a small force at Perryville. By first eliminating the enemy, Bragg now planned to order his force under Polk to assault what he still believed to be Buell's main army (Sill's diversionary force). Polk's attack would target the Federals' right flank as they advanced toward Frankfort/Versailles. Kirby Smith's army would attack the enemy head on.[33]

Options

As temporary commander of Bragg's Army of the Mississippi, Polk faced two choices: he could either obey Bragg's direct order to advance the army toward Frankfort, or he could disobey Bragg based on his own "better" perception of the situation at Bardstown. As briefly discussed above, a peripheral consideration here is Polk's history of deeming himself the better general.[34]

Option 1

In order for any military organization to function correctly, commanders and enlisted personnel must obey any and all lawfully given orders, generally regardless of how correct they may appear. Commanders at the upper levels may have information corroborating the validity of an order that is unavailable to those in the lower echelons. Only in extreme circumstances may a direct order be ignored. Therefore, even though neither Bragg, nor Polk, nor Kirby Smith apparently understood the locations and purposes of the advancing Union commands, Polk was obligated to follow his commander's orders. As Bragg directed, Polk had to swiftly put the Army of the Mississippi into motion.[35]

Option 2

Polk was stationed at Bardstown, and he received updated reports of increasing Union activity around his location. He could legitimately ignore Bragg's direct orders if this information was correct and verifiable. Polk could then oversee the army's movement in a more favorable direction, one better suited to its safety and overall performance.[36]

Decision

When a commander wanted to validate a momentous decision, calling for a council of war gave him a methodology to do just that. Polk convened a council of war on October 3 and persuaded his immediate subordinate commanders to ignore Bragg's direct orders. They agreed it was in the best interest of the Army of the Mississippi to retreat east to protect Camp Breckinridge (formerly Union Camp Dick Robinson), an easily defended position and the location of an important stockpile of supplies and munitions. The loss of Camp Breckinridge and its supplies would probably eliminate the Rebels' ability to remain in Kentucky. Polk ordered his troops to withdraw.[37]

Results/Impact

Polk initiated the retreat early on October 4. His right wing marched east toward Danville, while Hardee's left wing marched farther north toward Mackville and Harrodsburg. Advancing via separate roads eased the problem of congestion. It also kept both wings within about ten miles of each other for support in case of an unexpected attack. The line of march for Polk's right wing directed it right through the small town of Perryville. Unknowingly, Polk had determined the location of the major battle for the control of Kentucky: Perryville.[38]

Was Polk correct in disobeying Bragg's orders to advance on Frankfort? According to Perryville Battlefield expert Kenneth Noe, fellow historians Herman Hattaway, Archer Jones, Grady McWhiney, and Stephen Woodworth maintain that had Polk obeyed Bragg's orders and marched toward Frankfort, Bragg might have rendered Sill's part of Buell's army harmless, and possibly Dumont's part as well (see alternate scenario below). However, Noe further notes scholars Thomas Connelly's and Stanley Horn's contention that Polk correctly disobeyed his orders. The Army of the Mississippi was already confronting advance elements of Buell's main army, and Polk's left flank in particular was becoming extremely vulnerable to attack. Was Polk correct for once in disobeying orders?[39]

Alternate Scenario

Polk could have followed Bragg's direct order to march Bragg's Army of the Mississippi through Bloomfield to the Frankfort area. With Kirby Smith's Army of Kentucky confronting Sill's division, augmented by a flank and rear attack by Polk, Sill's division (and possibly eventually Dumont's) might have been eliminated as a force. Then Bragg and his combined armies might have confronted Buell's main force. Had Bragg remained on the defense forcing Buell to assault him, Bragg might have achieved a victory similarly to the Battle of Perryville, and stayed within Kentucky at least a while longer?[40]

Bragg Installs a Confederate Governor at Frankfort (October 4)

Situation

One reason the whereabouts of Buell's main army confused Bragg was that the Rebel general was distracted. During this time, Bragg searched for a way to entice Kentucky men to join his Army of the Mississippi. He saw that recruits were not readily enlisting, and those enlisting desired to join the cavalry. Contented Kentuckian men preferred waiting to see who would likely win the war, meanwhile enjoying the fruits of their labors. As a potential solution to the recruiting problem, Bragg could reinstall the Confederate governor of Kentucky, Richard Hawes (he had already been inaugurated). Hawes, had recently arrived back in the commonwealth and was available. Bragg intended to have Hawes reinstalled and then make conscription for the Confederacy legal, just as he had done in Tennessee. Would this act generate a wave of volunteerism as well?[41]

Bragg decided that the installation would take place on October 4 at the old capitol building in Frankfort, and he detailed Kirby Smith to escort Hawes there on the appointed day. The elaborate plans for the celebration included a dinner Bragg would host afterward.[42]

However, as the installation approached, some of Bragg's subordinates urged him to concentrate on confronting Buell and his large army. The officer was confronted with a dilemma.[43]

Options

Bragg could choose from three options: conduct the installation as planned, postpone the ceremony, or cancel it.[44]

Old Kentucky capitol building, Frankfort.
Library of Congress.

Option 1

The psychological and political value of reinstalling a Confederate Kentucky governor was obvious to Bragg and to all Confederate-leaning Kentuckians. Ideally this would help place the commonwealth firmly within the fold of Confederate states. More importantly for Bragg, and as noted above, this act would legitimize Rebel control of Kentucky. Legally, Bragg could advocate passing a conscription act to hopefully encourage some volunteerism and augment his ranks with Kentucky men. Bragg considered Kentucky men's failure to step forward and enlist as a major deterrent to success in making the state Confederate. The downside to this option was that it distracted Bragg from focusing on Buell's approaching army and how and where to confront it.[45]

Option 2

A compromise between Bragg and some of his subordinates, including Kirby Smith, dictated that postponing the installation would help the general better concentrate on confronting Buell. Bragg could reschedule the installation at a later time.[46]

Option 3

As a final option Bragg could cancel the installation until he had dealt with Buell and the situation had stabilized. Buell's advance required Bragg to determine the Army of the Ohio's destination and the best way to confront its troops. For the sake of the Confederacy, Bragg had to focus on this priority. He could deal with concerns such as the reinstallation after the looming battle. Indeed, if Bragg failed to maintain control over Kentucky, the state would revert to Union control, and no Confederate conscription would result.[47]

Decision

Bragg refused to postpone or cancel the installation, and he held it as scheduled on October 4.[48]

Results/Impact

Although it rained, Bragg insisted that the installation begin on time at the old capitol building in Frankfort. He started the ceremony with introductory remarks. As Governor Hawes then approached the speakers' stand, he received a huge ovation. The cheering apparently continued during his address, but the ominous sound of artillery firing suddenly resonated throughout the building, forcing a quick conclusion to the event. Sill's division had arrived just west of the city, yet Bragg was still confused. Assuming once again that this force was Buell's army, Bragg ordered bridges crossing the Kentucky River destroyed, then left for Harrodsburg.[49]

By concentrating on the installation, Bragg failed to focus on his real concern: the location of Buell's army. Had he made a better attempt to identify exactly what force was moving toward Frankfort, Bragg might have sooner discovered these troops to be a diversion. He might then have been better prepared to confront Buell at or near Perryville. By succumbing to his desire to install Hawes to obtain recruits, Bragg failed to adequately manage both Kirby Smith's army and his own. Kirby Smith was, indeed, a department commander. However, once out of his department, he was subordinate to the field commander, Bragg. Bragg's focus here made him order Polk at Bardstown to (unknowingly) confront almost all of Buell's army. As we will see, Buell himself helped save Polk and Hardee from sound defeat at Perryville.[50]

Polk Orders Hardee to Halt Buckner's Division at Perryville (October 7)

Situation

After departing Bardstown early on October 4, Hardee and his left wing began the march toward Harrodsburg via Mackville, while Polk and his right wing advanced southeast to Danville via Springfield. As previously noted, both forces moved generally east and were never more than ten miles apart, which allowed each to support the other in case of Federal attack on one. This common advance was designed to keep these units interposed between Buell and the critically important Confederate supply base at Camp Breckinridge (formerly Camp Dick Robinson), where Bragg had accumulated desperately needed supplies. Hardee was forced to shift more to the south as various cavalry fights took place around him. Further, because of the roads' poor condition, he obtained Polk's permission to march on the better but more southern Springfield Pike. However, the Springfield Pike connected with Danville via Perryville and did not lead to Harrodsburg. Hardee then followed behind Polk's Wing, which marched through Perryville and then northeast to Harrodsburg. On October 7 Hardee's command arrived in the vicinity of Perryville, where he made a fateful choice.[51]

Concerned about the pursuing Union force, Hardee believed that the best approach was to confront the Yankees near Perryville. As he stated, "With the view of inflicting a decisive defeat, or at least of pressing him back from any further advance against our line of communications in the direction of

Maj. Gen. William J. Hardee, CSA.
Library of Congress.

Danville and Cumberland Gap, I urged the concentration of our whole army at Perryville."[52]

Hardee graduated from West Point in 1838 and was breveted twice for service in the Mexican-American War. Before the war he wrote *Hardee's Tactics*, which was widely used by Union and Confederate officers. Most Rebels considered Hardee, nicknamed "Old Reliable," one of the Confederacy's best corps commanders. He appeared as a "fine looking old gentleman apparently about forty-eight years old," and he was a disciplinarian but not a martinet.[53]

Recent scholarship sheds a different light on Hardee, raising doubt as to his description as "Old Reliable." Gen. Joseph E. Johnston told Brig. Gen. St. John R. Liddell, "Hardee likes the show of war, but dislikes its labors and responsibilities. I believe that he was not intended by nature to be a great leader." Historian Steven Woodworth describes Hardee as "lackluster" and "one who never accomplished anything striking." Nevertheless, Hardee appeared to command reasonably well at the wing/corps level. Bragg himself reported just before the 1862 Kentucky Campaign that Hardee was the only "suitable" major general "now present." When not intriguing in politics, Hardee apparently worked well in the field.[54]

Hardee believed in four good reasons to concentrate in the terrain around Perryville. First, all soldiers in Kentucky faced extreme drought, so a source of water was critical for his men. While reports indicated that the nearby rivers and creeks were at all-time lows, at least some water was available in pools in Doctor's Creek, Bull Run, and the Chaplin River. It would be essential in order for Hardee's men to perform their duties and fight as necessary. A second reason to remain was the number of roads fanning out in all directions from Perryville, providing various avenues of escape or advancement, depending on the situation. Hardee had quickly noticed the rolling hills in and around Perryville, and he realized that the terrain would support defensive operations. Finally, this location again kept Hardee's wing interposed between Buell and supplies at Danville, as well as the Rebel supply base at Camp Breckinridge. Unable to make the decision himself, Hardee therefore recommended to temporary army commander Polk that Perryville would be an excellent position to confront the enemy.[55]

Options

As acting army commander, Polk had two options at this time: he could direct Hardee to remain at Perryville as requested, or he could tell Hardee to continue retreating as previously ordered.[56]

Option 1

Hardee had valid reasons for recommending confrontation with the advancing Union force as described above. Although still ignorant of the actual size of Buell's army pursuing the Rebels, Hardee and Polk certainly did not expect virtually the entire army. The Perryville location provided superb defensive positions if needed, plus critical access to water.[57]

Option 2

Continuing to march to Harrodsburg would safely reunite Bragg's and eventually Kirby Smith's armies, providing additional protection. This had been the latest plan, and it would comply with orders already in effect.[58]

Decision

Polk ordered Hardee to remain in the Perryville area with Buckner's Division, per Hardee's request.[59]

Results/Impact

That Hardee remained near Perryville established the location for the upcoming Battle of Perryville. Bragg remained confused as to exactly where Buell's army was located. As previously mentioned, Sill's diversionary force had fooled Bragg into believing that it was Buell's main army. Remember that because of the extreme drought, water for the soldiers was a very high priority for the commanders on both sides. Polk and Hardee certainly wanted to take advantage of its availability, even though limited, in the area around Perryville. This water supply would quickly attract the Union soldiers as well.[60]

However, Hardee had taken into consideration the other factors mentioned above, specifically the rolling hills that provided great defensive positions if needed. Unfortunately, these same hills would provide the Union with some good defensive locations. Polk's critical decision firmly established that an important battle would be fought at Perryville. Further, it would become the decisive battle for the Commonwealth of Kentucky to remain under Union control for the remainder of the war. At this time, Polk's somewhat offhanded communication to Bragg concerning the size of the enemy force—"I cannot think it large"—only perplexed Bragg even more.[61]

Bragg Orders Polk to March to Perryville and Attack the Approaching Union Force (October 7)

Situation

As noted above, Bragg was unclear as to the location and immediate objective of Buell's main army. Based on reconnaissance by Col. John Scott's cavalry, under the direction of Kirby Smith, and that general's own pickets, Bragg quickly assumed that the feint ordered by Buell and carried out by Sill's and Dumont's divisions was actually Buell's entire army, or at least the majority of it. Acting on this latest intelligence, Bragg expected Buell's "army" to continue advancing east of Shelbyville and directly toward the commonwealth capital of Frankfort. Once reaching this conclusion, Bragg decided to finally confront Buell. Please realize that Bragg changed his mind several times during these days as to how to challenge Buell.[62]

Polk added to the confusion by characterizing the size of the Union force pursuing him in the following statement to Bragg: "I cannot think it large." Then Polk turned right around and ordered Maj. Gen. Patton Anderson's division, which had just arrived in Harrodsburg, to march back to Perryville, along with Brig. Gen. Patrick Cleburne's brigade and Wharton's Cavalry.[63]

Bragg quickly began to develop a plan of battle. Brig. Gen. Humphrey Marshall's even smaller Rebel force still eluded him, but now that he had finally assumed command of Kirby Smith's small army, Bragg could reasonably assume the defensive and prepare to confront Buell somewhere near Frankfort. Bragg personally determined that this clash would occur somewhere near the town of Versailles, west of Lexington and south of Frankfort.[64]

September 29–October 7, 1862

Maj. Gen. Edmund Kirby Smith, CSA. Library of Congress.

Confused somewhat by reports of other Union forces south of his position, Bragg decided that he must take action. Both of his wing commanders were fighting the occasional rearguard action, especially by their respective cavalry brigades. Bragg thus realized that one or more of these forces needed to be dealt with. Based on the available reconnaissance or the lack thereof, he then began to formalize a plan of battle most favorable to him.[65]

Options

Bragg considered four reasonable courses of action predicated on his limited understanding of the situation. His first option was to unite as many troops from his and Kirby Smith's armies and prepare to confront Buell directly as the Federals advanced toward Frankfort. Another option was to challenge and render harmless the force following either Polk or Hardee, or both forces. A third course of action was to order Polk and Hardee to assault Buell's right flank as it continued toward Frankfort. Finally, Bragg could eliminate whoever was following Polk and Hardee as above, then have these Rebels attack the right flank of Buell's army as it advanced east to Frankfort.[66]

Option 1

Kirby Smith obviously preferred independent command to serving under Bragg. Therefore, he made every effort to remain apart from Bragg for as long as possible. However, after Bragg confronted the Munfordville garrison, he rode ahead of his two wings to Lexington and formally assumed command of Kirby Smith's army. The general now commanded a force somewhat close in size to Buell's approaching army. Bragg knew that Buell was undoubtedly under orders to drive the Rebels out of Kentucky, forcing Buell to go on the offensive. If Bragg could unite his two armies and find a good defensive position, he could realistically expect Buell to assault that position. Bragg would expect to successfully exploit the advantages of remaining on the defensive and defeat Buell. Successful use of this option would allow the Rebel armies to remain in Kentucky at least a while longer, hoping to realistically bring the commonwealth into the Confederacy.[67]

Option 2

Although unsure about the size and direction of the Union force or forces pursuing his two wings as they marched east from Bardstown, Bragg could eliminate these troops prior to confronting what he thought was Buell's main army marching directly to Frankfort. Of course, Bragg would eventually discover his intelligence was incorrect. He had the option to order Hardee and/or Polk to turn and attack these Federals with the intent of eliminating them from the upcoming battle. The enemy forces advancing on the small town of Perryville actually consisted of Buell's three corps minus two divisions—almost his entire army. Apparently, Bragg remained largely unaware of this information.[68]

Option 3

Bragg could catch the Union force off guard by ordering Polk to march his two wings north from the Perryville area and attack Buell's exposed right flank as Buell's army marched east toward Frankfort. Bragg might also place Kirby Smith's army to block Buell's advance, potentially confronting him on front and flank. Of course, it was assumed that this option would defeat Buell decisively.[69]

Option 4

Bragg could combine Options 2 and 3, first having Polk/Hardee defeat the "small" force in pursuit, and then attacking what he perceived as Buell's right.[70]

Decision

Based on his limited and incorrect assessment of the situation, Bragg chose Option 4. He ordered Polk to march to Perryville and assume overall command over both his and Hardee's Wings. Polk was then to defeat the local Federal force before conducting the flank attack on Buell's army.[71]

Results/Impact

Bragg's decision dictated that the ultimate battle for control of Kentucky would take place near the small town of Perryville. Accordingly, at 5:40 p.m. Bragg ordered Polk to take Cheatham's Division, recently arrived at Harrodsburg, and return to Perryville, attack the Union force there, and then march to the Versailles area to help defeat Buell's army. Polk left as ordered. Hardee received additional reinforcements, as Brig. Gen. Daniel Adams's and Col. Samuel Powel's brigades of Brig. Gen. Patton Anderson's division also arrived at Perryville. Bragg had now concentrated a significant force at and near Perryville that was prepared to confront whatever soldiers Buell had stationed there. Inadvertently, Bragg had set the stage for the Battle of Perryville.[72]

Alternate Scenario

Had Bragg concentrated all of his commands near Frankfort or Versailles, no Battle of Perryville would have occurred. Would a similar battle eventually have taken place? Still, Bragg likely would have chosen to abandon Kentucky, as we will discuss below.[73]

CHAPTER 3

INITIATING THE BATTLE OF PERRYVILLE, OCTOBER 8, 1862

Beginning very early on the morning of October 8, just prior to the Battle of Perryville, four additional critical decisions—Confederates and Federals each made two—formed the battle. Had these choices not been made, the Battle of Perryville would have turned out much differently.

McCook's Brigade Is Sent Forward to Search for Water (October 8, 3:00 a.m.)

Situation

We must remember that the extreme drought constantly and significantly affected operations on both Yankees and Confederates. Soldiers at all levels had to obtain water for themselves and their comrades, as no central water source existed in either army. Military maneuvering and discipline continued to suffer because troops' thirst overrode their minds. As the Union corps continued their advance ultimately to the Perryville area, Union and Confederate commanders were left with two questions: Where was the enemy? Perhaps more importantly, where was the water?[1]

On October 7, Maj. Gen. Alexander McD. McCook's First Corps marched southwest and encamped that evening around the small hamlet of Mackville. On the morning of the eighth his corps would resume the march to a point north of Perryville and become Gen. Braxton Bragg's target for assault. Maj. Gen. Thomas L. Crittenden's Second Corps marched south from Springfield to Haysville and then was to turn east toward Perryville. However, as they were so lacking in water, Maj. Gen. George H. Thomas, Buell's second-in-command, ordered the corps to continue south another two miles past Haysville to a fork of the Salt River. As the troops reached their destination later in the evening, this decision by Thomas delayed the Second Corps' arrival at Perryville on the morrow. "Acting Maj. Gen." Charles C. Gilbert's Third Corps left the Springfield area and marched under the hot sun directly toward Perryville. Encountering Rebel cavalry commanded by Col. Joseph Wheeler, Gilbert's corps nonetheless continued to advance almost to the outskirts of Perryville along the Springfield Pike. Along with Buell, Gilbert's men were the first to arrive at Perryville. As a result, Gilbert naturally wanted to ascertain what he faced.[2]

At this time in the late afternoon, Buell suffered an injury that would affect his view of the upcoming battle. When he stopped to deal with some insubordinate soldiers, one of them grasped his bridle, scaring his horse. The horse fell backward, throwing off the general. Buell's resulting injuries forced him to be transported by ambulance, severely reducing his ability to visit the battlefield.[3]

Buell was already planning for an assault on whatever Confederate forces awaited him in the Perryville area. He made sure that his commanders required all soldiers to fill their canteens with water before any movement on September 8. Buell rightly assumed that the next likely chance for his troops to refill their canteens would be in the waterways around Perryville.[4]

On the morning of the seventh, Maj. Gen. William J. Hardee, commanding Gen. Braxton Bragg's left wing, placed Brig. Gen. St. John R. Liddell's Rebel brigade west of the rest of his command on Bottom Hill. Named for local farmer Samuel Bottom, the hill stood just north of the Springfield Pike. Hardee also realigned Brig. Gen. Bushrod R. Johnson's and Brig. Gen. Sterling A. M. Wood's brigades north of Liddell. Though his men occupied Bottom Hill, Liddell desired better reconnaissance and eventually sent first the Fifth, and then the Seventh Arkansas, across Bull Run and onto Peters Hill to the west. Liddell could appreciate the Yankees' desire to maneuver to Bull Run for what little water remained there.[5]

October 8, 1862

Options

Buell had two choices as to how and when he could probe the Confederate force apparently arrayed before him. One option was to wait until all three of his corps were in position near Perryville before beginning a serious advance. The other was to order a probe to feel out the enemy's presence.[6]

Option 1

Buell's safest option was to wait until all three of his corps were positioned where he desired them. Remember that the general remained cautious and preferred to outmaneuver the enemy if possible. Then, with virtually his entire army present, he could order either a probe or an assault on the Rebel force near Perryville, and be confident that he had sufficient manpower to succeed. Of course, by postponing his desired attack, Buell would allow the Confederates facing him to potentially erect a strong defensive position, making it harder for the Federals to emerge victorious. If chosen by Buell, this option assumed that the enemy would simply await him without further maneuvering on its own.[7]

Option 2

Buell could also order a probe farther east to seek out any Rebel presence and attempt to locate and secure a source of water for his men, who needed it soon. A reconnaissance of this nature could quickly update Buell as to the locations of both water and the enemy. Even if it failed, this course of action would likely lose only a small portion of the general's manpower.[8]

Decision

From his headquarters tent next to the Dorsey House, in the evening Buell ordered a probe of Peters Hill. Named for the farmer whose house was located on its western side, Peters Hill stood just west and across Bull Run from Bottom Hill. This decision in effect opened the Battle of Perryville, which would determine the Confederacy's success or failure in bringing the Commonwealth of Kentucky into its fold.[9]

Results/Impact

Buell ordered "Acting Maj. Gen." Charles Gilbert to send one of his brigades east to capture Peters Hill. Gilbert directed Brig. Gen. Philip Sheridan to supply a brigade for this purpose, and Sheridan gave the assignment to Col. Daniel McCook's brigade of new soldiers. McCook's Brigade had not yet

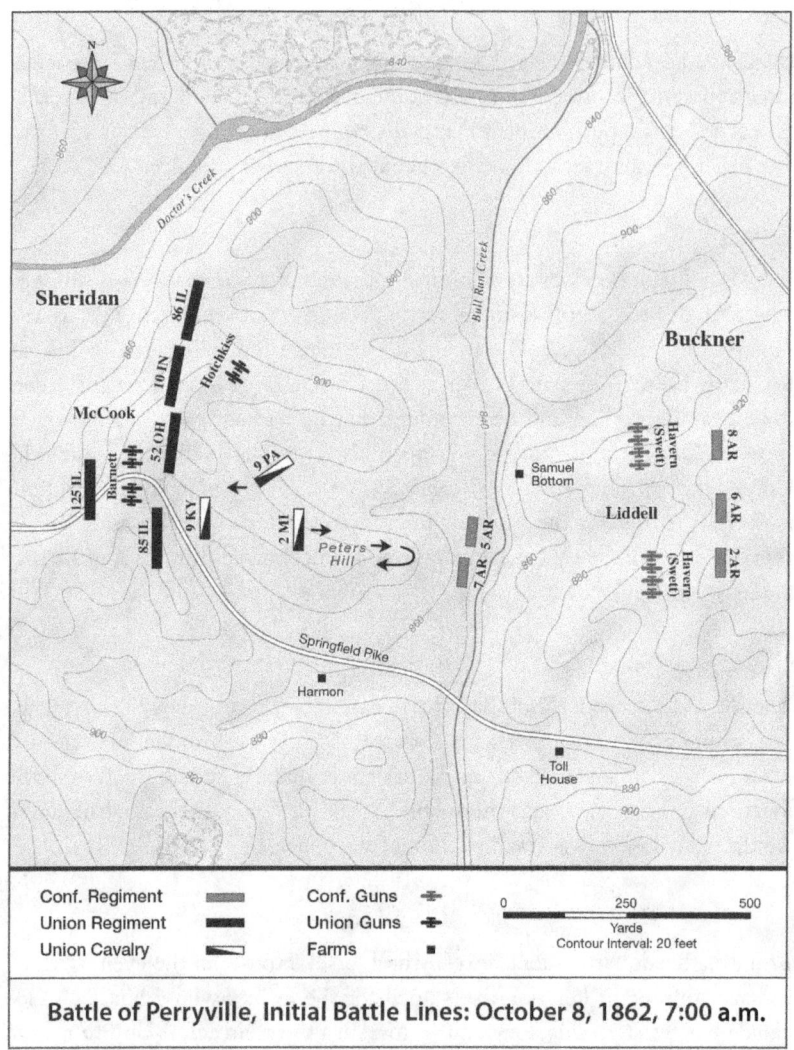

Battle of Perryville, Initial Battle Lines: October 8, 1862, 7:00 a.m.

seen combat, so Sheridan apparently considered this an opportunity for the troops to receive a taste of combat prior to a significant battle.[10]

Liddell's Seventh Arkansas quickly discovered the Federals advancing onto the hill, and fighting broke out. Assisted by Capt. Charles M. Barnett's artillery battery, McCook's men soon forced Liddell's troops off the hilltop. Liddell immediately sent the Fifth Arkansas to support the Seventh Arkansas just west of Bull Run. An artillery duel ensued, then McCook's regiments

October 8, 1862

Brig. Gen. Philip H. Sheridan, USA.
Library of Congress.

advanced. Sheridan ordered Lieut. Col. Bernard Laiboldt's brigade and Capt. Henry Hescock's Battery G, First Missouri Light Artillery to augment McCook. Acting Brig. Gen. Ebenezer Gay also received orders to attack the woods in front, backing McCook. The Federals' Colt revolving rifles made quite an impact. In addition, Buell had ordered Brig. Gen. Speed S. Fry's brigade to search for water, and it, too, joined the fray to repel the Rebels. Around 8:00 a.m. Liddell rushed to obtain assistance from Maj. Gen. Simon B. Buckner, his division commander. While coordinating with Buckner, Polk sent orders to fall back to join the rest of the Confederate line. This decision yielded Bottom Hill to the Yankees, resulting in the opening of the Battle of Perryville, both a major event in Bragg's Kentucky Campaign and a part of the Confederate high tide.[11]

Polk Refuses to Attack per Bragg's Direct Order and Assumes the "Offensive-Defensive" (7:00 a.m.)

Situation

Bragg was finally confident that Hardee and Polk, along with most of his army, faced a small force at Perryville. After first eliminating these Federals, Bragg then planned to use Polk's soldiers to assault what he still believed to be Buell's main army (Sill's diversionary force) on its right flank as it advanced toward Frankfort/Versailles. Kirby Smith's army would attack the enemy head on.[12]

Polk arrived at Perryville with reinforcements, apparently late in the evening, and was ready to lead the Rebels who had congregated there in battle. He even informed Bragg early the following morning, "Understanding it to be your wish to give them battle, we shall do so vigorously."[13] Following his formulation of the above message, Polk rode out to examine the tentative line of battle set by Hardee and his subordinates. As he did so, Polk grew concerned that more than a small Yankee force was situated west of his position. Evidently unaware of exactly how large this enemy was, Polk, who was not a combat general like Maj. Gen. Ulysses S. Grant, became somewhat fearful that these opponents could be problematic. We previously discussed Polk's tendency to challenge or ignore orders. He would often view an order from Bragg with skepticism.[14]

Options

Early on the morning of October 8, Polk considered two options. His first alternative was to conform to Bragg's orders and attack the "small" Union force at Perryville. Only a few days before, Polk himself had described the enemy unit to Bragg as follows: "I cannot think it large." Polk's other option would be to call off the assigned attack until he had a better idea of the actual size of the Union force facing him across the Chaplin River.[15]

Option 1

Polk's orders from Bragg were explicit—attack! Bragg fully expected to have Polk take care of the Union force at Perryville before completing his plan to strike Buell's main army near Frankfort or Versailles. These Federals needed to be eliminated as a concern to the Rebels. There was no simple way to avoid these orders; Bragg expected them to be carried out. However, as he was not on scene, Bragg could not accurately evaluate the situation.[16]

Option 2

As the senior Confederate commander present, Polk dictated the movements of the Rebel troops there. He had full responsibility for his men's actions. Knowing this, Polk needed to act cautiously and not commit his units indiscriminately. He could at least temporarily refrain from ordering an assault on the Union forces at Perryville.[17]

October 8, 1862

Decision

Polk quickly decided not to attack the Federals at Perryville. He called a council of war, a favorite method for sharing the responsibility for such decisions, to line up support for his choice.[18]

Results/Impact

Not surprisingly, those at Polk's council of war concluded that the Rebels would adopt the "offensive-defensive" methodology for the moment in order to better comprehend the size and direction of the Union force present. Troops taking this course of action simply wait and see how the enemy is going to maneuver, then respond appropriately. Adoptees of the "offensive-defensive" remain on the defense and protect their forces while preparing to resist an attack. Providing that the situation indicates a providential outcome, these troops might undertake a more precise offensive movement as the situation unfolds.[19]

As soon as he and his commanders accepted the offensive-defensive plan, Polk ordered Brigadier General Liddell's brigade to leave its advanced position and rejoin the rest of the Rebel line generally east of the Chaplin River. Polk then continued to observe any Union movements across the way. What he did not do was inform Bragg of his decision to cancel the assigned attack. On the morning of the eighth, Bragg, only ten miles away at Harrodsburg, strained to hear sounds of the assault he had recently ordered and Polk had promised to carry out. Hearing no battle sounds, Bragg and his staff hurried southwest to Perryville to ascertain just what action was taking place. Upon his arrival, Bragg discovered that no fighting was occurring, in violation of his direct orders.[20]

Historians generally fall into two distinct sides when evaluating Polk's response on the morning of the October 8. Some castigate him for failing to attack as ordered. Historian Kenneth Noe states that historians Stanley F. Horn and Joseph H. Parks generally favor Polk but do not specifically comment on the general's decision. Noe himself believes that Polk made the correct choice, as does Chris Kolakowski. Larry J. Daniel and James Lee McDonough, two of the more recent Perryville historians, support Polk. However, I read McDonough as actually opposing Polk's decision, and scholars Thomas L. Connelly, Grady McWhiney, Steven E. Woodworth, and Huston Horn also taking a position against the general's decision to wait. Early in the morning, only the initial units of Maj. Gen. Alexander McD. McCook's First Corps were arriving on what would become the battlefield. Attacking the Federals at this earlier time would have made Confederate victory even more likely, compared to what actually occurred later in the day. Yet in fairness to Polk, other historians agree that he was unsure of the size of the Union force opposing him. Polk also had no other reinforcements immediately available to him if they were necessary to either secure victory or prevent annihilation of his own remote force.[21]

We must also consider that Buell's intention early on the eighth was to attack the Rebel force present near Perryville. He was not yet aware that his corps were somewhat delayed in arriving on the line of battle he had designated. Also, when the enemy was known to be in the area, all commanders would have cavalry, scouts, pickets, etc. on the fringes of their commands specifically looking for any sign of the enemy to prevent a surprise assault. Especially with the arrival of the Third Corps very close to the First Corps, and with no orders not to engage at the time, an assault by Polk might actually have faced increased risk. Nonetheless, Polk's refusal to cooperate with Bragg in general was apparently reflected in, or it contributed to, his decision not to carry out Bragg's direct orders to attack.[22]

Bragg Realigns Cheatham's Division and Orders the Assault (10:00 a.m.–2:00 p.m.)

Situation

Bragg and his aides arrived in the Perryville area in midmorning, specifically finding his subordinates at the John Crawford House, located northeast of Perryville on the Perryville–Harrodsburg Road. Needless to say, he was once again infuriated at Polk's failure to obey his orders to attack. At Bardstown Bragg had delegated command of his army to Polk. Here Polk offered to turn over direct command of the Confederate force present to Bragg, but Bragg refused. In this instance, as Lieut. Gen. Ulysses S. Grant did later in the war, when he "accompanied" Army of the Potomac commander Maj. Gen. George. G. Meade, Bragg would issue orders to Polk, who would then carry them out. Then Bragg decided to evaluate Polk's line of battle. He quickly discovered a serious situation—Polk had left his right flank unattached to any kind of a physical barrier and simply dangling by itself.[23]

Options

Bragg had quickly realized the urgency of the situation. He felt that he could not simply accept the status quo, but must act. His first option was to have his entire line advance before the opposing Union force could attack. A second option was to advance only Hardee's Command on the northern (right) flank in order to forestall any attempted Federal assault on his vulnerable right.

October 8, 1862

John Crawford House, Bragg's headquarters, near Perryville, Kentucky. Photo by Chuck Lott.

Third, Bragg could try to change the location of his right flank to render it much less susceptible to attack. Finally, he could combine one or more of these options.[24]

Option 1

By sending his entire line forward, Bragg could apply pressure to the Union command and force it to focus on resisting this movement, not conducting a flanking attack on his vulnerable right flank. Although Bragg did not know that nearly all of Buell's army was in the area, this plan did assume an element of risk. The Rebel commander did not even correctly understand what Union force or forces were present. Yet this movement would compel the Federals to react to him instead of the reverse.[25]

Option 2

Another possibility was for Bragg to advance Hardee's Command, which was defending the northern, or right, part of the Rebel line. This course of action would occupy the enemy's attention, distracting the Federals from possibly assaulting this flank. However, this advance would take some time to organize and carry out. In addition, it could potentially bring on fighting before Bragg and the Rebels would be ready.[26]

Option 3

The most obvious solution to fixing the exposed right flank was to relocate it to a more secure position. Bragg realized that this simple maneuver would nevertheless consume a significant amount of time, and he would have to hope that the Yankees would grant it to him.[27]

Option 4

Bragg's final alternative was to consider conducting two (or more) of the above maneuvers. Doing so might further confuse the enemy as to which direction he wished to move, and allow him the time required to carry out the necessary operations.[28]

Decision

Bragg chose Option 4. He sent Hardee's left wing across the Chaplin River in order to temporarily occupy the Yankees' attention, distracting them from his other movement. This other movement was to stabilize Bragg's right flank. He ordered Maj. Gen. Benjamin F. Cheatham's division to leave its position in Perryville on the south end of his line and march behind the Rebel line all the way to Walker's Bend, over two miles north.[29]

Results/Impact

Bragg had made a truly crucial decision to postpone the assault that he had previously ordered Polk to initiate. Instead of an early morning attack attempting to catch and eliminate whatever Union forces were present, Polk had effectively given the enemy time to prepare for just such a maneuver. By taking additional time to reposition Cheatham and cover his right flank, Bragg potentially exposed his command to a charge he was not totally prepared to resist.[30]

However, had Bragg not modified his right flank, it would have remained vulnerable to a Union assault, potentially allowing the Yankees to roll up Bragg's entire line after overrunning the Rebel right flank. Cheatham's Division marched north to its new location at Walker's Bend, where the Chaplin River made a very distinctive series of turns. Deploying Cheatham here would provide an anchor for his right flank and (Bragg thought) position it such that it would outflank the Union left. Many Federal soldiers noticed the dust that Cheatham's men churned up as they marched north, which they interpreted as Bragg's army retreating north to Harrodsburg. This incorrect interpretation would allow Bragg to catch the Union left off guard. Leaving Perryville about

October 8, 1862

11:00 a.m., Cheatham's Division was in position at Walker's Bend around 1:30 p.m. Yet upon observing new Union troops even farther north, Bragg realized he needed to shift Cheatham again in order to remain north of the Union left flank. This took additional time, and by about 2:00 p.m. Cheatham was in place for the long-awaited assault to begin. However, when Bragg finally ordered the assault to begin, formally initiating the battle, he would discover he had erred.[31]

Alternate Scenario

As we will discuss below, although Bragg thought that he had correctly identified the Union left flank, his recognition of it was, in fact, incorrect. Had he not repositioned Cheatham at Walker's Bend, an assault by Bragg's right flank would have been vulnerable to even more counterassaults by the actual Union left flank, and the likelihood of success would have been considerably diminished. Indeed, Bragg was wise to reposition Cheatham.[32]

Buell Postpones His Planned Attack (11:00 a.m.)

Situation

While Bragg had his hands full repositioning Cheatham, Buell faced his own problems. Remember that he fell on the seventh and had severely limited mobility. Therefore, he was essentially confined to his headquarters by the Dorsey House, located a few miles west of Perryville, just north of the Old Springfield Road (since realigned). Buell's lack of mobility would severely limit what we would today call his situational awareness. He had ordered his three corps to march to the Perryville area in preparation for an assault on the Rebel forces there. However, the drought had heavily impacted his schedule. Buell had never initiated battle previously and knew he must succeed in confronting Bragg's force. While Gilbert's Third Corps was positioned near Buell's desired location, and it had already secured Peters Hill from the Confederates, Buell realized that Crittenden's Second Corps was not likely to move into position until much later than planned. Also, McCook's First Corps appeared tardy in arriving.[33]

Options

Buell had two options to consider. Certainly he could temporarily postpone his desired morning attack until later in the day, giving his corps time to move into position. His other option was to delay the assault until the next day.[34]

Option 1

Although Buell felt that his timetable was not being met, this did not necessarily mean that he could not initiate his plan of battle. Rather, he would have to delay it slightly. Of course, the enemy might not simply await the eventual arrival of Buell's corps. However, Buell felt that, once his three corps (minus Sill's two divisions) were present, he would likely be numerically equal or superior to Bragg, and ready to finally confront him. Remember that Buell, like many of his peers, preferred to outmaneuver his enemy as opposed to confronting him in battle. He always attempted to maintain superiority in manpower, complete with all necessary supplies, in order to not fail in battle.[35]

Option 2

Concerned that there was simply not going to be enough time to get his corps into position and also conduct a potential battle before nightfall, Buell could postpone his planned attack until the next day. He would then order an assault with his corps in position to support one another and confidently move against the Rebel forces present. Buell might fear that the Confederates could change position, attack, or retreat, but he would deal with them with his army intact. As noted in Option 1, Buell would not be comfortable ordering an attack until he felt able to position his corps adequately to win the battle.[36]

Decision

Around 11:00 a.m. Buell made the very significant critical decision to put off his attack until the next day in order to allow his corps to all be present, properly aligned, and ready for battle. This choice would have many ramifications.[37]

Results/Impact

Late in the morning, Buell decided to postpone the assault until the next day, September 9. Yet Gilbert's Third Corps had long since been in position and had advanced onto Peters Hill. McCook's First Corps, originally seven miles away, was arriving on the field of battle brigade by brigade, and it would be mostly present by early afternoon. Therefore, Buell was apparently concerned for his Second Corps commanded by Crittenden. Because of the extreme drought, Thomas, second-in-command and accompanying Crittenden, had ordered the corps farther south past Haysville to obtain water. Although nominally out of position, the corps was nonetheless only about seven miles away, and it likely could have arrived within a few hours. In fact, it would challenge Wheeler's Cavalry during the eighth. But Buell apparently did not feel it feasible for the Second Corps to arrive in sufficient time to participate in the planned assault.[38]

Remember that both army commanders were greatly confused as to whom they were facing. Buell believed that he was confronting Bragg's combined armies and would need all of his corps present. His proposed line of battle stretched some six miles to accommodate all of his brigades. Not even counting Sill's division, which was en route from the Frankfort area (Dumont's division remained in the vicinity), Buell had some fifty-five thousand troops available to confront only three Rebel divisions, although he did not actually know about the discrepancy. Had he been more aware of this difference, perhaps he would have not postponed the attack. The problem for the Yankees was that he did. As we will see, because of this order to delay, Gilbert initially refused to come to the aid of McCook's corps after Bragg assaulted it. Only after McCook finally convinced Buell of the onslaught on his men did Buell order Gilbert to send help. As noted above, had Maj. Gen. William "Bull" Nelson been in command of the Third Corps, he likely would have ignored the order to postpone and sent aid to McCook.[39]

Of course, Bragg had no knowledge of Buell calling off the assault until the next day. Bragg maintained his erroneous assumption that this Union force was not Buell's main army. He would begin to question that concept later in the day, but until then he continued to make plans to assault the Yankee force present at Perryville. So we have the commanders on both sides of the fighting unaware of the size of their opponent.[40]

Alternate Scenario

Buell's deferment of his planned assault until the next day precluded Crittenden's Second Corps from actively engaging in the battle on the eighth. Had Buell not postponed his attack and ordered Crittenden to continue to advance, the Second Corps, some twenty-two thousand strong, would have easily pushed Wheeler's Cavalry out of the way and marched into Perryville. Continuing to march north, the Second Corps would then have been in position to begin to roll up the Confederate left flank. By late afternoon the Federals could well have closed in on Bragg's three divisions in a pincer movement and possibly soundly defeated them, resulting in the Battle of Perryville becoming a substantial Union victory! This would have forced Bragg to retreat even more quickly than he ultimately did, as he would have had to withdraw to protect his supply base at Camp Breckinridge. In consequence, Kentucky would have unmistakably been under Union control. [41]

CHAPTER 4

THE BATTLE OF PERRYVILLE, OCTOBER 8, 1862

The Battle of Perryville finally began in earnest on the afternoon of October 8, and the fighting evolved differently than either the Union or Confederate commanders had planned. Ten critical decisions dictated the eventual outcome of the battle, which determined the fate of Kentucky in the Civil War.

McCook Strengthens the Union Left (1:00 p.m.–2:00 p.m.)

Situation

While Maj. Gen. Don Carlos Buell contemplated and then postponed his planned attack on the Rebels present at Perryville, his corps continued advancing toward that town. Maj. Gen. Alexander McD. McCook's First Corps was behind schedule, but his troops continued to march from Mackville along the Mackville Road toward their destiny at Perryville. Maj. Gen. Thomas L. Crittenden's Second Corps was also tardy, as it had diverted off course for water late the previous evening under Maj. Gen. George H. Thomas's orders as second-in-command. Nevertheless, this corps finally began its march to Perryville via the Lebanon Pike. "Acting Maj. Gen." Charles C. Gilbert's Third Corps had already assumed position just west of the town and had sustained contact with Brig. Gen. St. John R. Liddell's Confederate brigade. Buell's postponement had not halted his corps' movements.[1]

Maj. Gen. Alexander McD. McCook, USA. Library of Congress.

As the morning progressed, McCook's First Corps continued to advance along the Mackville Road toward Perryville. However, the brigades were strung out along that road and behind schedule. Nonetheless, by 10:30 a.m. McCook's lead brigades had arrived in the general location where the upcoming battle would take place, abreast of Gilbert's Third Corps which was located south of the Mackville Road, along the Springfield Pike. An 1852 West Point graduate, McCook became the highest-ranking of Ohio's fourteen "Fighting McCook's." After serving garrison duty, he then was assigned to duty on the frontier before becoming an instructor in tactics at West Point. During the Civil War, McCook led the First Ohio as its colonel at the Battle of First Bull Run, or Manassas. He commanded a division at Shiloh after his promotion to brigadier general. In July 1862, he was then promoted to the rank of major general. Although young and portly, McCook was nonetheless an aggressive commander.[2]

At Perryville, Buell would need to focus McCook's energy on the correct location. McCook ordered division commander Brig. Gen. Lovell H. Rousseau to advance a portion of his infantry and cavalry and clear the area of any enemy soldiers. Although observing Rebel troops to the south, McCook marked out a line of battle and ordered Rousseau to form on it. Before leaving to report to Buell as ordered, McCook ordered assistant adjutant general Capt. J. A. Campbell to post the men under division commander Brig. Gen. James S. Jackson to the south of the Mackville Road. Jackson's men would be held in column and ready to march to where needed. McCook then rode off to Buell's headquarters by the Dorsey House.[3]

Options

Upon his return, McCook suddenly faced three possible courses of action. One was to place Brig. Gen. William R. Terrill's brigade of Jackson's division in a reserve line behind Rousseau's already established line of battle. A second option was to extend his left flank farther north, tying it to Col. George Webster's brigade of Jackson's division, which had arrived and been placed in the line of battle. Col. Leonard Harris and Capt. Beverly D. Williams, McCook's guide, presented McCook with a third choice: manning what became known as the "Open Knob."[4]

Option 1

McCook's initial option was to reinforce Rousseau's line as a precaution and retain a reserve component with which to confront the enemy. A reserve is defined as the "portion of a body of troops that is kept to the rear, or withheld from action at the beginning of an engagement, in order to be available for a decisive movement." Commanders had the flexibility to dispatch reserves to where they would be most useful. This was common practice in the Civil War. McCook would want the option to support Rousseau, whom he had previously aligned with Gilbert's Third Corps per Buell's orders. Then, if required, McCook would be able to quickly firm up any weak spots that might appear within Rousseau's line. However, Rousseau had disobeyed McCook's orders and advanced his brigades to obtain water in the nearby Chaplin River.[5]

Option 2

Another logical option was for McCook to extend his left flank farther north so the Confederates would not outflank his men. One of the constant fears of commanders was to be outflanked, and both Bragg and McCook were taking precautions against this possibility. By extending his line north from the position occupied by Terrell's brigade, McCook would reduce his chances of being outflanked. However, he would also reduce his available reserve.[6]

Option 3

An unanticipated option presented itself when Rousseau's brigade commander Col. Leonard Harris and McCook's guide Capt. Beverly Williams discovered an elevation some few hundred yards northeast. Quickly named the Open Knob, this eminence provided an excellent command of the surrounding terrain. Including this location in his line would force McCook to relocate at least part of his command. However, the Open Knob's command of the surrounding terrain demanded that it be properly manned by McCook's troops.[7]

Decision

Upon arriving at the Open Knob, McCook quickly realized the tremendous potential of stationing soldiers at this location. He ordered several regiments and Lieut. Charles Parson's eight-gun battery to guard the elevation. McCook's decision to fortify the Open Knob would significantly benefit the Union as the battle opened.[8]

Results/Impact

As just noted, McCook quickly fortified the Open Knob. Prior to this decision, Bragg's plan to reposition Cheatham's Division to begin his assault on McCook's First Corps seemed an excellent one, and it would eventually send Maj. Gen. Simon B. Buckner's and Brig. Gen. J. Patton Anderson's divisions to assist en echelon. However, McCook effectively extended his line on the left flank, changing the flank's actual location. Hence, Cheatham's Division would attack the center of McCook's corps and not its left flank. When Brig. Gen. Daniel S. Donelson's brigade led the offensive, the Confederates received fire on both flanks as well as the center, as will be discussed below. They were ultimately forced to retreat. McCook's decision to fortify the Open Knob was fortuitous in that it helped save his corps from annihilation and an even worse outcome for the Union![9]

Alternate Scenario

If McCook had not repositioned part of his corps to defend the Open Knob and located Parson's independent battery on it, Cheatham could have focused his division on attacking the Union left flank and rolling up the Union line from north to south per Bragg's plan. Augmented by Buckner's and Anderson's Divisions in an en echelon attack, Cheatham's men might have created a real Union disaster at the Battle of Perryville, essentially destroying McCook's First Corps and perhaps scaring off Buell and keeping Bragg in Kentucky for a longer period of time.[10]

Wharton Fails to Fully Discover the Union Left (2:00 p.m.)

Situation

Maj. Gen. Leonidas Polk accompanied Maj. Gen. Benjamin F. Cheatham's division as it marched to reposition on the north of the Confederate battle line. At approximately 1:00 p.m. near the Goodknight House within Walker's Bend, Polk and Cheatham aligned the division in a column of brigades in preparation for the attack ordered by Gen. Braxton Bragg. Cheatham designated Brig. Gen. Daniel S. Donelson's brigade of a little over one thousand men to lead the attack, and the brigades of Brig. Gen. Alexander P. Stewart and Brig. Gen. George Maney were to follow. Donelson's force was understrength because Cheatham had assigned two of his regiments, the Eighth Tennessee and the Fifty-First Tennessee, to protect Capt. William Carnes's battery, which was dueling with several Union batteries. While Donelson's veterans were shorthanded, Cheatham probably reasoned that they would nonetheless have an easy time rolling up the Union left flank. Yet as the assault commenced, Donelson would simply have lost additional men and been unable to sustain the assault. Col. John Savage, commanding the Sixteenth Tennessee in Donelson's Brigade, later wrote that he believed that this assault meant certain death for him and his men. Cheatham realized that Carnes's battery armed with smoothbores was ineffective. He replaced it with Capt. Thomas J. Stanford's rifled battery, initially keeping the same two regiments out of the upcoming attack while they protected Stanford.[11]

About this time Col. John H. Wharton and his cavalry brigade provided Polk an important update. Before the war Wharton practiced law in Texas. He joined Terry's Texas Rangers as a captain and, after the death of its commander, eventually became its leader. After being wounded at the Battle of Shiloh, and following the 1862 Kentucky Campaign, Wharton would eventually be promoted to brigadier general and major general. The ambitious officer generally performed well. After following Cheatham's men, Wharton had

Col. John H. Warton, CSA.
Photographic History, Vol. X.

just conducted a reconnaissance on the extreme Union left around the small Wilson's Creek, slightly north of the Mackville Road, when he observed additional Union troops there. Col. George Webster's brigade attached to Brig. Gen James S. Jackson was advancing along that road toward the Union line.[12]

Polk received Wharton's report with alarm, as Cheatham was already overdue to begin the attack. However, if Wharton's information was correct, Polk must further realign Cheatham for his assault to be successful and wait until Webster's men were in position. If Cheatham attacked from his present location, the Union force would outflank him, and he would likely fail. Therefore, Polk decided to disobey Bragg's command to attack until he could likewise reposition Cheatham and better align him for the upcoming strike. Of course, this consumed additional time and further irritated Bragg when he rode up to ascertain the reason for the delay. However, Bragg had to agree that shifting Cheatham was necessary in order to accommodate his plan of attack, which we will discuss in relation to the following critical decision.[13]

Options

After Wharton reported his discovery to Polk and Cheatham, Polk ordered him to determine the location of the Union left flank again, and off he went. Wharton now had two options: he could make a final observation before guarding the extended Confederate right flank, or he could continue to closely monitor the Union left flank for additional arrivals.[14]

Option 1

As discussed previously, orders were orders and Wharton had no choice but to obey them. Polk knew that he must ascertain the location of the Union left flank in order to attack it, as we will learn in discussion of the next critical decision. He had no reason to disobey Polk.[15]

Option 2

Wharton's second option was to proactively monitor the Union left flank for any changes. As noted, its location directly affected Bragg's proposed Rebel attack. Failure to identify the Federals' left would place Cheatham's Division in a vulnerable situation.[16]

Decision

Wharton chose Option 1 and decided to make a final observation before relocating to a position from which to observe additional Union reinforcements.[17]

Results/Impact

Wharton's decision caused Cheatham's attack to go astray. Wharton briefly headed north before turning south. As his command moved south, it forced back Union pickets on the ridge to the southwest, above Walker's Bend. Then the Rebels encountered two companies of the Thirty-Third Ohio that McCook had dispatched to the Chaplin River to obtain water. Although surprised, the Ohioans managed to fire at Wharton, who quickly changed direction once again and departed to the north. Believing that he complied with Polk's orders, Wharton led his men to a location on the Benton Road a mile and a half from the Dixville Crossroads. He eventually operated on Maney's right flank, protecting it. Bragg's two brigades of Rebel cavalry, commanded by Wharton and Col. Joseph Wheeler, were consistently underused to determine the exact size and location of his enemy during the campaign.[18]

Wharton apparently observed no more than a few men on the Open Knob as his command proceeded north. He was too early to observe Union reinforcements arriving to the north; these troops would fundamentally change the location and strength of the Union left flank. Historian Kenneth Noe attributes the failure of Wharton's final reconnaissance to "timing, topography, and perhaps fate." Therefore, had Wharton delayed slightly, he might have witnessed the changing position of the Union left flank and continued to monitor it. This information was crucial to Bragg, Polk, and especially Cheatham. Wharton's failure to update the Confederate command resulted in Cheatham's initial attack failing, as we will see next.[19]

Alternate Scenario

Had Wharton observed these additional Union troops reinforcing the new Union left flank and relayed that information to Polk and Cheatham, Cheatham could have once again realigned his attack directly at the new flank. His chances of success would have improved greatly had he directed his assault more accurately at the new Federal left flank. Wharton might well have much more quickly driven the Yankees back to what would be labeled Starkweather's Hill, perhaps allowing the final collapse of McCook's corps.[20]

Cheatham Orders Maney's and Stewart's Brigades to Assist Donelson (2:30 p.m.–4:00 p.m.)

Situation

Braxton Bragg had made the critical decision to engage the pursuing Union force on the night of October 7, when he ordered Polk to proceed back to

Perryville with Cheatham's Division and confront the enemy the next morning. Highly annoyed at Polk for disregarding his orders to attack, Bragg continued preparing for an assault on the Federals near the town. Further irritated by Polk's disposition of the troops, Bragg quickly realized that the Rebel right could easily be flanked. Therefore, he needed to first relocate Cheatham's Division to near Walker's Bend, which delayed the attack. Upon moving Cheatham from the town some two miles north to a point near Walker's Bend, Polk belatedly convinced Cheatham, based on updated observation, that his men had to further relocate to be able to strike the Union left flank. Once Cheatham was in position, Bragg, through Polk, ordered him forward.[21]

"Ben" Cheatham had served in the Mexican-American War and became major general of the Tennessee State Militia. He drank heavily, but his men adored him and still revered him as a soldier's soldier and a combat commander. Bragg planned for Cheatham to attack en echelon. Echelon is defined as "a formation in which its subdivisions are placed one behind another, with a lateral and even spacing to the same side." In this situation Cheatham's Division was the formation involved, and his three brigades under Donelson's, Stewart's, and Maney's Commands were the subdivisions. Once Cheatham attacked, he was to roll up the Union line brigade by brigade, and then Hardee would advance and attempt to kill, wound, or capture whoever was left.[22]

Meanwhile, the situation changed on the Union left. McCook had extended his line farther north and had fortified the Open Knob. As discussed

Maj. Gen. Benjamin F. Cheatham, CSA. Library of Congress.

Brig. Gen. Daniel S. Donelson, CSA. Photographic History, Vol. X.

above, Wharton had cleared an intervening ridge, but for one reason or another, he had failed to ascertain the extension of the Union left. Bragg's, Polk's, and Cheatham's plan was now jeopardized. Whereas Cheatham wanted to initiate his assault on what he thought was the Union left, the attack was actually directed to McCook's center.[23]

At approximately 2:15 p.m., following orders, Cheatham directed Donelson to initiate the attack. Although unhappy, Donelson complied. He was handicapped because he had been stripped of two of his five regiments, the Eighth Tennessee and the Fifty-First Tennessee, which had been ordered to protect Carnes's Tennessee battery while it engaged in an artillery duel with several of McCook's batteries. However, even if Donelson had regained his two missing regiments, they would not have significantly changed the result as the assault unfolded. Cheatham apparently expected Donelson's Brigade to easily roll up the Union left flank. Unfortunately for Cheatham and the Rebels, he was quite incorrect! Initially covered by an intervening ridge, Donelson's men encountered a terrible sight once they crested it: they quickly received fire as expected from the center, but also from both flanks. The Confederates were in an untenable situation.[24]

Options

While Donelson and the remainder of his brigade advanced into a maelstrom, Cheatham had to quickly deal with four options. He could not simply allow

Open Knob today, Perryville Battlefield State Historic Site. Photo by the author.

Donelson's Brigade to be shot to pieces. Cheatham could recall Donelson at once, before his unit was destroyed, or he could quickly reinforce Donelson with Stewart's and Maney's Brigades. Alternatively, Cheatham could order Stewart and Maney to assault the newly discovered force situated on and around the Open Knob. A final option was to attempt to reinforce Donelson while also attacking those units around the Open Knob.[25]

Option 1

Logically, Cheatham's first thought might be to recall Donelson before he lost a good portion of his remaining regiments. While this course of action would preserve at least some of Donelson's troops, it would obviously stall, if not stop, the designated plan Bragg had devised and ordered. With Bragg already displeased enough at his commanders, Cheatham probably wasted little time considering this option.[26]

Option 2

Standard practice would be for Cheatham to quickly order any and all reserve units to advance to aid those under fire. This option would not roll up the Union left flank, but the additional firepower would possibly help advance the Rebels into the midst of McCook's line and push it back. However, before that could happen the Confederates would take significant casualties.[27]

Option 3

Once Cheatham discerned the new location of the Union left, and particularly of Capt. Charles Parson's independent battery playing havoc with Donelson's right flank, an assault on this position might eventually result in the capture or retreat of the Union forces there. A successful assault here would eliminate the enfilading fire onto Donelson's Brigade. However, this offensive would also commit Cheatham's reserve.[28]

Option 4

Utilizing Options 2 and 3, Cheatham could attempt to support Donelson directly or indirectly while also trying to eliminate the Union left flank's ability to inflict such slaughter on Donelson. Although using all of Cheatham's Division that was present, this option might successfully accomplish both goals.[29]

Decision

Cheatham quickly chose Option 4 and ordered Maney's Brigade to march more northerly and assault the Open Knob from the west through to the

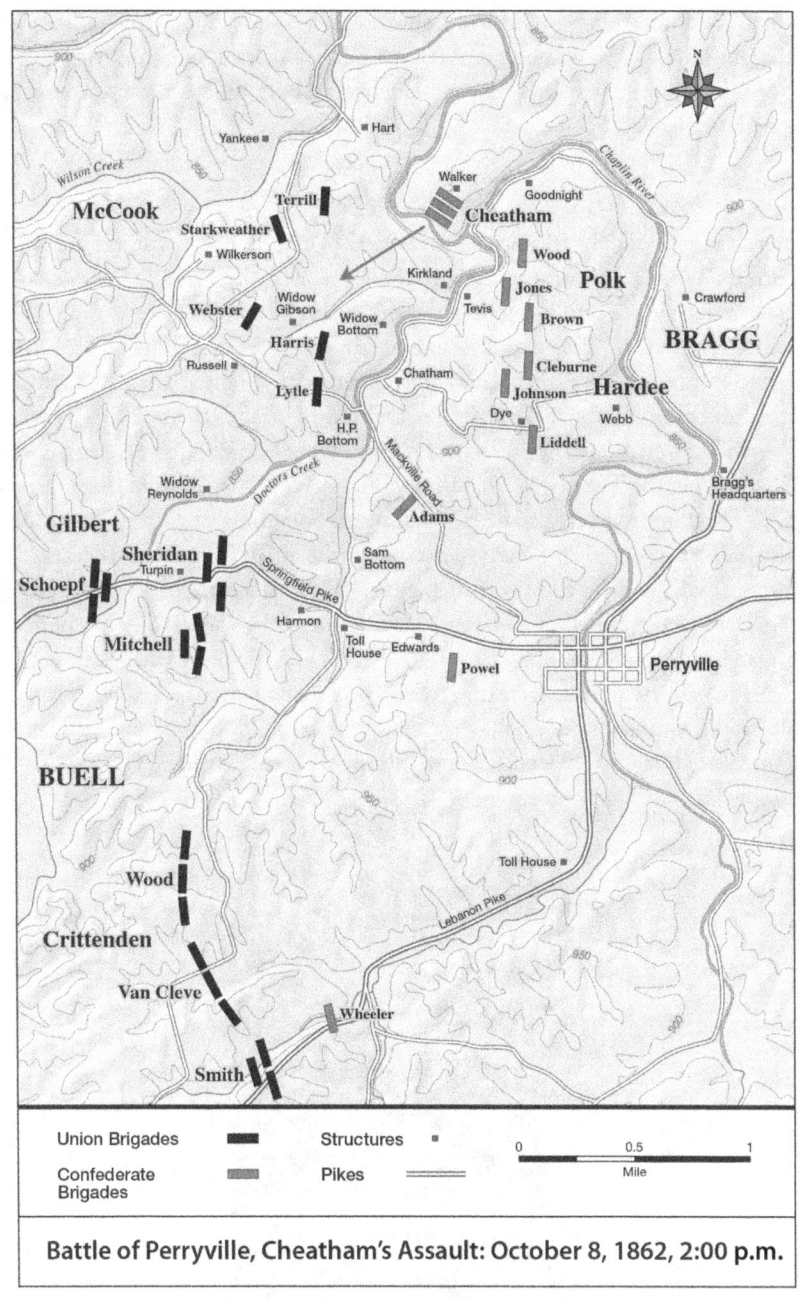

Battle of Perryville, Cheatham's Assault: October 8, 1862, 2:00 p.m.

north. Simultaneously, he ordered Stewart to advance to assist Donelson by plugging the gap that appeared between Maney's and Donelson's Brigades. Cheatham hoped that these movements would help relieve the fire concentrated at Donelson.[30]

Results/Impact

Stewart immediately advanced his brigade of almost 1,500 soldiers to support Donelson. Specifically, he marched the Fourth, Fifth, and Twenty-Fourth Tennessee into the gap between Donelson and Maney, keeping the Thirty-First and Thirty-Third Tennessee in reserve. The Fourth and Fifth marched toward the Open Knob and joined with Maney's men to capture Parson's battery and drive off the Federal forces located there. The Twenty-Fourth Tennessee, on Stewart's left, assisted Donelson's Sixteenth Tennessee in assaulting the Twenty-Fourth Illinois and driving it back from its position some two hundred yards south of the Open Knob. Stewart then directed the Thirty-Third Tennessee to advance next to the Fifth Tennessee and attack the Federals, and he commanded the Thirty-First Tennessee to also attack the Twenty-Fourth Illinois. Eventually supported by Donelson's regrouped brigade and Brig. Gen. Sterling A. M. Wood's brigade of Hardee's left wing, the Thirty-First and Thirty-Third Tennessee joined to attack Col. George Webster's Union brigade and eventually assisted in the capture of Capt. Samuel J. Harris's Nineteenth Battery, Indiana Light Artillery.[31]

Brig. Gen. Alexander P. Stewart, CSA.
Photographic History, Vol. X.

October 8, 1862

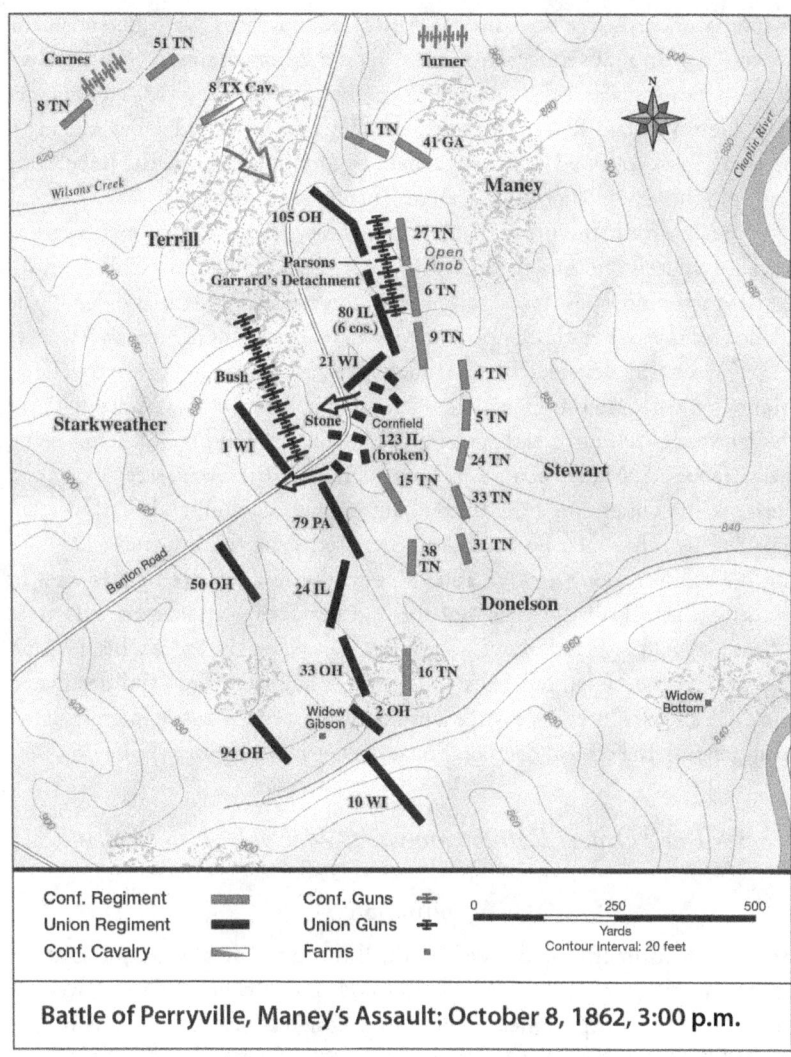

Battle of Perryville, Maney's Assault: October 8, 1862, 3:00 p.m.

Meanwhile, Maney led his brigade on his new assignment to eliminate the concentrated Federal force on and around the Open Knob. Once northwest of the Open Knob, he arranged his brigade with the Ninth Tennessee on his left, the Sixth Tennessee in the middle, and the Forty-First Georgia on his right, backed up with the First and Twenty-Seventh Tennessee. Capt. Melancthon Smith's Mississippi battery, consisting of four guns and temporarily commanded by Lieut. William B. Turner, joined in support on Maney's right. The brigade advanced steadily until reaching a wooden rail fence, where it stalled under heavy fire. The 123rd Illinois and 105th Ohio defended the Open Knob and moved forward of it. Union division commander Brig. Gen. James S. Jackson was killed during this combat, adding to brigade commander Brig. Gen. William R. Terrill's worries. After a concentrated volley, the 105th broke and ran, followed by Maney's men. By around 3:00 p.m. the Rebels had captured the Open Knob and seven of Parson's eight guns.[32]

After clearing the Open Knob of Yankees, Maney's men continued to advance southwest into the adjoining cornfield. However, Col. John C. Starkweather, now positioned southeast of this field on what would quickly be labeled Starkweather's Hill, opened fire with twelve cannon. The raw Twenty-First Wisconsin defended the cornfield. Yet after firing only two volleys, Maney's men routed it. Cheatham's Division continued to advance with all three brigades to Starkweather's position on and around his hill. After being twice repulsed, Maney sent Col. Hume Feild's First Tennessee to try and outflank the Union line. The third charge was successful, and Starkweather rounded up what men he could and prepared for a final defense. Deploying his soldiers along a ridge and stone wall a few hundred yards west of Starkweather's Hill, he prepared for another Rebel attack. By this time Cheatham had suffered about 40 percent casualties. However, his division had pushed the Union left back some twelve hundred yards and decimated McCook's First Corps. We will examine this part of the battle in more detail in addressing the critical decision Starkweather made later in the day.[33]

Buell Orders Reinforcements to McCook (4:00 p.m.)

Situation

Because of his injury the day before, Buell remained mostly immobile at his headquarters by the Dorsey House, located only a couple of miles west of Perryville on the Springfield Pike. Given Buell's location, historians find his inability to hear the battle raging a few miles north of Perryville, where McCook's First Corps initially fought frantically to resist Cheatham's attack, astonishing. Scholars attribute this lack of recognition to the phenomenon labeled acoustic shadow. Somehow, weather conditions can occasionally prevent sound from carrying, and it happened in this instance. Buell had heard some firing at first but dismissed it as of no concern. Before Cheatham assaulted his corps, McCook rode to Buell's headquarters around noon to report. McCook did not request support until later in the afternoon, and some historians criticize him for waiting so long to ask for help. According to McCook, at 3:30 p.m. he ordered staff officer Maj. Caleb Bates to ride to Buell's headquarters to call for reinforcements. McCook also ordered Capt. Horace Fisher to locate the nearest commander and request support, which turned out to be Brig. Gen. Albin F. Schoepf's First Division of Gilbert's Third Corps, followed shortly by another staff officer, Capt. W. T. Hoblitzell.[34]

At approximately 4:00 p.m. Captain Fisher notified Buell of the assault on McCook's First Corps. Needless to say, Buell was astonished! He had expected no major fighting after he had issued his postponement order earlier, as previously discussed. He now had to make a decision.[35]

Options

Faced with this new information, Buell must decide whether to believe the report and how to respond to it at some level. One option was to request further information before sending support. A second option was to send minimal reinforcements. A third possibility was to send a large command to reinforce McCook.[36]

Option 1

Perhaps still taken aback, Buell could request more information as to the magnitude of the fighting and, more specifically, exactly where it was taking place. He then could make a more rational decision as to what units should be ordered to support McCook. While Buell certainly had troops available, he was unaware of precisely how many McCook required. The drawback was that by seeking further information, Buell would waste precious time, which would only add to McCook's woes.[37]

Option 2

Based on McCook's message requesting assistance, Buell could immediately order some reinforcements to him. This would not require a large deployment of troops, and it might well give McCook all the support he needed. Sending backup troops would require minimal time and might be the difference between success and failure.[38]

Option 3

Possibly erring on the side of caution, Buell could order a significant force to immediately march to McCook's aid. Sending perhaps two divisions or more should eliminate any concern that McCook could not confront and defeat the Rebels attacking him. While this solution would consume some additional time, the end result might be a victory for the Union. However, it might upset Buell's plans for the all-out attack tomorrow.[39]

Decision

After a few minutes of deliberation, Buell chose the second option. He ordered Gilbert to send two brigades from Schoepf's division to reinforce McCook if McCook's men were actually involved in heavy fighting.[40]

Results/Impact

In spite of Buell's disbelief that McCook was fighting for his very survival, Buell directed to Gilbert to reinforce McCook with two brigades. Gilbert was concerned with the safety of his Third Corps (as discussed below), and he only reluctantly agreed, giving the assignment to Schoepf. Schoepf, in turn, gave the task to Brig. Gen. James Steedman's and then Col. Michael Gooding's brigades, both of which marched rapidly to assist their brothers in the First Corps. The reinforcements set off at about 4:45 p.m. and arrived at McCook's location by 5:30 p.m. This small relief force would make a significant difference in how the battle ended. Ultimately, these brigades shored up McCook's beleaguered defense and helped to form the final Union line as the fighting wound down for the day.[41]

After the fighting ceased for the evening, both brigades retreated slightly, remaining southwest of the Mackville Road and the Dixville Crossroads, forming the southern end of McCook's final line. The critical appearance of these two brigades, as well as Capt. Ebenezer Gay's cavalry, helped to stem what could easily have become a rout of McCook's corps. The units' participation in the early evening fighting solidified the Union position.[42]

Alternate Scenario

Had Buell refused to believe reports of significant fighting in McCook's part of the potential battlefield, he would not have dispatched reinforcements. Without Gooding's and Steedman's brigades in support, McCook might well have been overrun, losing more troops and suffering a much more significant repulse and an even greater tactical victory for the Rebels. Yet this circumstance probably would not have changed the overall outcome. Bragg would have quickly realized he was probably facing Buell's main army, which he could not hope to defeat with the limited force he had present at Perryville.[43]

October 8, 1862

Buckner Orders Adams to Break the Deadlock at the Bottom House (4:00 p.m.)

Situation

The two brigades of Col. Thomas M. Jones and Brig. Gen. John C. Brown, which belonged to Brig. Gen. J. Patton Anderson's division, were stationed just to the south, next to the left of Cheatham's Division. For whatever reason, Anderson positioned himself on the south end of the Rebel line monitoring his other two brigades, commanded by Brig. Gen. Daniel W. Adams and Col. Samuel Powel. Jones and Brown were thus left on their own. Jones covered the line between Cheatham to the north and Maj. Gen. Simon B. Buckner's division to the south. After observing Cheatham's departure from the plan of battle as he contended with the Union forces controlling the Open Knob, Jones advanced into the fray around 3:00 p.m., apparently under his own initiative. Brown followed him around 3:30. After moving forward and engaging in a brief fight against Col. Leonard Harris's Ninth Brigade and Capt. Peter Simonson's Fifth Indiana Light Battery, first Jones and then Brown were repulsed, and they retreated back out of range of Union fire. Interestingly, just before Jones and Brown advanced, Capt. Charles L. Lumsden's Battery F, Second Alabama Light Artillery fired on Simonson's battery located on Loomis's Heights. The shells hit an intervening ridge, causing no harm to Simonson.[44]

Likewise, observing Cheatham's desperate fighting for the Open Knob,

Henry P. Bottom House, Perryville Battlefield State Historic Site. Photo by the author.

Hardee, commanding the left wing, ordered Buckner to advance his division into the battle per Bragg's plan. Buckner commanded four brigades led by Brig. Gens. St. John R. Liddell, Patrick R. Cleburne, Bushrod R. Johnson, and Sterling A. M. Wood. His mission was attacking west up the Mackville Road, passing by Henry P. Bottom's house as he did so. Adams's Brigade of Anderson's Division, which was located south of the Mackville Road, was also available for this endeavor. Buckner launched his attack in a column of brigades. Johnson led the assault, Cleburne followed, and Wood's troops moved northwesterly to augment Brown's Brigade. Liddell's Brigade temporarily remained in reserve. The fighting quickly centered around the Bottom House, whose low stone walls provided some shelter to the advancing Rebels. Col. William Lytle's Seventeenth Brigade put up strong resistance, with some of his regiments running out of ammunition, as did some of the Confederates.[45]

Options

At this point the Confederate attack had come to a standstill. As the senior commander on scene, Buckner realized that he needed to do something. Buckner grew up in Munfordville, Kentucky, graduated from West Point in 1844, and had won two brevets in the Mexican-American War. Stuck with surrendering Fort Donelson after Gens. John Floyd and Gideon Pillow fled, he was nevertheless widely respected and a well-known Kentuckian. The Army of the Mississippi welcomed Buckner's presence. He assisted in Col. John

Maj. Gen. Simon B. Buckner, CSA. Library of Congress.

October 8, 1862

Wilder's surrender at Munfordville by showing him Bragg's entire army, which surrounded the Union position guarding the railroad bridge there. Buckner had the option of calling for a retreat in order to regroup and perhaps attack at a different location. He could also augment his attacking force. Finally, he could seek help and advice from Hardee as to what new action to take.[46]

Option 1

Although unsatisfactory to Rebel desires, one option was to retreat, regroup, and resupply the engaged Rebel brigades. Once these tasks were completed, the brigades could be relaunched in another attack on McCook's corps in anticipation of a more successful outcome. While this process would take time and effort, a revived large-scale attack might succeed where the original one had failed to break the Union lines.[47]

Option 2

Buckner realized that Adams's Brigade of Anderson's Division was available and located just south of the Mackville Road. He could order this unit to advance and potentially outflank the Union line positioned near and around the Bottom House. Assuming that Buckner could successfully direct them into a good offensive position, Adams's nearly two thousand men might provide just enough additional firepower to help break the entrenched Yankees.[48]

Option 3

Perhaps unsure of what else to do, Buckner could ask Hardee for assistance. This option would take time as well, and other than Liddell's Brigade and Brig. Gen. Preston Smith's brigade guarding Perryville itself, no fresh forces were available.[49]

Decision

Buckner quickly chose Option 2 and ordered Adams to assist in the assault around the Bottom House.[50]

Results/Impact

The addition of Adams's Brigade gave the Confederates just enough additional combat power to break the Union line of Lytle's brigade and force it back almost a mile to near the Dixville Crossroads. McCook's corps was in a dire predicament—if it could not somehow stop this Confederate advance, it might well be crushed. McCook tried to regroup.[51]

The Battle of Perryville

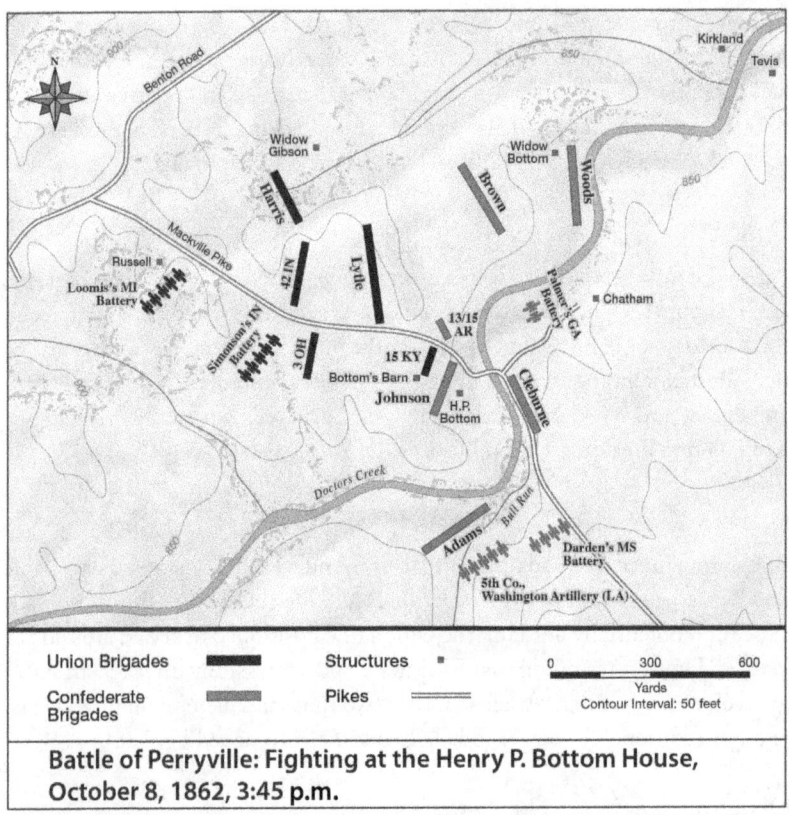

Battle of Perryville: Fighting at the Henry P. Bottom House, October 8, 1862, 3:45 p.m.

As Adams's Brigade advanced, it took fire from Sheridan's batteries and was forced to retreat. However, Hardee quickly ordered the brigade back into the assault. By 5:00 p.m. McCook desperately worked to set up some kind of defensive line. Buckner's use of Adams's Brigade broke the stalemate around the Bottom House, pushed the Union line back almost a mile, and greatly contributed to the Confederate tactical victory.[52]

Powel Is Ordered to Make a Reconnaissance in Force (4:15 p.m.)

Situation

While Cheatham's Division to the north and Buckner's Division just south of it fought extensively, so, too, did Anderson's Division. Jones's and Brown's

Brigades joined the battle just south of Cheatham, and Buckner dispatched Adams's Brigade of Anderson's Division to break the logjam at the Bottom House, as we just saw above. This left Anderson's last brigade, that of Col. Samuel Powel guarding Perryville and positioned west of the town on and just south of the Springfield Pike, other than Smith's, as the only one not yet involved in the battle. Adams was much annoyed, as he expected this unit to advance with his brigade. This would quickly change.[53]

As the afternoon wore on, Bragg received information from Wheeler, who was operating on the Lebanon Pike, that an additional concentration of the enemy might well be situated south and west of Perryville. As the battle continued, Bragg began to wonder whether he was indeed facing a larger Union force than he anticipated. He now needed to make a decision.[54]

Options

Bragg needed to ascertain whether additional Union forces were advancing to confront him. One option was to order Powel's small brigade to perform a reconnaissance west of Perryville. Bragg's second choice was to leave Powel in position in case a force of Yankees suddenly appeared. Powel could hold these enemy troops in place in order to protect Bragg's left flank.[55]

Option 1

Bragg's first option was to order Powel to make a reconnaissance in force west of Perryville in order to determine the presence of any additional Union forces in the area. This intelligence would provide Bragg with a more comprehensive vision of what enemy forces he faced, or would face. However, the reconnaissance would reduce protection on his left flank. Wheeler's small cavalry and Preston Smith's brigade in Perryville were the only units available if the Rebel left needed protection from a new advancing Union force.[56]

Option 2

Concerned over possible Union forces approaching his left flank, Bragg could keep Powel's Brigade in position as both a protective and a warning force in case additional Federals were advancing from that direction. Bragg needed additional time to finish off McCook's corps and did not want surprise in the form of a Union flank attack. He was not expecting any real opposition on his left.[57]

Decision

Around 4:00 p.m. Bragg decided to order Powel to conduct what amounted to a reconnaissance in force to the west along the Springfield Pike. Apparently the order was conveyed to Anderson, who in turn sent Powel westward.[58]

Results/Impact

Capt. Overton W. Barrett's (Confederate) Missouri battery had opened fire on Capt. Henry Hescock's Battery G, First Missouri (Union) Light Artillery, which belonged to Sheridan, on Peters Hill around 3:30 p.m. Buell, who was next to the Dorsey House, finally heard this action. Powel moved out about 4:15 to conduct his reconnaissance in force and silence Hescock's battery, believing it to be unsupported. Powel's Brigade consisted of three regiments: the Twenty-Ninth Tennessee advanced, centered initially on the Springfield Pike, while the Forty-Fifth Alabama pressed forward just south of the Twenty-Ninth, and the Twenty-Fourth Mississippi followed behind as a reserve. Powel's Brigade marched unknowingly into a huge trap.[59]

Totally unaware that they were marching directly toward Gilbert's Third Corps, the men of Powel's Brigade would soon confront fourteen Union regiments! Sheridan observed Powel's advance and realigned his division to better repel him. He relocated Hescock's battery and a section of Capt. Charles M. Barnett's Battery I, Illinois Light Artillery south of the Springfield Pike. In addition, Sheridan positioned Col. Daniel McCook's brigade near the crest of Peters Hill and shifted Col. Nicholas Greusel's and Lieut. Col. Bernard Laiboldt's brigades south of the road as well, accompanied by two additional batteries. Division commander Brig. Gen. Robert Mitchell also brought forward two of his brigades. As a result, Powel unknowingly advanced into a real firestorm.[60]

After trading several volleys with the Yankees and even bringing up the Twenty-Fourth Mississippi, Powel stood no chance of success. He quickly retreated, leaving a significant number of casualties. While Powel's reconnaissance in force certainly verified that additional Federal units were present west of Perryville, his confrontation with them in turn captured Gilbert's and Sheridan's undivided attention and forced them to focus on the possibility of further Rebel attacks against their position. This helped disrupt their awareness of the assault against McCook just to their left flank, and to further confuse them as to the strength of the Confederate force they faced. In turn, Powel's movement prevented Gilbert's and Sheridan's advance. In addition, Powel also prohibited the Federal officers' potential attack of the Confederate left flank from the south, which could possibly have overwhelmed Bragg's

October 8, 1862

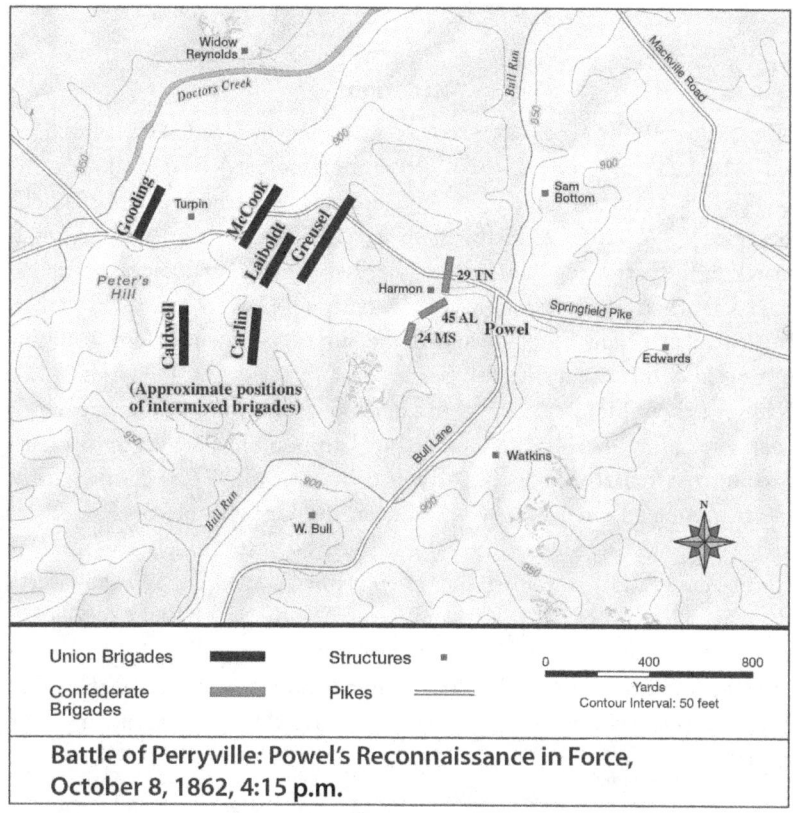

Battle of Perryville: Powel's Reconnaissance in Force, October 8, 1862, 4:15 p.m.

force, as discussed below. This could have changed the tactical winner of the battle.[61]

Alternate Scenario

If Bragg had held Powel in position to protect his left flank, the aggressive Sheridan and Mitchell could conceivably have convinced Gilbert to allow a reconnaissance of their own. As discussed next, Gilbert continued to insist on remaining in position per his orders from Buell. Yet the absence of additional Confederate brigades east of Gilbert's location might have changed his mind. Had "Bull" Nelson remained alive and in command of the Third Corps, the outcome might well have been much different. This Union force might then have been able to assault Bragg's left flank and roll it up, or it might have outflanked him, threatening his supply base at Camp Breckinridge.[62]

Starkweather Holds the Union Left (4:30 p.m.)

Situation

While Powel's Brigade advanced and became engaged with Sheridan's and Mitchell's divisions at the south end of the battlefield, Col. John C. Starkweather remained under constant fire on the northern end of the field. Because of a delay in receiving supplies, Starkweather's brigade began its march to the battleground after the other two brigades and joined the action after Cheatham's assault had begun. A practicing lawyer from Milwaukee, Starkweather originally commanded the First Wisconsin before assuming command of the Twenty-Eighth Brigade in Rousseau's Third Division. Little is known about him, but throughout much of the war his seniors apparently considered him a good brigade commander. This unit had not yet proven itself in combat. After arriving on the battlefield, Starkweather's men briefly assisted in attempting to repel Maney's assault on the Open Knob. Starkweather's Twenty-Eighth Brigade consisted of the Twenty-Fourth Illinois, the Seventy-Ninth Pennsylvania, the First and Twenty-First Wisconsin, and the Fourth Battery, Indiana Light Artillery, and Battery A, Kentucky Light Artillery, a total of approximately 2,500 men. However, the Twenty-Eighth had already suffered significant losses while trying to defend the area around the Open Knob. Instinctively, Starkweather placed his brigade on the Union far left on a small hill.[63]

Col. John C. Starkweather, USA.
Photographic History, Vol. X.

As Brig. Gen. William R. Terrill's Thirty-Third Brigade broke and fled off of and around the Open Knob, Starkweather quickly came under fire. His raw Twenty-First Wisconsin, positioned just east of the Benton Road at the western edge of a cornfield extending east toward the Open Knob, managed to get off a couple of volleys before being overrun by Maney's Brigade, now at reduced strength but augmented with Stewart's Fourth and Fifth Tennessee. Rebels soon occupied the cornfield, forcing Starkweather and Terrill back across the Benton Road. Starkweather had stationed Capt. Asahel K. Bush's Fourth Battery, Indiana Light Artillery and Capt. David C. Stone's Battery A, Kentucky Light Artillery on a ridge or small hill just west of the Benton Road, quickly labeled Starkweather's Hill. With six cannon each, these two batteries fired canister as fast as possible at the attacking Rebel force. Joined by remnants of his regiments, Starkweather briefly held his hill. Adding to the chaos was Rebel Capt. William W. Carnes's Tennessee battery, which moved near the Benton Road and provided counter–battery fire. By 3:45 p.m., after several Union assaults, Starkweather was forced to retreat from his hill.[64]

Options

As the Rebel assaults against Starkweather's position on and around his hill finally compelled him and his men to retreat, he could choose from two options. The colonel could continue to retreat to a safe location far enough in the rear where he could attempt to regroup his shattered brigade, or he could try and make another stand against the ever-persistent Rebels.[65]

Option 1

Starkweather had been heavily engaged for well over an hour and had sustained significant casualties in the fighting. Forced to withdraw, he logically needed to move far enough west to remain disengaged from the enemy while attempting to regroup and refit his men. Also, the colonel needed to guard what artillery he had managed to remove from Starkweather's Hill in order to keep it from falling into the Rebels' possession.[66]

Option 2

Starkweather's second option was to once again relocate to a defensible position and attempt to hold the Union left flank. This was a riskier choice, but if the Union left was driven back far enough, the Dixville Crossroads could eventually fall into Confederate hands. In that case, Union supplies could potentially be cut off, and McCook's First Corps might possibly be destroyed.

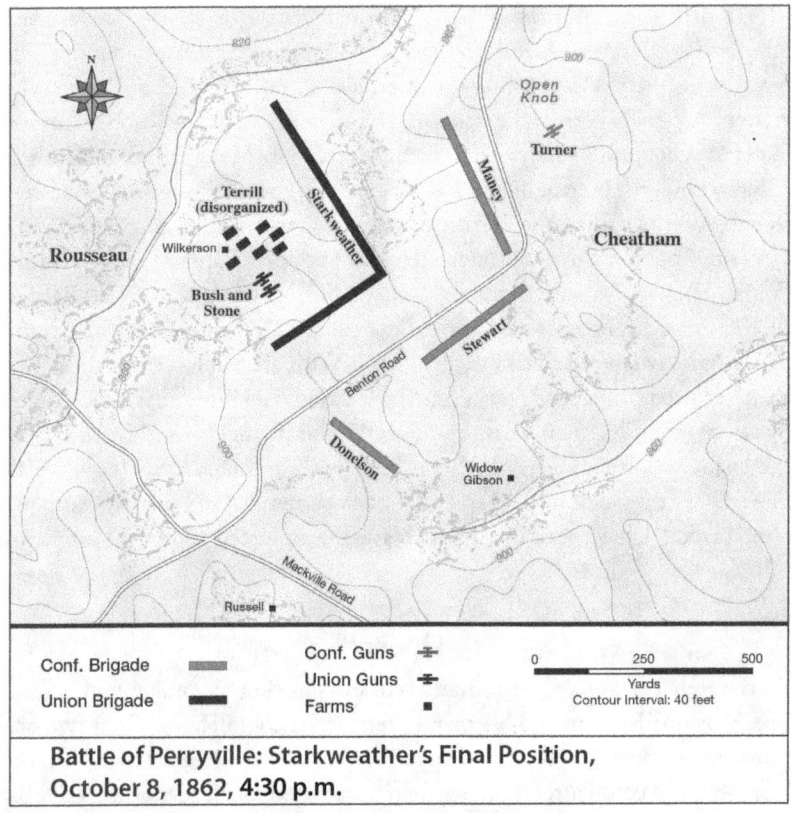

Battle of Perryville: Starkweather's Final Position, October 8, 1862, 4:30 p.m.

Fortunately, the local terrain provided good additional defensive positions for another stand.[67]

Decision

As Starkweather fell back off of his hill, he discovered the remnants of Terrill's brigade regrouping some three hundred yards west, along another small ridge and partially along a low stone fence. He decided to have his men join with Terrill's and attempt to hold that position. Hopefully, the combined brigades could withstand at least one more Rebel charge.[68]

Results/Impact

By 4:30 p.m. Starkweather and his remaining fighters joined Terrill and then managed to repulse Maney's Brigade and part of Stewart's Brigade. The

Confederate units were charging the third position held by the Union far left that afternoon. Resistance from Federals, coupled with the thorough fatigue of Maney's and Stewart's Confederates, resulted in the Rebels being unable to carry the position. The Confederate assault on the Union left flank was over: even though the Union would temporarily lose control of the Dixville Crossroads, Starkweather had held on and saved the Federal left flank![69]

Starkweather paid a heavy price for his defense of the Union left flank. The Seventy-Ninth Pennsylvania and First and Twenty-First Wisconsin all suffered 50 percent casualties, while the Twenty-Fourth Illinois escaped with only 30 percent casualties. However, Starkweather had saved McCook from disaster, for which McCook was grateful. The Confederate losses in Maney's and Stewart's Brigades were almost as terrible. Many historians label Starkweather's ability to stop the Rebels, along with the assistance of Gooding and Steedman discussed below, as the "high-water mark" of the western Confederacy. Whether or not the reader agrees, while Bragg technically won the battle tactically, this was as far as his troops would take him in Kentucky.[70]

Alternate Scenario

Had Starkweather abandoned the battle in order to save his brigade from more casualties, McCook's corps would have faced disaster. If the Rebels had overrun Terrill's damaged brigade, McCook, losing control of the Dixville Crossroads, could have been cut off from the rest of the Union army and possibly forced to surrender. This outcome would have been at best a disaster, thereby furthering Bragg's tactical victory.[71]

Gilbert Refuses to Let Mitchell Advance into Perryville (5:00 p.m.)

Situation

After Powel's advance and retreat, Sheridan returned his attention to the continued fighting done by McCook's corps. However, Mitchell advanced in pursuit of Powel and rapidly moved toward Perryville. Remember that around 11:00 a.m. Buell postponed his planned attack until the next day. Gilbert had lunch with Buell, so Gilbert was well aware of his orders to hold his position until the Second Corps arrived, meaning that the coordinated attack would not take place until the next morning, September 9.[72]

Brig. Gen. Robert D. Mitchell was a territorial legislator from Kansas, and as colonel leading the Second Kansas he was severely wounded at the Battle

Brig. Gen. Robert D. Mitchell, USA.
Library of Congress.

of Wilson's Creek. He considered himself an aggressive commander and now maintained that he could capture Perryville. Mitchell ordered Col. William P. Carlin to lead his brigade (of Mitchell's division) east in pursuit of Powel, who had retreated back across Bull Run into the town of Perryville. When Carlin reached the western edge of Perryville, he ordered Capt. William Hotchkiss's Second Battery, Minnesota Light Artillery to open fire on downtown, further encouraging Powel's soldiers to hustle through town. Carlin then ordered his Twenty-First and Thirty-Eighth Illinois into Perryville. However, Rebel resistance stiffened as Brig. Gen. Preston Smith's brigade, in reserve defending Perryville, opened fire. Barrett's Missouri and Capt. Henry C. Semple's Alabama batteries opened up against Hotchkiss's men, resulting in a noisy confrontation. Also, the Thirty-Eighth Illinois captured a wagon train of ammunition destined for Capt. Cuthbert H. Slocomb's Fifth Company, Washington Artillery, belonging to Adams's Brigade. Mitchell thus saw more opportunity.[73]

Options

While he actually had three options at this time, Mitchell foresaw the opportunity to wreak havoc on Bragg's left flank. Therefore, his first possible course of action was to continue maintaining control over Perryville, then advance. Other available options included stopping and retaining Perryville, or retreating to the main Union line around Peters Hill.[74]

October 8, 1862

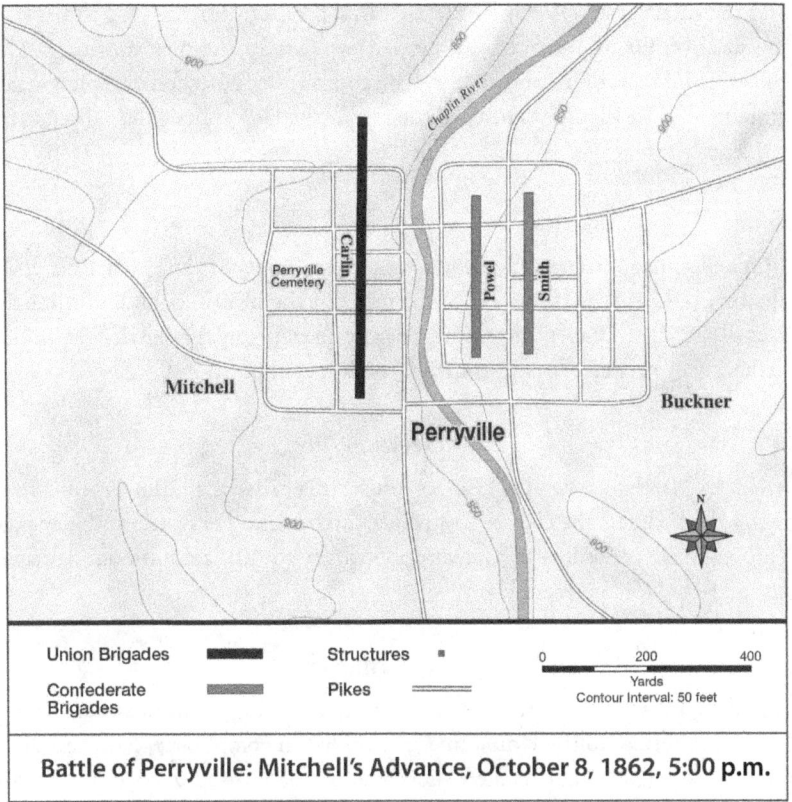

Battle of Perryville: Mitchell's Advance, October 8, 1862, 5:00 p.m.

Option 1

As an aggressive commander with combat experience, Mitchell anticipated a great chance to bring the battle to Bragg, who was concentrating on fighting McCook. Although darkness was settling in, Mitchell believed that, if properly reinforced, his troops could completely overrun Powel's tentative line, control Perryville, and advance on Bragg's left flank and begin to roll it up. As the commander actually present at the town of Perryville, Mitchell understood the current picture there more than other Union commanders, especially his immediate superior Gilbert. He felt confident that the Federals could safely advance farther. Of course, Mitchell still was unaware of the actual size of the Confederate left.[75]

Option 2

With night almost fallen, Mitchell could logically stop where he was with Carlin's brigade, now reinforced with Col. William W. Caldwell's brigade, and retain at least western Perryville. This position provided a good starting location for movement beginning after daylight the next morning. Although confident of his ability to defend this terrain, Mitchell occupied what amounted to a salient far ahead of the rest of the Union line, and salients are vulnerable targets.[76]

Option 3

Mitchell's final option would be to retreat to the safety of the Union line. This choice would ensure the safety of his men. In the morning, and with much better visibility, Buell's three corps finally present on the battlefield could make a coordinated effort to confront the Rebel opposition.[77]

Decision

Much to Mitchell's disgust, Gilbert refused his calls for reinforcements, denying the Federals the chance to advance farther into Perryville and beyond. This resulted in the loss of a great opportunity to inflict additional damage on the Rebel force present.[78]

Results/Impact

Needless to say, Mitchell was livid upon receiving written orders from Gilbert to retreat to the Union line. Somewhat in compliance, Mitchell sent Caldwell's brigade back to the Union line, but he refused to order Carlin to retreat. The Federals had once again lost an opportunity to inflict damage on Bragg and possibly change the outcome of the battle. Although Buell obviously failed to understand that he did not face Bragg's entire army, updated information from a division commander on the scene was ignored. Had Mitchell been allowed to capture all of Perryville, and had Buell provided additional men to block the road leading east, Mitchell would have potentially compromised Bragg's ability to protect his supply base at Camp Breckinridge. This would have forced Bragg to immediately fall back through or near Danville, remaining on the defensive.[79]

From Bragg's perspective this was a lucky break. Other than Preston Smith's brigade, which was still held in reserve while guarding Perryville, Bragg had committed all of his brigades and had no others available to counter an advance by Mitchell. Therefore, the Confederate general was able to concentrate on his fight with McCook's First Corps. As we will see, this resulted in a tactical victory for Bragg, although it was short-lived.[80]

October 8, 1862

Alternate Scenario

Had Gilbert provided reinforcements for Mitchell and allowed him to continue to advance through Perryville and further confront Powel, Smith, and any other Rebel units guarding Bragg's left flank, Bragg would likely have realigned at least a few of his brigades, especially Liddell's, to confront Mitchell's force. As a result, Liddell would not have contributed to the Confederates' final advance to a site near the Dixville Crossroads. While Bragg still could declare a tactical victory, it would not have been as significant. Depending on Mitchell's success in confronting enough Confederate brigades, and accounting for the fact that darkness was becoming a major factor, this alternate scenario could potentially have changed the outcome of the battle to a draw.[81]

Hardee Orders Liddell to Make a Final Assault (5:45 p.m.)

Situation

After Adams's Brigade helped to break the stalemate around the Bottom House, McCook was in peril as his brigades were forced back toward the Dixville Crossroads. The Confederates had repelled the Union lines almost a mile, and could thus smell victory. Wood's Brigade had advanced by around 5:00 p.m. and assaulted Capt. Ebenezer Gay's cavalry and Lytle's brigade defending the Mackville Road near the Dixville Crossroads. Gooding's brigade arrived in time to eventually repulse Wood. The Rebels needed to somehow break the Union line here and capture the crossroads.[82]

However, as discussed previously, reinforcements from Gilbert's Third Corps, Gooding's and Steedman's brigades, arrived along the Mackville Road around dark. Quickly supporting a grateful McCook, the forces went into action. As Gooding moved into position to replace McCook's worn fighters, he repulsed Wood. Sunset was at 5:32 p.m. By around 6:30 p.m. Gooding had finally situated his brigade along the southwest side of the Mackville Road, with Steedman's brigade falling in behind. By 6:450 p.m. Steedman was in line southeast of Gooding, with Gooding's left flank anchored near the Dixville Crossroads. It was fully dark with a full moon providing some illumination.[83]

Options

What options were left for the Confederates? They were almost totally fought out. One alternative was to cease fighting, concede the present battle line, and accept tactical victory. The other option was to order Brig. Gen. St. John R. Liddell's brigade, apparently the only one with any fight remaining, into the fray. (Preston Smith's brigade had not been involved in actual combat, but it was maintaining watch on Perryville.)[84]

Option 1

With the battlefield shrouded in darkness and McCook's original line forced back almost a mile, Bragg could rest on his laurels. He had already achieved a tactical victory, so it was not particularly necessary for him to continue fighting. However, this meant not achieving a more complete triumph.[85]

Option 2

Having fought this long and hard, the Confederates might only need to make one final assault on McCook's line to cement victory. Assuming the Rebels could find a brigade or two still able to fight, a last successful assault might completely annihilate McCook.[86]

Decision

Hardee realized that it might take only one more assault to break McCook's line and ensure a Rebel victory, but he saw the Confederates' momentum beginning to fade. Therefore, he sent his aide Col. Hardin Perkins to a surprised Liddell with the following orders: "General Hardee wishes you now to move upon the enemy where the firing is hottest." Liddell complied. However, to Liddell the location where the firing was hottest seemed to be everywhere![87]

Brig. Gen. St. John R. Liddell, CSA.
Photographic History, Vol. X.

October 8, 1862

Results/Impact

Starting near the Chatham House, Liddell commenced marching toward the fighting. After crossing Doctor's Creek he advanced on a Union battery (Nineteenth Battery, Indiana Light Artillery) he considered critical to silence. Arriving at the now abandoned battery on the left flank of Cheatham's Division, currently positioned along the Benton Road, Cheatham himself rode up to Liddell and encouraged him to join the fight. However, when Liddell requested Cheatham's help in positioning his brigade, the division commander simply said that Liddell would find the line.[88]

Liddell eventually stationed his brigade in a single line just northeast of the Mackville Road with his far left regiment, the Second Arkansas, pointed right at the Dixville Crossroads. About 6:45 p.m. he advanced into the fight. However, events would preclude Liddell from moving very far, as will be discussed next. At this time, further Confederate success seemed likely, ensuring a tactical victory.[89]

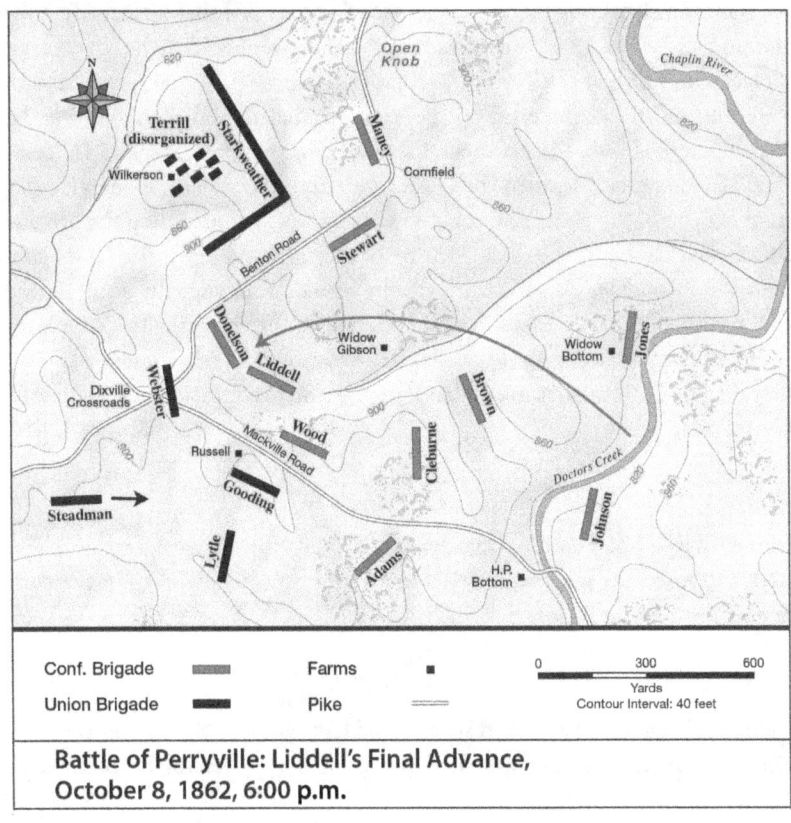

Battle of Perryville: Liddell's Final Advance, October 8, 1862, 6:00 p.m.

Polk Orders All Fighting to Cease (7:15 p.m.)

Situation

As Liddell's Brigade advanced against Gooding and Steedman's brigades per the above narrative, suddenly the noise of the fighting all but stopped. Concern arose as to whether the force ahead of Liddell was friendly. Remember that it was now pitch-dark except for the full moon. In daylight the firing of thousands of rifles and cannon produced immense thick smoke, often reducing visibility to almost zero. Compounding this problem was the fact that a normal-sized regiment might stretch out over the length of a football field, and a brigade might be perhaps three times as wide. Command and control was always difficult, but nighttime made it even more challenging, and this was why night fighting was rare during the Civil War.[90]

At this time Polk rode up to Liddell, pleased to see him in action. Liddell confided to Polk that his soldiers were concerned that the line of troops they faced might be friends. Polk quickly took it on himself to investigate, riding through Liddell's line and approaching the unknown line only some twenty-five yards away. Riding up to an officer, Polk demanded that he identify himself and his command. Surprisingly, the officer replied that he was Lieut. Col. Squire Keith of the Twenty-Second Indiana! Realizing his predicament, Polk told Keith to cease firing or be court-martialed, and then, bluffing, he rode along the Yankee line a short distance before galloping back to Liddell's line. Liddell quickly learned the truth when Polk exclaimed, "General, every mother's son of them are Yankees. I saw the colonel commanding the brigade and looked closely at the dark clothing of the men and am sure of not being mistaken." Liddell's Brigade immediately opened fire, virtually annihilating the Twenty-Second Indiana, which suffered 65 percent casualties, the largest rate of any unit present at the battle. After only a few minutes of firing, Gooding and Steedman retreated, leaving Liddell in command of the Dixville Crossroads.[91]

Options

Liddell wished to continue to advance, driving the Yankees farther back. Polk had to decide whether the Rebels should continue fighting in the dark or end the fighting for the day.[92]

Option 1

Liddell's Brigade had achieved success and had captured the significant Dixville Crossroads, which dominated the flow of supplies to the battlefield.

October 8, 1862

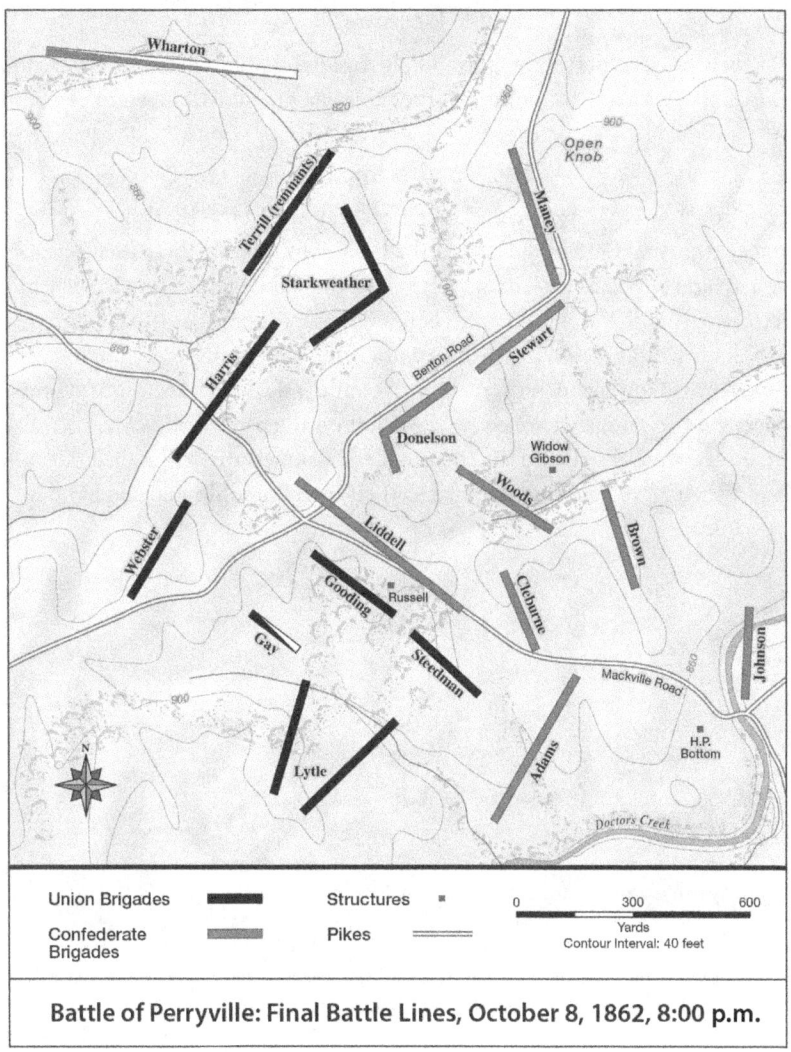

Battle of Perryville: Final Battle Lines, October 8, 1862, 8:00 p.m.

Would continuing to advance lead to further success? The drawbacks of this plan were that it was dark and ammunition was low.[93]

Option 2

Polk's other option was to cease firing for the day (evening). The Rebels had already achieved a major tactical victory, and as Polk had already demonstrated to himself, confusion reigned and would likely worsen as the evening progressed. Yet Liddell was successfully advancing.[94]

Decision

Likely because of his recent "scare," Polk decided that further fighting was too risky and a waste of ammunition. Therefore, he ordered all firing to cease.[95]

Results/Impact

Polk's decision to order a cease-fire effectively ended the Battle of Perryville and set the final lines of the battle. The Union would hold these lines until after daylight while, as we will discuss below, the Confederates would stealthily retreat during the night, quickly abandoning all of their hard-won efforts.[96]

Liddell disagreed with Polk's decision to cease firing but complied. He set about having his men care for the wounded, deal with the captured prisoners, and acquire abandoned weapons left on the battlefield.[97]

Meanwhile, Buell and his commanders assumed that the fighting would begin again at daybreak and prepared their men for additional combat.[98]

CHAPTER 5

AFTER THE BATTLE: OCTOBER 8–24, 1862

After the Battle of Perryville each commander made one critical decision with very significant ramifications for his side, and one officer eventually lost his command.

Bragg Decides to Retreat (October 8, 9:00 p.m.)

Situation

After the fighting finally ceased in the early evening, the troubled Gen. Braxton Bragg called for a council of his commanders around 9:00 p.m. The good news was that he had won a tactical victory over Buell, forcing Maj. Gen. Alexander McD. McCook's First Corps back more than a mile and nearly ruining it as a fighting unit. Unfortunately, even as Bragg reveled in his victory, he had received concerning reports addressing which Union forces were present and in what numbers, and just whom he would likely engage on the morrow. Information from his cavalry commander on his left flank, Col. Joseph Wheeler, indicated a large Union force was positioned along the Lebanon Pike just southwest of Perryville. Likewise, Bragg worried about the quick repulse of Col. Samuel Powel's brigade on the southern end of the battlefield: What size force caused that repulse? The loss of Capt. Cuthbert H. Slocomb's Confederate ammunition train in Perryville concerned Bragg as well. The

Rebel commander now worried that all three of Maj. Gen. Don Carlos Buell's corps were near or on the battlefield. Furthermore, Bragg considered the loss initially reported as about 30 percent of his command in achieving victory. These were irreplaceable soldiers.[1]

Additionally, while Bragg evaluated the present situation on the battlefield, he already had serious concerns about the campaign he was waging. The men of Kentucky men had not enlisted by the thousands as Col. John H. Morgan had so confidently predicted. Bragg had attempted to circumvent the lack of volunteerism by installing Confederate governor Richard Hawes and initiating the Confederate draft, but that measure failed as Hawes and the Rebels were driven out of the capital at Frankfort. Even though he had won today's contest, Bragg already predicted that Buell could certainly attempt to outflank him and capture the main source of Rebel supplies at Camp Breckinridge (formerly Camp Dick Robinson) near Bryantsville.[2]

Options

As Bragg paced the floor at the Crawford House, he considered three options. First, he could remain with his army, such as it was, and continue the combat in the morning. Second, he could retreat to Harrodsburg and consolidate his two armies. Finally, he could withdraw directly to Bryantsville in order to protect his supplies.[3]

Option 1

His men fully expected to continue the fight early in the morning and add to their hard-earned victory. However, with the loss believed to be some 30 percent of his command, the general's force was considerably reduced, and it would most likely be fighting an even larger Union force if, in fact, most of Buell's army was now present. Bragg was finally realizing that he might well be confronting all of Buell's command. To the Rebel general, the odds increasingly favored Buell.[4]

Option 2

If indeed essentially Buell's entire army was now present at Perryville, Bragg was severely outnumbered. In order to achieve better odds, he could unite his two armies and perhaps give battle on more equal terms. Retreating to Harrodsburg and joining forces with Maj. Gen. Edmund Kirby Smith would increase his numbers. At the same time, Bragg could observe whether Buell would try to outflank him. However, withdrawing to Harrodsburg required Bragg to vacate the Perryville Battlefield and surrender his success there, which would not be good for his troops' morale. Another consideration was that the badly wounded would be surrendered to the Yankees, while the dead might not receive proper burial.[5]

Option 3

Retreating directly to Bryantsville and Camp Breckinridge would protect Bragg's main source of supplies. Kirby Smith could march there and unite with Bragg's men. Then, while protecting his supplies, Bragg might confront Buell again on more equal terms. Of course, surrendering the battlefield to the Yankees would dispirit the Rebels, and the badly wounded and dead would be left to the enemy.[6]

Decision

Based on the likely increase in Buell's force, Bragg knew he would have to fight if he remained. In addition, the Rebel commander needed to protect his supplies at Camp Breckinridge. Thus Bragg chose Option 2, abandoning the Perryville Battlefield to Buell.[7]

Results/Impact

While Bragg's soldiers could not understand why they were withdrawing, that was indeed what they did. Taking turns and cautiously moving back to the original line just east of the Chaplin River, Bragg had removed his force from Perryville by dawn and retreated to Harrodsburg, arriving later on October 9. Kirby Smith joined Bragg there on October 10, after a short fight with elements of Brig. Gen. Joshua W. Sill's division, and both armies were united for the first time in the campaign. Bragg positioned his combined force south and west of Harrodsburg, ready for combat.[8]

Realistically, Bragg really had no choice but to order the retreat to Harrodsburg. His only other option, retreating directly east to Bryantsville and Camp Breckinridge, would likely have resulted in Buell taking advantage of the fact that Kirby Smith's other separated Rebel forces were cut off from Bragg. In fact, Buell eventually ordered an advance southeast of Perryville with the additional plan to cut off Bragg from his escape route to Cumberland Gap. When Buell began cautiously advancing, Bragg realized that protecting his source of supplies at Camp Breckinridge near Bryantsville was imperative. After a discussion with Kirby Smith, he ordered his men to march in that direction. Bragg's combined force reached its destination on October 11 and discovered more bad news: only about four days' rations for the general's armies remained.[9]

On October 12, Bragg called together his senior commanders and announced that the Army of the Mississippi and the Army of Kentucky would

After the Battle

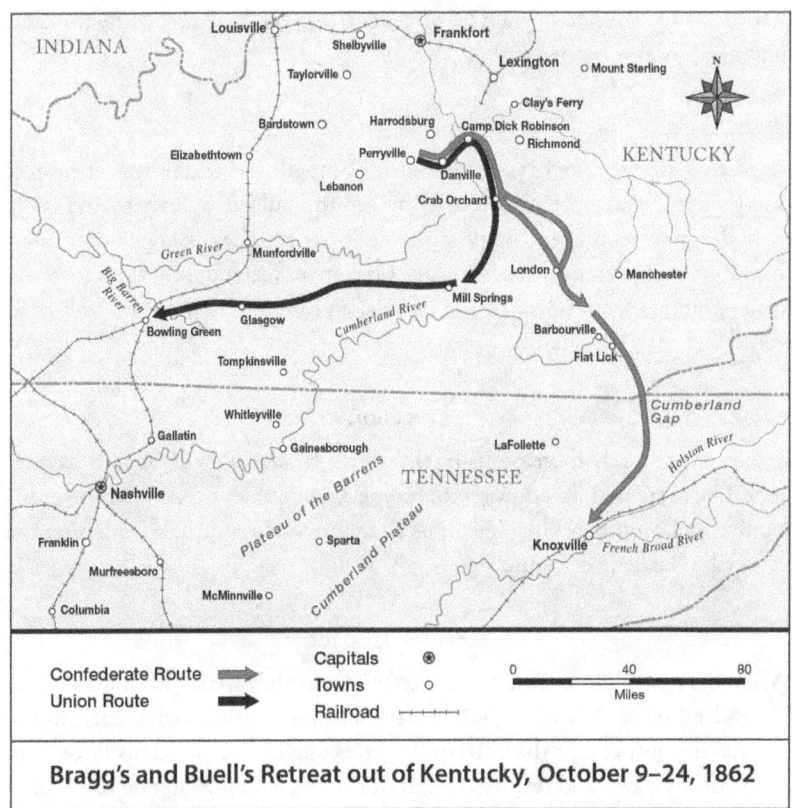

Bragg's and Buell's Retreat out of Kentucky, October 9–24, 1862

leave Kentucky. This critical decision augmented Bragg's earlier decision to retreat from the Perryville battlefield. The retreat out of Kentucky was an 1862 Kentucky Campaign critical decision and was not directly connected to the Battle of Perryville. We will discuss this choice in chapter 6, "Aftermath and Conclusions."[10]

Buell Initially Fails to Aggressively Pursue Bragg (October 9)

Situation

Union skirmishers advanced at daylight on October 9 in preparation to receive the expected Confederate attack. To their amazement, Bragg's force had abandoned the battlefield! The battle was over.[11]

Options

While Buell would naturally want to begin pursuing Bragg's tattered force as it retreated to Harrodsburg, he faced a terrible situation. He had to deal with hundreds of wounded and dead soldiers, both his own and Bragg's. Therefore, Buell could either pursue Bragg immediately, pursue him with a limited force while caring for his casualties, or first take time to care for his own casualties and refit his men.[12]

Option 1

Buell would want to pursue Bragg, but his superiors in Washington, DC, also expected him to fight to regain full control of the Commonwealth of Kentucky. With virtually his whole army present and Sill on his way to join it, and even with the horrendous losses in McCook's corps, Buell's force significantly outnumbered Bragg's. Literally running down Bragg would give Buell the decisive victory that he needed and remove some of the sting of the Battle of Perryville. While most historians concede the tactical victory to Bragg, Buell was the strategic winner as he remained on the battlefield while Bragg retreated. Buell knew he must not waste this opportunity.[13]

Option 2

As a compromise, Buell could send part of his command after Bragg while keeping the other part on the battlefield to care for the Federal and Rebel dead and wounded. Bragg did not have time to look after his own casualties beyond taking the lightly wounded with him. This option would allow Buell to at least keep Bragg under observation until the Union troops could initiate a full-time pursuit. Attending to the thousands of casualties on both sides of the fighting required a substantial amount of time.[14]

Option 3

Confronted with the overwhelming task of caring for all of the dead and wounded, Buell was morally obligated to remain with at least part of his command in order to provide the necessary coverage. Bragg's hasty retreat forced him to leave his dead and more seriously wounded servicemen behind, hopefully in the care of the Yankees, thus placing an unanticipated burden on Buell. Burying the dead and placing the wounded in nearby homes and other structures where they could receive proper care would consume at least a day of the Federals' time.[15]

Decision

Unfortunately for Buell's military career, he selected Option 2. While he did send several divisions and some cavalry, including two divisions of Gilbert's corps destined for Crawford Springs, in pursuit on the road to Harrodsburg, he did not aggressively pursue Bragg. As was his nature, Buell cautiously waited for Bragg to signal his next move. He discovered that Bragg had indeed retreated to Harrodsburg, not Danville. Buell apparently didn't recognize how severely McCook's First Corps suffered at the hands of Bragg's veterans until the next day, when the list of McCook's casualties was made known to him.[16]

Results/Impact

The casualties from the fighting on September 8 were indeed horrendous. While many soldiers who had fought the day before regrouped or left in pursuit, others removed the wounded to whatever shelter could be found and buried the dead. The Rebels had attempted to preserve their slain comrades by placing them in piles surrounded by logs in order to keep animals, especially hogs, from eating them. However, since the Rebels had stripped many Union soldiers of clothing, the disgusted Yankees left many Confederates where they lay. Many Northern soldiers commented on the tremendous number of dead left rotting. Ultimately, it fell to the local inhabitants to bury the dead and care for the wounded of both sides.[17]

Buell began a unified pursuit the next day, but he was behind Bragg, who beat him to the well-fortified Camp Breckinridge. As noted above, Bragg notified his command of his decision to leave Kentucky, and the Rebels began their retreat on October 13. The Confederate commander generally managed to keep ahead of Buell, as will be discussed in chapter 6, and then Buell called off the pursuit. This did not bode well for him.[18]

Alternate Scenario

President Lincoln and the Washington establishment strongly expected Buell to defeat Bragg in Kentucky. Although such action was contrary to Buell's normal methodology, what would have happened had he aggressively pursued and cut off Bragg's route of escape? The elimination of the Confederate Army of the Mississippi this early in the war would certainly have changed future events in the Western Theater, not to mention Buell's career![19]

CHAPTER 6

AFTERMATH AND CONCLUSIONS

The Battle of Perryville provides students of the Civil War with a most interesting dynamic. Gen. Braxton Bragg, with a force on the battlefield of around sixteen thousand men, unknowingly decided to assault Maj. Gen. Don Carlos Buell's Army of the Ohio, with fifty-eight thousand or more soldiers present in the area. Conversely, Buell, with a force over three times the size of Bragg's, postponed his attack out of concern that he was outmanned! The lack of military intelligence provided by the cavalry of both sides was a factor in this engagement.[1]

The actual Battle of Perryville featured Bragg's Command, consisting of three infantry divisions and two cavalry brigades totaling some sixteen thousand men, assaulting only Buell's First Corps, without Brig. Gen. Joshua W. Sill's division, of about thirteen thousand soldiers, and making one small foray (by Col. Samuel Powel's brigade) against Brig. Gen. Charles C. Gilbert's Third Corps. This was essentially even odds, and the Confederate force present successfully assaulted and pushed back the First Corps approximately a mile, a tactical victory. Yet Bragg, finally recognizing that Buell's entire army (less Brig. Gen. Joshua W. Sill's division) was present, decided he had no choice but to retreat. In so doing, he yielded strategic victory to Buell. Bragg retreated to join up with the rest of his army and that of Maj. Gen. Edmund Kirby Smith's Army of Kentucky to eventually gain full strength, as well as to protect his supply depot at Camp Breckinridge, near Bryantsville.[2]

This was a nasty battle—both sides suffered horrific casualties! Bragg wrote in his report of the fighting, "For the time engaged it was the severest and most desperately contested engagement within my knowledge." Pvt. Sam Watkins, infamous author of *Company Aytch or, A Side Show of the Big Show and Other Sketches*, stated, "I was in every battle, skirmish and march that was made by the First Tennessee Regiment during the war, and I do not remember of a harder contest and more evenly fought battle than that of Perryville." While casualty numbers tend to vary depending somewhat on how they are interpreted, and while the Confederate military often did not issue reports, the Union suffered 845 killed, 2,851 wounded, and 515 missing, for a total of 4,211 losses, the vast majority of them in the First Corps. This figure equates to about 7 percent of Buell's command.[3]

However, a fairer comparison would be within McCook's First Corps, consisting of 13,121 soldiers, with 700 killed, 2,235 wounded, and 384 missing, resulting in a casualty rate of 25 percent. On the Confederate side, inaccurate records do indicate that 510 men were killed, 2,635 wounded, and 251 missing, for a total of 3,396 casualties, or 21 percent of those present. Not surprisingly, Maj. Gen. Benjamin F. Cheatham's division suffered the most with 305 killed, 1,140 wounded, and 79 missing, for a total of 1,524 losses, or 23 percent. According to another source, the Battle of Perryville ranked twenty-third in terms of casualties with 4,226 Union and 3,401 Confederate, for a total of 7,627, compared to the 7,607 above. It was a bloody fight![4]

As briefly mentioned above, all of these casualties completely saturated the area's ability to handle them. The Yankees saw that the Union and Confederate wounded were distributed to virtually any structure for miles around. Many of those with injuries eventually died, thereby contributing to problems with the final statistics. The Rebels stacked some of their dead in protected log enclosures, but they otherwise had no time to conduct burials. The Yankees proceeded to bury their own, but upon discovering that the Rebels had stripped many of the Union dead of clothing and personal objects, Federal soldiers left many of the Rebel bodies to rot. It fell to the landowners to bury them.[5]

In 1865 burial parties exhumed 969 Union bodies and reinterred them on top of Peters Hill. By 1868 all of these bodies had been reinterred once again at a newly established Federal cemetery at Camp Nelson, located near Nicholasville, Kentucky. Because of all of the Confederate dead left around his house and on his property, Squire Bottom established a Confederate cemetery on his property and buried some 400 Rebels there. He managed to build a stone wall around the graveyard as well. On the fortieth anniversary of the Battle of Perryville, a twenty-eight-foot-tall Confederate monument was dedicated within the cemetery. On the sixty-ninth anniversary of the battle, a similar-sized monument nearby was dedicated to the Union dead. Today, the Perryville Battlefield State Historic Site visitor center is located close to the cemetery.[6]

The Battle of Perryville involved twenty-two critical decisions. Far and away, and as expected during a battle, the dominant critical decisions were tactical. Commanders made fifteen such choices. In addition, the fighting witnessed four strategic critical decisions and one operational, one logistical, and one personnel decision. Buell made six critical decisions, Bragg five, and Polk four. McCook, Wharton, Cheatham, Buckner, Starkweather, Gilbert, and Hardee made one each.[7]

The loss of Maj. Gen. William "Bull" Nelson resulted in Buell replacing him with "Acting Maj. Gen." Charles C. Gilbert. Battle historians, especially Kurt Holman, strongly believe that had Nelson been present in command of the Third Corps, he would have ignored orders not to fight, and would have aggressively entered the battle instead. He would likely have disrupted Bragg's assault at least to some degree. Fortunately for Bragg, his foe was limited largely to McCook's First Corps, which he soundly drove back a mile or more, inflicting heavy casualties.[8]

Bragg decided to retreat from the Perryville Battlefield during the evening of October 8, and many historians believe that this choice applied to more than the just-finished battle. Rather, these scholars contend that by this time Bragg had also decided to abandon the Commonwealth of Kentucky itself. Even if this assumption is incorrect, Bragg quickly determined that his situation was dire. Many factors contributed to his choice. First, upon reaching his supply location at Camp Breckinridge, the general was shocked to discover that only four days' rations were available for his armies. A lack of foodstuffs, coupled with the pervasive drought, provided little opportunity for his soldiers to remain in Kentucky. The upcoming rainy season loomed as well. Moreover, as previously discussed, Bragg was heartily disgusted with the lack of Kentucky men willing to volunteer to join his army. On October 12 he reported, "The campaign here was predicated on a belief and the most positive assurances that the people of this country would rise in mass to assert their independence. No people ever had so favorable an opportunity, but I am distressed to add there is little or no disposition to avail of it. Willing perhaps to accept their independence, they are neither disposed nor willing to risk their lives or their property in its achievement."[9]

Several other factors influenced Bragg's decision to abandon Kentucky. Rumors abounded that additional reinforcements were marching to join Buell, and Brig. Gen. Gordon Granger was in fact leading the Army of Kentucky south from Cincinnati. Bragg had counted on having the small armies of Maj. Gen. Earl Van Dorn and Maj. Gen. Sterling Price join him, but he learned that they had been defeated at a battle at Corinth, Mississippi, and would be unable to join up. With Corinth again in Union control, Chattanooga was increasingly vulnerable to another Union advance, which originally motivated Bragg to protect it prior to the Kentucky Campaign itself. Maj. Gen. John C. Breckinridge of Kentucky, originally promised to Bragg, would not leave Tennessee. Aware that Buell was already in the process of attempting to cut his probable line of retreat, Bragg foresaw that he and his men could not remain. A final deciding factor was that Pres. Jefferson Davis had warned Bragg that the Confederacy could not afford to lose his army. On October 13 the armies of Bragg, Kirby Smith, and Brig. Gen. Humphrey Marshall, who had joined late in the campaign, began their retreat to Tennessee, essentially the reverse of Kirby Smith's original advance.[10]

Although there was loud clamor to remove Bragg from command, after conferring with the general, Davis kept him in command. Bragg would remain in command until after Maj. Gen. Ulysses S. Grant's victory at Chattanooga in November 1863.[11]

Meanwhile, Buell advanced with the rest of his army on October 10. He initially tried to cut off Bragg's line of retreat and then pursued him to no avail. Realizing that chasing Bragg through desolate country was impractical, Buell called off his troops. Unfortunately, he intentionally disobeyed Pres. Abraham Lincoln's wishes and direct orders. Lincoln had concerned himself with the welfare of citizens of Eastern Tennessee who supported the Union. He wished for a Union army, specifically Buell's, to cover that area and protect its residents. Buell refused to advance there, knowing that the lack of supplies in that region precluded sustaining his army. Lincoln and the administration in Washington, DC, seemed not to grasp the magnitude of the supply problem. Nonetheless, Lincoln was the commander in chief, and defying his orders was a bad course of action.[12]

Buell decided that Bragg's ultimate destination was Nashville, and he eventually moved his army directly there after calling off the pursuit. Having been defied one time too often, Lincoln relieved Buell of his command and replaced him with Maj. Gen. William S. Rosecrans.[13]

The Battle of Perryville ultimately led to the Confederates leaving the Commonwealth of Kentucky, never to return in force. Along with most of the other actions described in chapter 1, the Confederacy failed to win the 1862 Kentucky Campaign—the Confederate high tide had come and gone. While technically a Confederate victory, this most important battle for control of the commonwealth quickly squandered any Rebel gains, as Bragg felt he was forced to retreat immediately.[14]

Aftermath and Conclusions

The consequences of the Battle of Perryville were immense for both the Union and the Confederacy. Bragg fell back to the Murfreesboro area, a few miles south of Nashville. Not contemplating further fighting until the roads became passable in the late spring, he spread his units out for better foraging. Rosecrans was another methodical general who went to work rebuilding and refitting his army, renamed the Army of the Cumberland. Hounded by officials in Washington, DC, he advanced to Murfreesboro the day after Christmas and caught Bragg off guard. Hurriedly gathering his troops, Bragg attacked early on the morning of January 31, and in a true slugfest he almost, but not quite, cut Rosecrans's supply line. After a day of cautious rest, Bragg assaulted Rosecrans's right, but he was heavily repulsed. The enemy's response included a large assembly of cannon and eventually forced him to retreat. This Battle of Stones River or Murfreesboro gave Lincoln an important victory.[15]

For many Civil War buffs and historians the Battle of Gettysburg in early July 1863 was the turning point of the war. In reality, while this engagement was the largest of the war, it changed little while resulting in some fifty thousand casualties, preventing Gen. Robert E. Lee from generally assuming the offensive in the future. The other well-known action occurring at that same time was Grant's ultimate capture of Vicksburg. While this was a tremendous psychological victory and goal, little Rebel traffic crossed the Mississippi River by then, and northwestern crops were moving up the Ohio River instead.[16]

A third operation, the Tullahoma Campaign, was conducted at the same time but is often overlooked. After a colossal rebuilding of his Army of the Cumberland, Rosecrans completely outmaneuvered Bragg over ten days in late June and early July and at a cost of only six hundred men. The Confederate commander was located south of Murfreesboro, and Rosecrans forced him back to Chattanooga. After regrouping again, Rosecrans maneuvered to cut Bragg off from Chattanooga, forcing him to abandon that city. The Union general divided his corps, sending troops over Lookout Mountain and giving Bragg the chance of defeating them individually. However, due to command failures, this did not occur. Bragg then tried to sever Rosecrans's supply line back to Chattanooga. Fortunately for Bragg, this attempt resulted in the only win for the Army of Tennessee (formerly the Army of the Mississippi) at the Battle of Chickamauga, second only to Gettysburg in terms of casualties.[17]

Bragg's failure to follow up this victory resulted in a minisiege of Chattanooga. Grant replaced Rosecrans, and in late November, in a series of movements ultimately resulting in his men's assault of Missionary Ridge, Grant broke the siege and made Chattanooga the jumping-off point for 1864.

With Grant appointed to command all Union armies and repositioned to the Eastern Theater, Maj. Gen. William T. Sherman conducted the Atlanta Campaign, successfully capturing the city in early September. Many credit Sherman's victory with ensuring Lincoln's reelection and the successful pursuit that won the war. Sherman then made his March to the Sea, demonstrating complete dominance of the Confederate interior. From Savannah, Georgia, he marched north to join Grant but arrived too late. Grant had surrounded Lee's army at Appomattox Court House, where Lee surrendered on April 9, 1865.[18]

The Battle of Perryville ultimately removed any chance for the Confederacy to retain Kentucky. Over time, the battle also led to generally consecutive Federal victories in the Western Theater, a major contribution to eventual Union victory. This was an important battle in our history, and we should remember it as such.

APPENDIX I

DRIVING TOUR OF THE CRITICAL DECISIONS OF THE BATTLE OF PERRYVILLE

This driving tour consists of ten stops generally located where critical decisions were made during the Battle of Perryville. The tour is mostly chronological with a few exceptions for sightseers' convenience. Please drive cautiously and park safely out of the way of traffic. Please do not read while driving unless a passenger can do so for you.

Due to its rural location and the long-term efforts of the American Battlefield Trust (formerly the Civil War Trust), the Perryville Battlefield is one of the most completely preserved Civil War battlefields. The trust has augmented the original small state historic site by purchasing and donating to the Commonwealth of Kentucky some 1,150 acres of land so far. As you drive and walk within the site, enjoy this well-maintained chunk of Civil War history!

Some of the critical decisions were made at a distance from the battlefield—for instance, Buell's replacement of Nelson with Gilbert to command his Third Corps while in Louisville. It is impractical to include Louisville in the tour, so that critical decision, along with a few similar ones, will be discussed at Tour Stop 1.

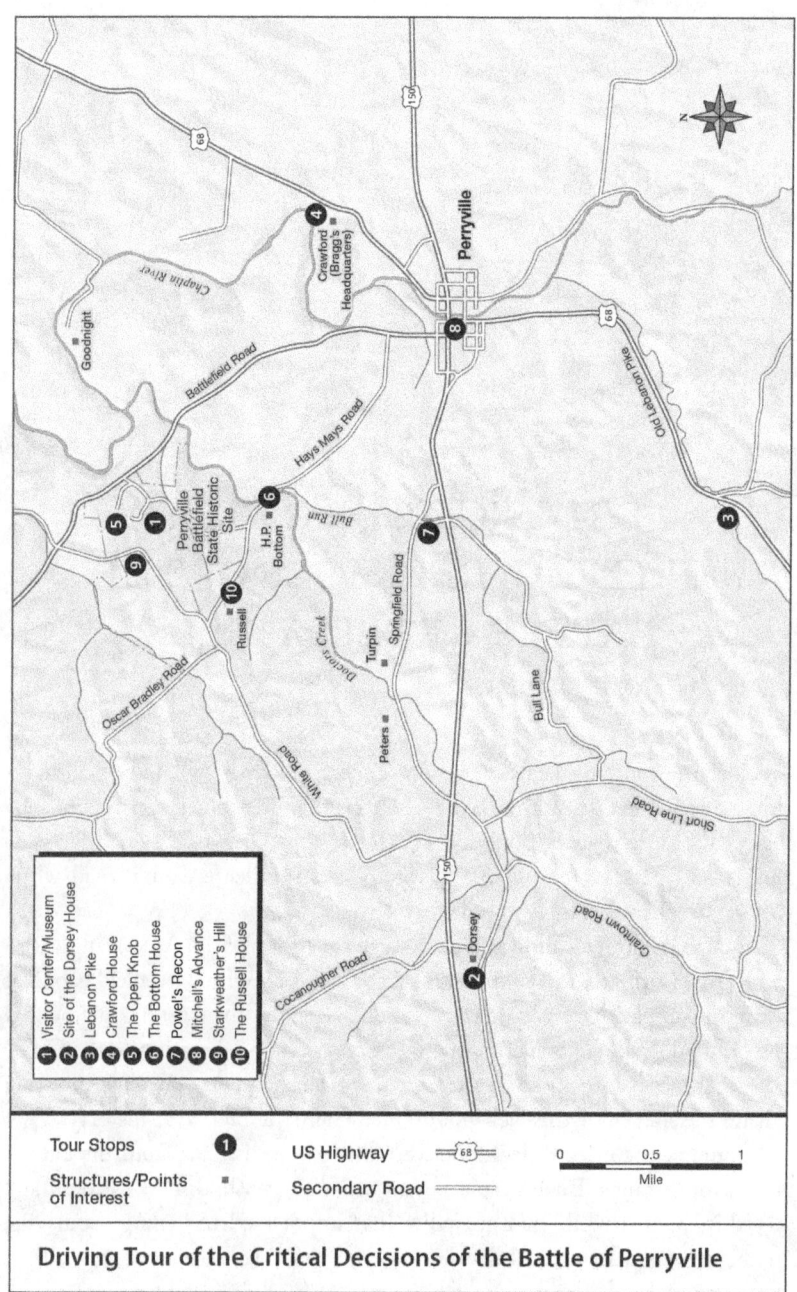

Driving Tour of the Critical Decisions of the Battle of Perryville

Driving Tour of the Critical Decisions of the Battle of Perryville

Begin the tour at the Perryville Battlefield State Historic Site, located about two miles north of the town of Perryville, Kentucky. From downtown Perryville, drive west on Second Street to the intersection with North Jackson Street. Turn right (north) onto North Jackson Street, which becomes State Highway 1920, also labeled Battlefield Road. Drive about two miles and turn left into the entrance to the battlefield, then drive a short distance to the visitor center / museum and park. Explore that facility. Then walk a few hundred feet east to the small Confederate cemetery.

Stop 1—Perryville Battlefield Visitor Center / Cemetery

Critical Decisions: (1) Buell Replaces Nelson with Gilbert, (2) Buell Orders an Advance Supplemented with a Diversionary Movement, (3) Polk Disobeys Bragg's Orders to Advance Toward Frankfort, (4) Bragg Installs a Confederate Governor at Frankfort, (5) Polk Orders Hardee to Halt Buckner's Division at Perryville, (6) Bragg Orders Polk to March to Perryville and Attack the Approaching Union Force

Notice that, per the Stop 1 map, you are standing just northwest of where Donelson's Brigade passed on its assault around 2:30 p.m., initiating the Battle of Perryville. Donelson's Sixteenth Tennessee led the attack and was followed by the Fifteenth Tennessee, whose right flank marched past this

Visitor center, Perryville Battlefield State Historic Site. Photo by the author.

Appendix I

Confederate cemetery, Perryville Battlefield State Historic Site. Photo by the author.

position, with his Thirty-Eighth Tennessee on its left. Face left, northwest, and you can see the Open Knob, the location of Parson's battery, which directed terrible enfilading fire on Donelson's men. (The Open Knob is Stop 5, although for the sake of convenience you can visit it next if desired).

Maj. Gen. Don Carlos Buell made the first critical decision. As he reassembled his Army of the Ohio at Louisville, he designated three corps. Unfortunately, his choice for command of the Third Corps, Maj. Gen. William "Bull" Nelson, had to be replaced because Brig. Gen. Jefferson C. Davis of Indiana murdered him. Buell chose "Acting Maj. Gen." Charles C. Gilbert, whose performance at the Battle of Perryville was uninspired at best.

> **Narrative of Earl J. Hess, *Banners to the Breeze***
>
> The most serious consequence of Nelson's death was the need for a new commander for the III [sic] Corps. Buell unwisely chose Gilbert, who had been a captain only a month before and had relatively little combat experience. Gilbert had done well in picking up the pieces from the Richmond battle and in dealing with administrative matters in Louisville, yet he was unprepared to command a corps in an important campaign. His battlefield promotion to major general had not yet been recognized by the Senate, a fact that apparently escaped Buell's notice. Most important, he did not have the confidence of

Driving Tour of the Critical Decisions of the Battle of Perryville

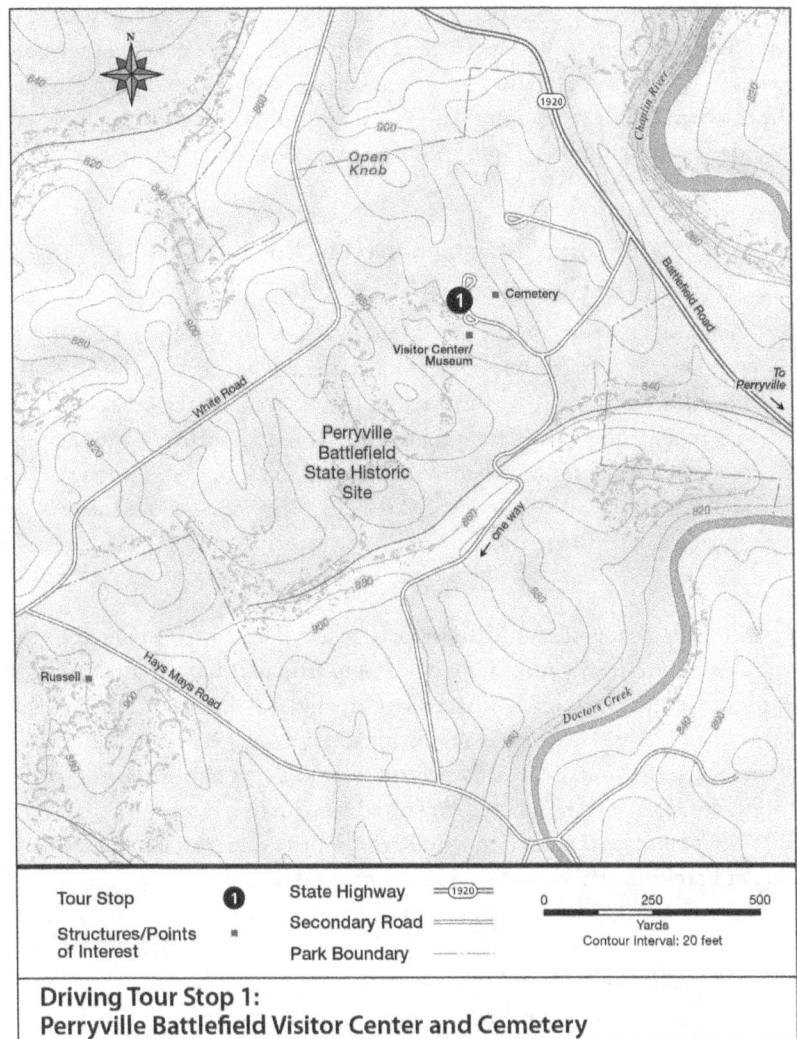

**Driving Tour Stop 1:
Perryville Battlefield Visitor Center and Cemetery**

the III [*sic*] Corps. Gilbert became infamous for bullying soldiers on the march when they took fence rails to build fires or fresh fruit to eat. Rumors circulated throughout the corps that a silly martinet had been given command because of his personal connections with influential people. Neither McCook nor Crittenden would prove to be extraordinary corps commanders, but Gilbert was certainly in a situation that was far above his abilities.[1]

Appendix I

Maj. Gen. Don Carlos Buell also made the second critical decision. As its results unfolded, he wisely not only marched his three corps via separate routes to Bardstown, but also sent a diversionary force of two divisions under the command of Brig. Gen. Joshua W. Sill. This distracting force completely fooled Gen. Braxton Bragg into believing that it was Buell's main army.

> ### Report of Maj. Gen. Don C. Buell, USA, Commanding Army of the Ohio
>
> The army marched on the 1st ultimo in five columns. The left [Sill and Dumont] moved toward Frankfort, to hold in check the force of the enemy which still remained at or near that place; the other columns, marching by different routes, finally fell respectively into the roads leading from Shepherdsville, Mount Washington, Fairfield, and Bloomfield to Bardstown, where the main force of the enemy under General Bragg was known to be.[2]

After his Army of the Mississippi reached Bardstown, Bragg traveled to Lexington to finally meet with Maj. Gen. Edmund Kirby Smith and his Army of Kentucky. Bragg left Maj. Gen. Leonidas Polk in command of the Army of the Mississippi. Planning on attacking Brig. Gen. Joshua W. Sill's diversionary divisions marching toward Frankfort, Bragg made the third critical decision when he ordered Polk to advance in that direction and charge Sill's right flank, in conjunction with Kirby Smith's direct attack, somewhere west of Frankfort. Polk disobeyed this command.

> ### Report of Gen. Braxton Bragg, CSA, Commanding Army of the Mississippi
>
> I ordered Major-General Polk in writing, dated Lexington, 1 p.m., October 2, and sent it by two routes, to move from Bardstown with his whole available force by way of Bloomfield toward Frankfort, to strike the enemy in flank and rear, and informed him that Major-General Smith would attack in front. When received at Bardstown on the 3d the general submitted this order, which is not mentioned in his report (see Exhibit No. 1), to a council of wing and division commanders, and determined to move as originally instructed by me on leaving Bardstown. Fortunately notice of this determination reached me at Frankfort in time to prevent the movement against

the enemy's front by General Smith, but it necessitated an entire change in my plans, the abandonment of the capital, and the partial uncovering and ultimate loss of our stores at Lexington. Not doubting but that some imperative necessity unknown to me existed with the general for this departure from instructions I conformed at once to his movements, and put General Smith's command in motion to form the junction farther south, still covering the supplies at Lexington as far as practicable.[3]

Polk glossed over his disobedience in his report.

Report of Maj. Gen. Leonidas Polk, CSA, Commanding (Temporarily) Army of the Mississippi

At Bardstown, on September 28, the Army of the Mississippi, by order from General Bragg, was placed under my command. Up to that time I had command of the right wing only, General Hardee having command of the left. My orders from the general commanding, who was called on public duty to the capital at Frankfort, were to press in the enemy's pickets upon Louisville and to maintain my position. If the enemy advanced upon me in moderate force, to attack him; if in large force, I was to fall back upon Harrodsburg, marching in two columns via Perryville and Mackville respectively. The enemy having made a general advance, I moved upon Harrodsburg, and in consequence of the state of the roads marched the whole column by the Springfield and Perryville pike. The object of this movement was to form a junction with the Army of the Kentucky under General Kirby Smith, who was to move for that purpose upon Harrodsburg also from the north side of the Kentucky River. Another object was to cover our base, which after the evacuation of Cumberland Gap by the enemy was established at Camp Dick Robinson, in the forks of the Dick and Kentucky Rivers.[4]

As Buell marched after Bragg, rather than focusing on confronting Buell's Army of the Ohio, Bragg made critical decision number four, to (re)install the Confederate governor of Kentucky. While appointing the governor was certainly a political coup, Bragg's real motivation was legally instituting Confederate conscription of Kentucky's men in order to voluntarily or involuntarily rebuild his Army of the Mississippi. However, by focusing on this event he failed to keep track of Buell.

> ### Report of Gen. Braxton Bragg, CSA, Commanding Army of the Mississippi
>
> Arriving in Lexington on October 1, I met the Provisional Governor of the State, who had previously been invited to accompany me, and arranged for his installation at the capital on the 4th. The available forces of General Smith, just returned to Lexington, were ordered immediately to Frankfort.[5]

Due to terrible roads, Polk allowed Maj. Gen. William J. Hardee, commanding the left wing of the Army of the Mississippi, to follow Polk's right wing as it marched through Perryville. Desiring to confront Buell's pursuing force, Hardee asked Polk, who was temporarily the army commander, whether he could do so at Perryville, where the terrain was conducive to fighting and water was available. Polk acquiesced to Hardee's request, making critical decision five, which set the scene for the Battle of Perryville.

> ### Report of Maj. Gen. William J. Hardee, CSA, Commanding Left Wing, Army of the Mississippi
>
> On the 7th I informed General Bragg [also Polk], who was at Harrodsburg, that the enemy was moving in heavy force against my position. With the view of inflicting a decisive defeat, or at least of pressing him back from any farther advance against our line of communications in the direction of Danville and Cumberland Gap, I urged the concentration of our whole army at Perryville.[6]

> ### Report of Maj. Gen. Leonidas Polk, CSA, Commanding (Temporarily) Army of the Mississippi
>
> On arriving at Perryville I communicated with the general commanding the forces then at Harrodsburg, informing him that the right wing, under command of General Cheatham, had been ordered forward to take a position on the farther side of that town, and as there was a scarcity of water I had ordered General Hardee to halt Buckner's division near Perryville and to post Anderson's on

Salt River between the two towns. These dispositions were carried into effect and I reported to the general commanding in person.[7]

Bragg made the sixth critical decision when he decided not only to confront whatever size of force Buell had nearing Perryville, but also to send support to his own soldiers stationed there. The Confederate commander dispatched Anderson's and Cheatham's Divisions as reinforcements, with Polk in overall command.

Report of Gen. Braxton Bragg, CSA, Commanding Army of the Mississippi

This presented an opportunity which I promptly seized of striking him [Buell] in detail. Accordingly written orders were given to Major-General Polk, dated Harrodsburg, October 7, 5.40 p.m. (see Exhibit No. 4), to move Cheatham's division, now at Harrodsburg, back to Perryville, and to proceed to that point himself, attack the enemy immediately, rout him, and then move rapidly to join Major-General Smith, as before ordered, and, it was added, "no time should be lost in this movement."[8]

Report of Maj. Gen. Leonidas Polk, CSA, Commanding (Temporarily) Army of the Mississippi

Information having been received through General Hardee that the enemy was pressing with heavy force upon his position it was resolved by the general commanding the forces to attack him at that point. He accordingly directed me on the evening of the 7th to order Anderson's division, of Hardee's wing, to return to Perryville and also to order General Cheatham, with Donelson's division [brigade] of his wing, to follow it immediately, and to return myself to that place, to take charge of the forces and attack the enemy next morning. I urged the strong expediency of concentrating all our forces upon the point to be attacked, and at all events the necessity of having the remaining division of the Army of the Mississippi (Withers') placed at my disposal. To this the general objected, upon the ground that General Kirby Smith had informed him that the enemy was in force in his front and that his troops could not be spared from that

> part of the field, nor could the division of Withers be spared, as he thought the force in front of Smith made it necessary for him to be re-enforced.⁹

The next stop is the Dorsey House, the site of Buell's headquarters during the battle, located about five miles southwest. Leave the visitor center parking lot and return to the park entrance. Turn right (southeast) onto Battlefield Road / State Highway 1920, and return to Perryville. At the intersection of Jackson Street and US Highway 150, turn right (west). Drive about 2.4 miles to the second intersection with the Old Springfield Road, turn left (southwest) onto the Old Springfield Road, and follow it about 1.0 mile to just past the intersection with Cocanougher Road. Pull over and park safely on the right, where the road begins to curve to the southwest. Stand by your vehicle and look north. The Dorsey House stood just north of this road. Please do not trespass, as the site is on private property.

Stop 2—The Dorsey House—Buell's Headquarters

Critical Decisions: (7) McCook's Brigade Is Sent Forward to Search for Water, (10) Buell Postpones His Planned Attack, (14) Buell Orders Reinforcements to McCook, (22) Buell Initially Fails to Aggressively Pursue Bragg

After Buell injured himself, he was confined to his headquarters in a tent next to the Dorsey House, only about three miles from the fighting on the Union left. Amazingly, apparently due to the phenomenon labeled acoustic shadow, he could not hear the noise of the battle. He made four critical decisions while at the Dorsey House. The first was to ascertain whether water was available for his men, as the drought was a serious detriment to their ability to fight. Therefore, he ordered a probe to seek a site or sites for his men to obtain water.¹⁰

> **Report of Maj. Gen. Don C. Buell, USA, Commanding Army of the Ohio**
>
> The center corps arrived on the afternoon of the 7th, and was drawn up in order of battle about 3 miles from Perryville, where the enemy appeared to be in force. The advance guard, under Captain Gay,

Driving Tour of the Critical Decisions of the Battle of Perryville

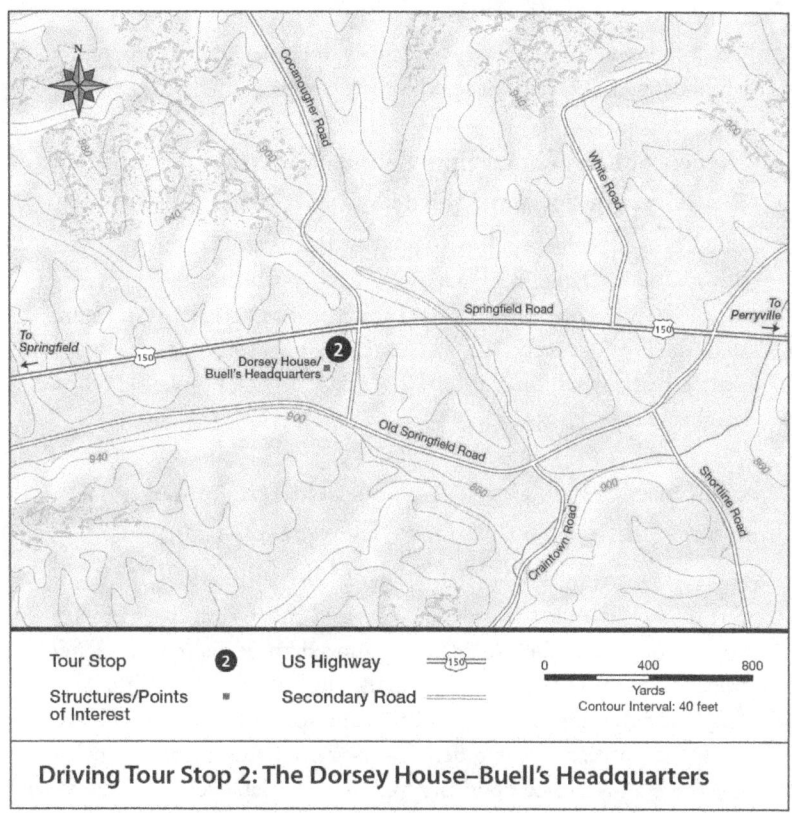

Driving Tour Stop 2: The Dorsey House–Buell's Headquarters

consisting of cavalry and artillery, supported toward evening by two regiments of infantry, pressed successfully upon the enemy's rear guard to within 2 miles of the town against a somewhat stubborn opposition.

The whole army had for three days or more suffered from a scarcity of water. The last day particularly the troops and animals suffered exceedingly for the want of it and from hot weather and dusty roads. In the bed of Doctor's Creek, a tributary of Chaplin River, about 2.5 miles from Perryville, some pools of water were discovered, which the enemy showed a determination to prevent us from gaining possession of. The Thirty-sixth brigade, under the command of Col. Daniel McCook, from General Sheridan's division was ordered forward to seize and hold a commanding position which covered these pools. It executed the orders that night, and a supply of bad water was secured for the troops.[11]

Report of Brig. Gen. Philip Sheridan, USA, Commanding Eleventh Division, Third Corps, Army of the Ohio

In accordance with the instructions of the general commanding I directed Col. Daniel McCook, with his brigade and Barnett's battery, to occupy the heights in front of Doctor's Creek, so as to secure that water for our men. This was done very handsomely after a sharp skirmish at daylight in the morning, giving us full possession of the heights [Peters Hill].[12]

Report of Col. Daniel McCook, USA, Commanding Thirty-Sixth Brigade, Eleventh Division, Third Corps, Army of the Ohio

Sir: In obedience to the orders of General Buell, conveyed through you, at 2 a.m. of the 8th instant I moved three regiments of my brigade, viz, the Eighty-fifth Illinois, the Fifty-second Ohio, and the One hundred and twenty-fifth Illinois, to the foot of Peters' Hill, the position I was ordered to carry. At this point, discovering the enemy's force upon the hill above, I deployed the Eighty-fifth Regiment Illinois upon the right of the Perryville road and the Fifty-second Regiment upon the left, throwing skirmishers to the front, enveloping my flanks. The skirmishers had scarcely taken intervals when a severe and galling fire was opened on them. As soon as sufficient ground was gained to the front I deployed the One hundred and twenty-fifth Regiment Illinois upon both sides of the road as a reserve. Although all my regiments were fresh from their homes they moved steadily up the hill driving the enemy, who contested warmly every step, and occupied the crest of the heights, which gave us a commanding position over the surrounding country and one of vast importance at a subsequent part of the day.[13]

By late morning, realizing that all three of his corps were not in his desired position to launch an attack, Buell made the critical decision to postpone the attack until the next day. While the Dorsey House is no longer extant, its location remains very important to the study of the battle. Note that it is close to the battlefield. Logically, it seems unlikely that Buell could not hear the fighting. Yet the phenomenon of acoustic shadow left him unaware of the battle.

> **Report of Maj. Gen. Don C. Buell, USA,**
> **Commanding Army of the Ohio**
>
> The disposition of the troops was made mainly with a view to a combined attack on the enemy's position at daylight the following morning, as the time required to get all the troops into position after the unexpected delay would probably make it too late to attack that day.
>
> The cannonading, which commenced with the partial engagement in the center, followed by the reconnaissance of the cavalry, under Captain Gay, extended toward the left, and became brisker as the day advanced, but was not supposed to proceed from any serious engagement, as no report to that effect was received.[14]

After Buell had postponed the attack until the next day, he was astounded to learn of Bragg's assault on McCook's First Corps, only finding out when McCook finally requested reinforcements. Buell then made the critical decision to provide limited support to McCook.

> **Report of Maj. Gen. Don C. Buell, USA,**
> **Commanding Army of the Ohio**
>
> At 4 o'clock, however, Major-General McCook's aide-de-camp arrived and reported to me that the general was sustaining a severe attack, which he would not be able to withstand unless re-enforced; that his flanks were already giving way. He added, to my astonishment, that the left corps had actually been engaged in a severe battle for several hours, perhaps since 12 o'clock. It was so difficult to credit the latter that I thought there must even be some misapprehension in regard to the former. I sent word to him that I should rely on his being able to hold his ground, though I should probably send him re-enforcements. I at once sent orders for two brigades from the center corps (Schoepf's division) to move promptly to re-enforce the left. Orders were also sent to General Crittenden to move a division in to strengthen the center and to move with the rest of his corps energetically against the enemy's left flank.[15]

Appendix I

The following day after the battle, Buell and his soldiers were surprised to discover that the Rebels had abandoned the battlefield, leaving their dead and severely wounded for the Yankees to handle. Caught off guard, Buell made the critical decision to order a limited pursuit of Bragg and his men while contending with both sides' casualties. Thus he lost the ability to quickly hinder Bragg's retreat or to attempt to block him from his all-important supply base at Camp Breckinridge (formerly Union Camp Dick Robinson).

Report of Maj. Gen. Don C. Buell, USA, Commanding Army of the Ohio

No doubt was entertained that the enemy would endeavor to hold his position. Accordingly orders were sent to the commanders of corps to be prepared to attack at daylight in the morning. They received instructions in person at my headquarters that night, except General Crittenden, for whom instructions were given to Major-General Thomas, second in command. General McCook supposed, from indications in his front, that the enemy would throw a formidable force against his corps, in pursuance of the original attempt to turn our left. He represented also that his corps was very much crippled, the new division of General Jackson having in fact almost entirely disappeared as a body. He was instructed to move in during the night and close the opening between his right and General Gilbert's left. His orders for the following day were to hold his position, taking advantage of any opportunity that the events of the day might present. The corps of Generals Crittenden and Gilbert were to move forward at 6 o'clock and attack the enemy's front and left flank.

The advance the following morning, in pursuance of these orders, discovered that the enemy's main body had retired during the night, but without any indications of haste or disorder, except that his dead and many of his wounded were left upon the field. The reconnaissance during the day showed that his whole force had fallen back on Harrodsburg, where the indications seemed to be that he would make a stand. It will be impossible to form any correct judgment of the operations from this time, particularly without considering the condition of the two armies and the probable intentions of the enemy.[16]

While the Dorsey House is no longer extant, its location remains very important to the study of the Battle of Perryville. Note that it is close to the battlefield—logically, it seems unlikely that Buell could not hear the fighting.

Driving Tour of the Critical Decisions of the Battle of Perryville

Yet the phenomenon of acoustic shadow prevented him from being aware of the battle.

The next stop is where Wheeler guarded the Lebanon Pike, located about four miles away. Carefully turn your vehicle around, and drive east along the Old Springfield Road back to the intersection with US Highway 150. Turn right (east) on US 150 and drive back to Perryville. Once in town, drive a couple of blocks to the first traffic light at the intersection with US Highway 150 and Buell Street. Turn right (south) onto Buell Street. Continue south, noting the historic old Merchant's Row to your left (east). Buell Street becomes US Highway 68. As you pass the intersection with West Fifth Street, note your mileage. Continue farther south, eventually veering southwest 1.8 miles to the intersection with the Brumfield Road / State Route 1984 on the left, and park just past the intersection. Leave your vehicle and face southwest down US Highway 68, which generally follows the same route as the Old Lebanon Pike.

Stop 3—The Lebanon Pike

Critical Decision: (10) Buell Postpones His Planned Attack

Note per the Stop 3 map how close the various units of Crittenden's Second Corps were to Perryville, and how easily they might have overwhelmed Wheeler's small command. The Stop 3 map indicates Wheeler's and Crittenden's approximate positions about 2 p.m.

View along the Old Lebanon Pike, near Perryville. Photo by Chuck Lott.

Appendix I

Wheeler and his brigade guarded this approach during the day of the battle. In the morning he advanced southwest along the Lebanon Pike, forcing back some advanced Federal units. Later on, Crittenden's advancing Second Corps, numbering some twenty thousand soldiers, repelled Wheeler. As discussed above, Buell's order to postpone the attack until September 9 contributed much more to holding back Crittenden's Second Corps than did Wheeler's small brigade. More importantly, Wheeler notified Bragg around 3:00 p.m. that he believed that he was facing a sizeable force. Had Crittenden's Second Corps aggressively advanced to Perryville, brushing Wheeler out of the way, the Second Corps could potentially have rolled up the Rebel left, changing the outcome of the battle, or at least initially blocking Bragg from his supply base at Camp Breckinridge. In his report, Wheeler took full credit for holding Crittenden back.[17]

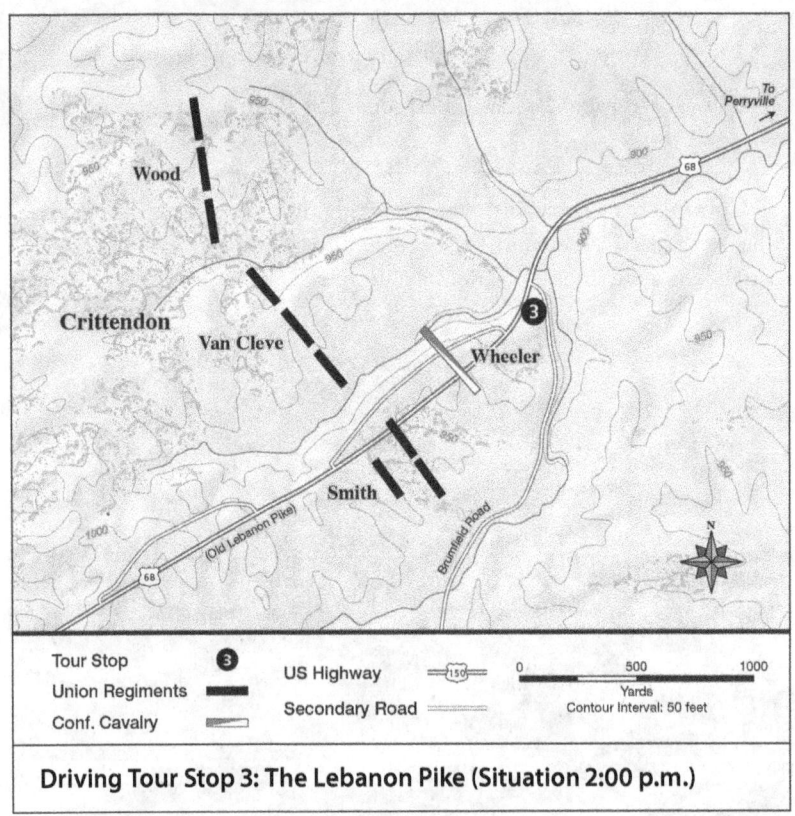

Driving Tour Stop 3: The Lebanon Pike (Situation 2:00 p.m.)

Report of Col. Joseph Wheeler, CSA, Commanding Wheeler's Cavalry Brigade, Buckner's Division, Hardee's Left Wing, Army of the Mississippi

During the night I received orders to place my brigade on the left of our general line of battle for the engagement which was to take place the following day.

At daylight the skirmishing again commenced, and at about 8 o'clock my brigade was deployed as directed. Pickets and scouts were immediately thrown out on all the approaches to Perryville from the south and southwest as far as the Lebanon and Danville road and all precaution taken to prevent a flank movement of the enemy.

Seeing myself confronted by a large body of troops of all arms deployed in line of battle and gradually increasing their front my line was advanced to hold them in check sufficiently to prevent their farther advance.

About 10 a.m. my pickets on the Perryville and Lebanon road were pressed in by a large body of cavalry, which proved to be the First Kentucky and Seventh Pennsylvania Regiments, which were moving down the Lebanon and Perryville road with a large force, partly dismounted, deployed on each side. At this moment, receiving orders from General Polk to clear that road of the enemy, we charged the enemy, throwing their entire force of cavalry into confusion and putting it to flight.

We pursued them at full charge for 2 miles, capturing many prisoners and horses in single combat and driving the remaining under cover of their masses of infantry. The enemy also fled terror-stricken from a battery placed in advance of their general line and left it at our disposal. The charge, one of the most brilliant of the campaign, was made in column; detachments of the First and Third Alabama Cavalry with the gallant Cols. [W. W.] Allen and [James] Hagan being in advance. Colonel Hart, who had just come up with a body of about 400 cavalry, followed for a short distance, but owing to some mistake turned off the road, carrying all his own command, together with all in his rear, thus leaving the combat to the few brave men of the First and Third Alabama Regiments. With these few, who, after sending our prisoners to the rear, numbered only about 80 men, we were confronted by such forces that we were prevented making any farther advance. I therefore withdrew a short distance

> and again deployed our line, engaging the enemy with both cavalry and artillery until night, and prevented this large force from taking any other part in the contest of that day. Early in the day I sent a battalion under Major Adrian to re-enforce the picket on the Perryville and Mitchellsburg road, the enemy having pressed upon us at that point with apparent indication of an attempt to gain our rear. Major Adrian skirmished with them and held them at bay until we retired the following morning.[18]

The next stop is Bragg's headquarters, located at the Crawford House, which is about three miles northeast. Carefully turn around and drive back to Perryville. Continue to the intersection with Second Street (US Highway 150), turn right (east), and drive two blocks to the intersection with South Bragg Street. Turn left (north) onto South Bragg Street, which becomes North Bragg Street in one block. Drive north, then northeast on North Bragg Street, which becomes the Harrodsburg Road, and continue 0.9 mile from downtown to the Crawford House on the left (west). Park, leave your vehicle, and face the house. Although located on the battlefield, the building is currently privately owned, unsafe, and closed to the public.

Stop 4—The Crawford House: Bragg's Headquarters

Critical Decisions: (8) Polk Refuses to Attack per Bragg's Orders and Assumes the "Offensive-Defensive," (9) Bragg Realigns Cheatham's Division, (21) Bragg Decides to Retreat

When he failed to discern any sounds of the battle he had ordered Polk to initiate, Bragg rode southwest from Harrodsburg on the morning of October 8. He chose the Crawford House for his headquarters. Although Bragg was undoubtedly on the battlefield when he made some of these critical decisions, since this house was his official headquarters, we will discuss his choices here.

On the battlefield, Polk told Bragg that he, with his commander's support, had made the critical decision to adopt the "offensive-defensive."

Driving Tour of the Critical Decisions of the Battle of Perryville

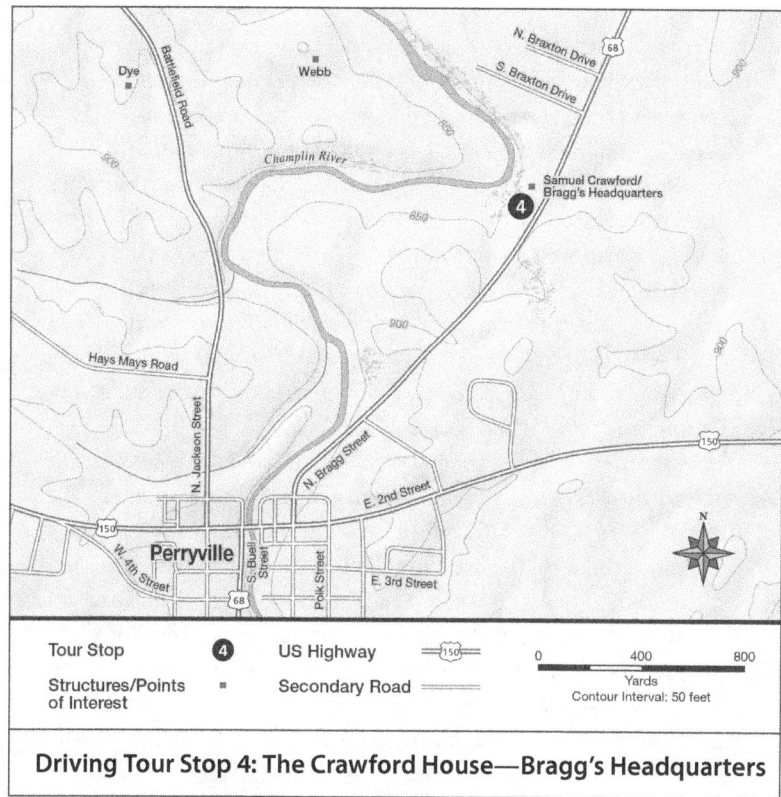

Driving Tour Stop 4: The Crawford House—Bragg's Headquarters

Report of Maj. Gen. Leonidas Polk, CSA, Commanding (Temporarily) Army of the Mississippi

Information having been received through General Hardee that the enemy was pressing with heavy force upon his position it was resolved by the general commanding the forces to attack him at that point. He accordingly directed me on the evening of the 7th to order Anderson's division, of Hardee's wing, to return to Perryville and also to order General Cheatham, with Donelson's division [actually Brigade] of his wing, to follow it immediately, and return myself to that place, to take charge of the forces and attack the enemy the next morning. I urged the strong expediency of concentrating all of our forces upon the point to be attacked, and at all events the necessity of having the remaining division of the Army of the Mississippi (Withers') placed at my disposal. To this the general objected, upon

> the ground that General Kirby Smith had informed him that the enemy was in force in his front and that his troops could not be spared from that part of the field, nor could the division of Withers be spared, as he thought the force in front of Smith made it necessary for him to be re-enforced. He therefore proposed to order Withers to the support of Smith and to take charge of those combined forces himself in person. Generals Anderson and Cheatham proceeded to Perryville and reported to General Hardee as ordered, and on arriving were posted by that officer in a line of battle which he had selected. I followed as soon as practicable, arrived during the night, and reconnoitered the line of battle early on the following morning.
>
> At a meeting of the general officers, held about daylight, it was resolved, in view of the great disparity of our forces, to adopt the defensive-offensive, to await the movements of the enemy, and to be guided by events as they were developed. The line of battle selected was indicated by the course of the Chaplin Fork of Salt River, on the banks of which our troops were posted. The division of General Buckner, of the left wing, occupied the extreme right; that of General Anderson the center; that of General Donelson, of the right wing, under General Cheatham, the left. General McCown, who reached the field by a forced march with a cavalry force at an early hour, was directed, by order of General Bragg, to turn over his command to Colonel Wheeler and to report to him for orders. The whole of our force, including all arms, did not exceed 15,000. We have good reason to believe that the force of General Buell immediately in front of us, consisting of the corps of Generals McCook and Gilbert, each about 18,000 strong, and that General Crittenden, with a corps of about the same number, was within 8 miles of the field at the opening of the attack.[19]

Apparently quite annoyed that his orders had not been carried out, Bragg proceeded to tour the Rebel line and then made the critical decision to re-align Cheatham's Division on the battlefield into a more favorable position protecting his right flank.

Report of Gen. Braxton Bragg, CSA, Commanding Army of the Mississippi

Having on the night of the 7th learned that the force in front of Smith had rapidly retreated, I moved early the next morning to be present at the operations of Polk's forces. The two armies were formed confronting each other on opposite sides of the town of Perryville. After consulting with the general and reconnoitering the ground and examining his dispositions I declined to assume the command, but suggested some changes and modifications of his arrangements, which he promptly adopted.[20]

Narrative of Christopher Losson,
Tennessee's Forgotten Warriors

An irritated Bragg rode to the scene and arrived around 10 a.m. While he surveyed the setup, McCook's corps moved into position on Gilbert's left. Bragg was determined to strike the Federals at Perryville but feared being overlapped on the right. He altered his battle formation in response to McCook's arrival, but still remained unsure that the force represented an entire corps. About an hour after Bragg reached the field, [following Bragg's orders] Polk ordered Cheatham to shift from the left side of the Rebel line to the right. The move was soon underway, the hot sun beating on Cheatham's men as they marched northward for more than a mile. The movement attracted sporadic artillery fire, but Cheatham's men were periodically sheltered by the undulating hills along Chaplin's Fork. When the shift was completed, Cheatham's division and a Texas cavalry unit under John A. Wharton anchored the Rebel right flank. To Cheatham's left were two divisions of Hardee's wing, one led by Simon Bolivar Buckner and the other by Patton Anderson.[21]

After the battle concluded, at the Crawford House, Bragg had to decide whether to remain and fight or retreat. Finally realizing he was actually confronting Buell's entire army, Bragg made the critical decision to retreat. Additionally, he needed to protect his supply base at Camp Breckinridge, formerly known as Union Camp Dick Robinson.

> ### Report of Gen. Braxton Bragg, CSA, Commanding Army of the Mississippi
>
> Ascertaining that the enemy was heavily re-enforced during the night, I withdrew my force early the next morning to Harrodsburg and thence to this point. Major-General Smith arrived at Harrodsburg with most of his forces and Withers' division the next day (10th), and yesterday I withdrew the whole to this point, the enemy following slowly but not pressing us. My future movements cannot be indicated, as they will depend in a great measure on those of the enemy.
>
> The campaign here was predicated on a belief and the most positive assurances that the people of this country would rise in mass to assert their independence. No people ever had so favorable an opportunity, but I am distressed to add there is little or no disposition to avail of it. Willing perhaps to accept their independence, they are neither disposed nor willing to risk their lives or their property in its achievement. With ample means to arm 20,000 men and a force with that to fully redeem the State we have not yet issued half the arms left us by casualties incident to the campaign.[22]

The next stop is at the Open Knob, about three miles away. Depart the Crawford House and return to downtown Perryville. Turn right (west) on US Highway 150 / Second Street, and continue three blocks. Turn right (north) onto North Jackson Street and drive two miles back to the Perryville Battlefield State Historic Site. Turn left into the entrance, drive to the visitor center, and park. Walk to the Confederate cemetery and proceed through it. Take the trail that begins on the northwest side, and walk about 270 yards up to the Open Knob.

Stop 5—The Open Knob

Critical Decisions: (9) Bragg Realigns Cheatham'sDivision and Orders the Assault, (11) McCook Strengthens the Union Left, (12) Wharton Fails to Fully Discover the Union Left, (13) Cheatham Orders Maney's and Stewart's Brigades to Assist Donelson

This is a unique stop in that only one part of one critical decision (McCook strengthening his left) was actually made here. However, the three other crit-

Driving Tour of the Critical Decisions of the Battle of Perryville

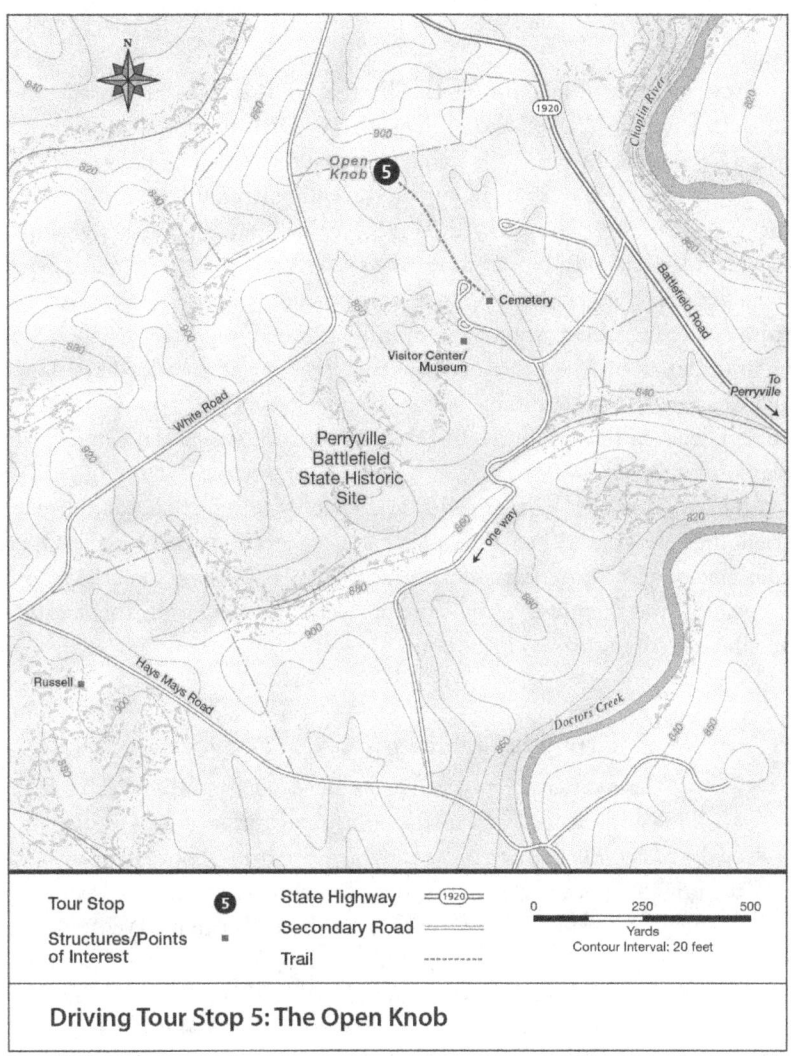

Driving Tour Stop 5: The Open Knob

ical decisions plus McCook's partial one referenced above were all reached because of this location and its ramifications on the decision-makers. The exact sites of these choices are not known.

On the Open Knob, first face southeast. You are standing at the location of Parson's eight cannon, which were in a perfect position to enfilade Donelson's Brigade as it made its original assault, initiating the main portion of the

Battle of Perryville. Note how easily these cannon could inflict harm on his brigade.

Now face northeast toward the Battlefield Road. After crossing the Chaplin River at Walker's Bend, Cheatham's Division initiated its assault with Donelson's Brigade in the lead, down past the cemetery. However, realizing that Donelson was not rolling up the Union left flank, in order to save that brigade, Cheatham ordered Maney's Brigade to charge this position. The 123rd Illinois, positioned just northwest on Parson's battery, was ordered to halt Maney's attack; however, the 123rd was quickly routed. Likewise, the 105th Ohio, initially to your right, eventually failed to protect Parson's battery. The units of Maney's Brigade eventually overcame Federal resistance and captured this location, including seven of Parson's cannon. Cheatham's critical decision to capture the Open Knob greatly assisted the Confederate plan of attack.

As McCook's various brigades arrived on the field, he continued to strengthen his left. When a couple of his officers showed him the Open Knob, he quickly recognized its value as a valuable position to occupy, both defensively and offensively. You can appreciate the view from this location and its value to the armies involved.

Narrative of Kenneth W. Noe, *Perryville*

Seat-of-the-pants improvisations continued on the Federal left as McCook next decided what to do with Terrill's brigade, still waiting on the Mackville Road near the Dixville Crossroads. Should he place the brigade in a reserve line behind Rousseau as he had originally intended, or instead use the brigade up front to extend Webster's line further to the left, taking full advantage of the terrain? [Col.] Leonard Harris and Capt. Beverly D. Williams, McCook's guide, argued for a third option. They insisted that the ideal position for the brigade lay a few hundred yards further along the ridge to the northeast, on Harris's left. At the northern end, they counseled, the high ground of the ridge rose to an imposing crest on a high, open knob [the Open Knob] overlooking Walker's Bend to the east and a deep valley to the north. Riding over to the area they had indicated to see for himself, a delighted McCook found the spot and immediately agreed that troops placed there would command the Chaplin River and especially the pools of water sighted in the river's bend six hundred yards below. The site was ideal ground, save for the fact that it threw any troops occupying it would be well forward of

Harris's and Lytle's line, not to mention Webster's. As fate would have it, those troops would belong to the corps' least-experienced brigade. McCook, however, could not pass up occupying such imposing ground.[23]

Report of Maj. Gen. Alexander McD. McCook, Commanding First Corps, Army of the Ohio

Having been informed by my guide, Capt. Beverly D. Williams, acting assistant quartermaster on General Jackson's staff, and also by Col. L. A. Harris, commanding the Ninth Brigade, that by moving a short distance to the left of the Perryville road I could get high commanding-ground for a portion of my line, I went forward in person to the high ground overlooking a portion of Chaplin River, advanced to within 600 yards of the river, and saw the water. Having previously ordered a portion of the Thirty-third Ohio Volunteers into the woods on the right as skirmishers to ascertain if any enemy was present in that vicinity, I then sent for Generals Jackson and Terrill, showed them the water, marked their line of battle, and ordered a battery to be posted on this line, with strong support. General Terrill was ordered to advance a body of skirmishers cautiously down the slope of the hill to the water as soon as the line was formed.[24]

Col. John A. Wharton made a final reconnaissance around 1:45 p.m., just before, under directions from Bragg and Polk, Cheatham ordered Brig. Gen. Donelson's brigade to begin the attack on the Union left. Unfortunately, for all involved in the ensuing attack, Wharton failed to discern the additional Union troops around the Open Knob and farther north. As a result, Donelson's Brigade attacked the middle of McCook's corps and not its left flank. Union fire enfiladed Donelson on both of his flanks, quickly causing large casualties.

Narrative of Earl J. Hess, *Banners to the Breeze*

But the attack was unfolding much more slowly than Bragg intended. Polk crossed his divisions to the west of the Chaplin River but then learned from Wharton that many more Union troops were marching toward Perryville along the Mackville Road than anyone had expected. Their obvious intention was to extend the Federal left. Bragg's tactical plan was based on the assumption that his enemy's left rested at the Russell house. If Wharton's report was true, Polk would be unable to outflank the Federals and might even be hit in his own flank when he began to wheel to the left. Bragg concluded that his corps [wing] commander was right. Cheatham's division, which was on the far right, had to move farther north. The only way it could do so was to recross the Chaplin River and reassemble at Walker's Bend, formed by the river bulging westward around a plot of mostly flat land. From here, it could cross the shallow water, ascend the sixty-foot-high bluffs, and form on a flat shelf of land. Then the Confederates could move up the higher ground that the Federals were beginning to occupy. A crude road leading from Walker's Bend had to be partially dug out to accommodate the artillery. This repositioning would take time, but it was necessary. Unfortunately for the Confederates, Bragg failed to use Wharton's cavalry to determine exactly where the forming Union line would end. As a result, Cheatham would still not be able to outflank it.[25]

Narrative of Kenneth W. Noe, *Perryville*

In a larger sense, however, Wharton's reconnaissance failed miserably. It was not all his fault, but rather a function of timing, topography, and perhaps fate. The entire basis of the Confederate attack was a surprise flanking movement against an unanchored Federal left. Had Wharton ridden out five minutes later, he would have seen the first of Starkweather's and Terrill's brigades moving onto the northern hilltops and might have concluded that the northern flank extended much farther to the north. Wharton, however, rode out when he did, and so saw only a few mounted men—conceivably cavalry, but in fact several generals with their staffs—on top of the Open Knob.[26]

Maj. Gen. Benjamin F. Cheatham received the assignment to launch the attack against the Union left. Unfortunately, soon after his initial brigade, Donelson's, began the assault, Cheatham recognized that Donelson was not striking the actual Union left flank. Instead, Donelson was headed toward the center of McCook's hastily deployed corps. Cheatham knew he must rectify the situation quickly. He ordered Brig. Gen. Alexander P. Stewart's brigade to support Donelson, while he directed Brig. Gen. George Maney's brigade to deploy more to the northwest and assault the Federal position atop and near the Open Knob.

> ### Report of Maj. Gen. Leonidas Polk, CSA, Commanding (Temporarily) Army of the Mississippi
>
> I awaited until the re-enforcements got into position. The attack was then ordered. Wharton charged the enemy's extreme left with great fury, passing on over stone walls and ravines and driving back the enemy's infantry several hundred yards. This movement placed in our possession a skirt of woods and an eminence of great importance to our success on our right. It was quickly followed by the brigades of General Cheatham, under Brigadier-Generals Donelson, Stewart, and Maney. These mounted the steep and difficult cliffs of Chaplin River in gallant style and moved forward upon the enemy's position with a most determined courage. Their approach was met by a storm of shot, shell, and musketry from several batteries strongly posted and supported by heavy masses of infantry. Their progress was nevertheless steadily onward, and although mowed down by well-directed volleys of musketry and well-served artillery the gaps thus produced in our lines were promptly filled and our troops pressed forward with resistless energy, driving the enemy before them and capturing three of his batteries. In this movement the enemy's left was forced back about a mile until his three lines were pressed into one. Here, being heavily re-enforced, he recovered one of his batteries, but did not attempt to regain any of the ground he had lost. This charge of these brigades was one of the most heroic and brilliant movements of the war. Considering the disparity of the numbers of the troops engaged, the strength of the enemy's position, the murderous character of the fire under which they had to advance, the steadiness with which they endured the havoc which was being made in their ranks, their knowledge that they were without any supporting force, the firmness with which they moved upon the enemy's masses of infantry and artillery, it will compare favorably with the most brilliant achievements of historic valor. In this charge General James S. Jackson, who commanded a division of the enemy, was killed amid the guns of one of the batteries [Parson's] that was taken.[27]

Appendix I

The Forty-First Georgia belonged to Maney's Brigade and fought heavily per Cheatham's orders to help capture the Open Knob. Capturing Lieut. Charles Parson's independent battery of eight guns was necessary to relieve the fire on Donelson's Brigade as it advanced.

> ### Report of Maj. John Knight, CSA, Commanding (Temporarily) Forty-First Georgia, Maney's Brigade, Cheatham's Division, Right Wing, Army of the Mississippi
>
> On the 8th instant this regiment participated in a battle with the Federals at Perryville, Ky. Being on the right of General Maney's brigade, was led into the battle by a flank movement across a creek in the direction of the battle guided by the sound, and brought into line of battle by filing to the right through a brush-wood under heavy cannonading, being protected by an eminence in front where the line was formed, composed of the Forty-first Georgia, Sixth and Ninth Tennessee Regiments, and moved forward. As it emerged from the woods it came in view of the enemy's battery [Parson's], situated on an eminence in a cleared field, supported by a heavy force, where it instinctively halted. In an instant the brigade was ordered forward by the brigade commander, and as it moved forward, owing to the situation of the enemy, the Forty-first Regiment was first exposed to the fire, and as soon as it was in view the enemy opened upon them a most terrific and deadly fire, when our regiment responded and baited for several minutes. It was a fearful time. At this critical moment General Maney passed down our line, encouraging the men by his personal presence and urging them forward. Just at this place our regiment sustained one-half, if not two-thirds, of their entire loss during the battle. Finally this suspense was relieved by the enemy's lines giving way, which was closely followed up by our troops, who seemed to vie with each other in seeing who could do the most to drive the enemy from the field. Never perhaps did troops fight more desperately than did these on this occasion. Our regiment lost 6 men bearing aloft the colors (2 killed and 4 wounded). Our colors had six holes shot through them. Our noble colonel (Charles A. McDaniel) fell late in the evening, severely wounded, in the corn field beyond the belt of woods we passed through after going out of the old field.[28]

The next stop is in the heart of the fighting at and around the H. P. Bottom House, which is just over a mile away to the southwest. Depart the

Driving Tour of the Critical Decisions of the Battle of Perryville

visitor center parking lot, drive a few hundred yards, and turn right onto the gravel road labeled Bottom Lane. (Do not drive all the way to the main entrance to the park; if you do, you have missed the turn.) Follow Bottom Lane approximately a mile as it climbs up and passes along Loomis's Heights. Carefully park on the gravel road near its intersection with the paved highway, formerly the Mackville Road, now designated the Hayes-Mays Road.

Stop 6—The H. P. Bottom House

Critical Decision: (15) Buckner Orders Adams to Break the Deadlock at the Bottom House

This is Position 6A. Leave your vehicle, walk to the edge of the Hayes-Mays Road, and face southeast, viewing the H. P. Bottom House just east of the road as the road descends to Doctor's Creek.

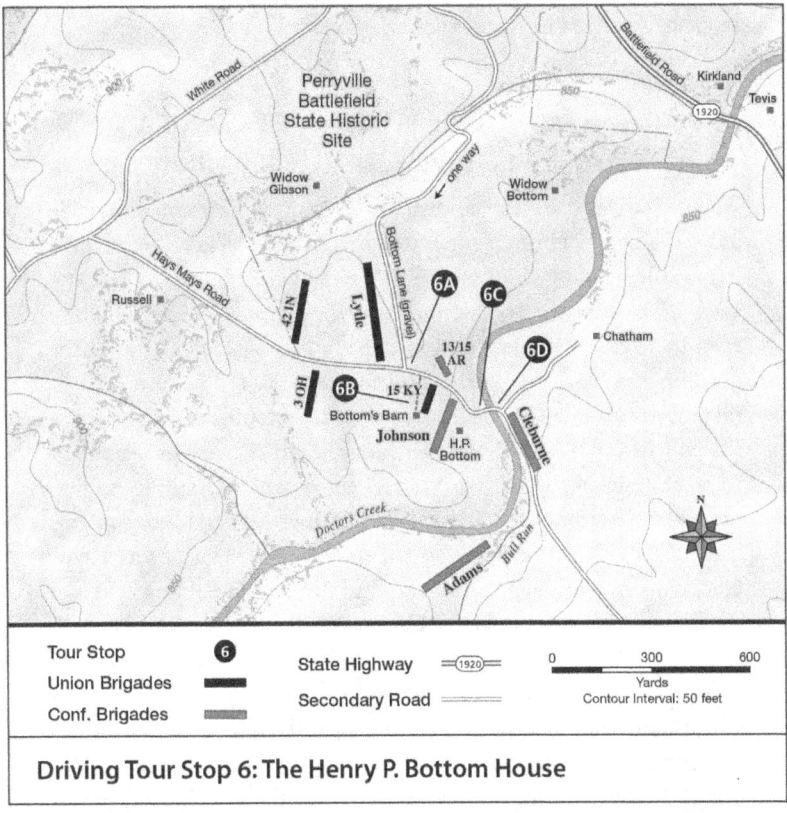

Driving Tour Stop 6: The Henry P. Bottom House

Appendix I

Per the Stop 6 map, note the location of the various Union and Confederate units engaged in the heavy combat at each of the four positions within this stop. Decisive fighting took place at this location from around 1:00 p.m. until about 5:00 p.m. The Stop 6 map displays the action at the time Adam's Brigade advanced in action around 3:45 p.m.

After Cheatham's Division became heavily engaged around the Open Knob, the brigades of Col. Thomas M. Jones and Brig. Gen. John C. Brown, belonging to Brig. Gen. Patton Anderson's division and positioned just south of Cheatham, were ordered to attack McCook. After Anderson's two brigades were repulsed north of this location, Maj. Gen. Simon B. Buckner ordered the four brigades of his division to attack in a column of brigades. Brig. Gens. Bushrod Johnson, Patrick Cleburne, Sterling A. M. Wood, and St. John R. Liddell led their brigades toward the Bottom House, except that Wood moved north to support Brown. The fighting at and around the residence was terrific. The Bottom House, which you see in the distance, was a major focal point of Confederate attacks that the Yankees strongly resisted. Buckner's critical decision to force the Yankees back from the H. P. Bottom House greatly assisted in Rebel victory.

Report of Maj. Gen. William J. Hardee, CSA, Commanding Left Wing, Army of the Mississippi

About 1 o'clock in the afternoon General Cheatham's division crossed Doctor's Fork on our extreme right and engaged the enemy's left on the heights with great vigor. Immediately I ordered General Buckner to advance his division and attack the salient angle of the enemy's line where the Mackville road crosses Doctor's Fork. The position was a strong one. The enemy was posted behind a natural parapet afforded by the character of the ground and some stone fences [surrounding the Bottom House], which were enfiladed by their batteries on their right and swept by another strong battery posted in their rear. The brigade of Brigadier-General Johnson gallantly led the advance, with Brigadier-General Cleburne's as a support, while the brigade of General St. John B. Liddell was held as a reserve. The brigades of [John C.] Brown and Jones, of Anderson's, and [S. A. M.] Wood, of Buckner's division, had been detached to occupy the interval between the right of Buckner and the left of Cheatham, and the two remaining brigades of Anderson's division, under command of General [D. W.] Adams and Col. [Sam.] Powel, [Twenty-Ninth Tennessee], covered the extreme left of our

> line. By this time, Cheatham being hotly engaged, the brigades of Johnson and Cleburne attacked the angle of the enemy's line with great impetuosity near the burnt barn, while those of Wood, Brown, and Jones dashed against their line more to the right, on the left of Cheatham. Simultaneously the brigades of Adams and Powel, on the left of Cleburne and Johnson, assailed the enemy in front, while Adams', diverging to the right, united with Buckner's left. The whole force thus united then advanced, aided by a crushing fire from the artillery, which partially enfiladed their lines. This combined attack was irresistible, and drove the enemy in wild disorder from the position nearly a mile to the rear. Cheatham and Wood captured the enemy's battery in front of Wood, and among the pieces and amid the dead and dying was found the body of General James S. Jackson, who commanded a division of the enemy at that point.[29]

Carefully cross the Hayes-Mays Road, and walk south along the fence line a few hundred yards to Position 6B, near the Bottom barn site. Face east and then south, looking at the area around the Bottom House. This is the location of the burnt barn mentioned above.

Report of Col. John Beatty, USA, Commanding Third Ohio, 17th Brigade, Tenth Division, First Corps, Army of the Ohio

> At 11 o'clock a.m. my regiment was ordered to take the advance of the brigade to which it belongs, and proceeded to the crest of the hill overlooking a branch of Chaplin Creek, when the enemy in front opened upon us from a battery and we were ordered to retire to the foot of the hill, some hundreds of yards in the rear. There we formed in line of battle and remained for more than an hour while the batteries were replying to those of the enemy.
>
> About 2 p.m. the enemy were seen advancing toward our position, and my regiment was ordered to the crest of the hill. A battery, known as the Washington Battery, at once opened upon us, and I ordered my men to lie down and wait the approach of the enemy's infantry. The latter advanced under cover of a house upon the other side of the hill and reaching a point 150 yards distant, deployed behind a stone fence which was hidden from us by standing corn. At

this time my left wing rested upon a lane known as the — road, my line of battle extending along the crest of the hill and passing near to and somewhat beyond a large barn filled with hay. In this position, with a well-handled battery playing upon us, our first fire was delivered, the enemy replying with destructive effect. Capt. H. E. Cunard, Company I, was one of the first to fall, shot through the head, while gallantly performing his duty. A little later Capt. Leonidas Mc-Dougal, Company H, while waving his sword and cheering his men, fell pierced by a ball through the breast. Later still First Lieutenant Starr, Company K, died like a soldier in the midst of his men. About 175 of my regiment were killed and wounded upon the crest of the hill. Our line was steadfastly maintained until the barn on our right was fired by a shell from the enemy's batteries, and in a few minutes the heat became so intense that my right was compelled to fall back. After rallying we were relieved by the Fifteenth Kentucky, Col. Curran Pope, and our ammunition being nearly exhausted, we retired to the bottom of the hill. Soon after I sent Companies A, D, and F to act in conjunction with two companies of the Fifteenth Kentucky in endeavoring to hold a fence which ran along the side of a field in which we had been fighting and perpendicular to our former line, but the fire of the enemy's battery, combined with that of his infantry, was so deadly that these men were again ordered to retire. The Fifteenth Kentucky having by this time left the crest of the hill and the enemy opening from a new battery on our right a fire which completely enfiladed our line, I concluded, after consultation with Colonel Pope, to leave the ravine, filed off into the — road and was marching toward the rear, when I perceived the enemy emerging from the woods upon our right and coming in great force toward the ground we had just been holding. I immediately ordered my regiment to face about and advanced to meet the enemy, intending, in the absence of ammunition, to charge him with the bayonet. I was met here, however, by Lieutenant Grover, of Colonel Lytle's staff, with an order from him to retire. Accordingly we turned into a ravine on the right of the road and were supplying ourselves with ammunition when, hearing that Colonel Lytle, my brigade commander, was killed, and being separated from the other regiments of the brigade, I reported to Colonel Harris, commanding the Ninth Brigade, for further duty. Night soon came on, however, and the engagement ceased.[30]

Narrative of Kenneth A. Hafendorfer, *Perryville*

Now suddenly the log barn filled with hay, located on the right of Colonel Beatty's line, was hit by one of [Capt. Cuthbert H.] Slocomb's [5th Company, Washington Artillery] shells and caught fire. As flames burst from the roof, windows, doors and openings between the logs, the men of the 3rd Ohio in that vicinity were temporarily thrown into confusion. But despite the intense heat and smoke, they closed up on the left and continued to fight. Beatty's men, however, by now were about out of ammunition. Colonel William Lytle, who was with the regiment, ordered Beatty to retire the 3rd Ohio back down the hill in its rear and sent orders for Colonel Curran Pope to move his 15th Kentucky Regiment up to replace it. The 3rd Ohio was almost broken as it now fell back. It had gone into action with 500 men and had lost around 175.[31]

Narrative of Chris Kolakowski, *The Civil War at Perryville*

Just to the right of the battle line stood H. P. Bottom's large barn; shellfire set it ablaze, killing many wounded of both sides that had crawled there for safety.[32]

Walk back to and cross the Hayes-Mays Road, then return to your vehicle. Carefully turn left (southeast) onto the Hayes-Mays Road and drive several hundred yards down to Position 6C, located near the Bottom House, and park. Leave your vehicle and observe the house and surrounding area. The house is private property; please do not trespass.

Brig. Gen. Bushrod Johnson wrote a very long, detailed account of the action surrounding the H. P. Bottom House. Although somewhat edited here, it remains lengthy.

Report of Brig. Gen. Bushrod R. Johnson, CSA, Commanding 3rd Brigade, Third Division, Left Wing, Army of the Mississippi

In front of the right wing of the brigade and just below the crest of the undulation was a farm-house, with outhouses, orchard, and inclosed grounds. A rail fence ran nearly parallel with the crest of the undulation and to the left of the farm-house. Below this fence about

200 yards was the east bank of the Doctor's Fork, along a portion of which in front of my brigade was a stone fence, and the bank itself was nearly vertical, of solid rock, and from 3 to 5 feet high. Behind this bank the enemy were in position, with skirmishers advanced to the rail fence and farm-house on the undulation above. On the opposite or west bank and running parallel to the general direction of the stream was another stone fence, inclosing in part the yard of a farm-house, and a fence on the west side of this yard was also of stone. Beyond this last fence was the house or barn which was burned during the conflict of my brigade with the enemy. The Mackville and Perryville road descended the slope on the north side of the farm-house, leaving a yard in its front partly inclosed on that side by a stone fence and partly by a rail one. On the north side of the Mackville road and to the right of the farm-house last referred to was an elevation commanding the open fields and grounds on the west, south, and north, and much of the slope on the east of the creek. This height, the three stone walls (each commanding the one more advanced toward our position), and the crest of the hill above them all were occupied by the enemy or held within their lines. The position was a very strong one. There was perhaps none stronger in the enemy's lines.

While the Third Brigade was in position, as just described, the right section of Captain Darden's battery kept up a fire on the enemy in front, and Capt. [William W.] Carnes' battery on our right, posted on a spur of the same hill, and a battery of the enemy on our left, kept a very brisk fire on each other and on the infantry within their reach. Their shots passed immediately in front of the Third Brigade in a direction very nearly parallel to its line of battle, so that an advance from our position upon the enemy in front seemed likely to expose the brigade to an enfilading fire from the enemy's battery on our left. Some of the enemy's shots fell among the men of the Thirty-seventh Tennessee Regiment without injury to the men.

Between the hours of 1 and 2 p.m., when the troops of the right wing of our army were seen advancing to the attack on my right and in a line of battle approaching a perpendicular to that on which we were formed, I was ordered to move my brigade in conjunction with the right wing by changing my front obliquely to the left. By this means the enfilading fire of the enemy's battery was avoided and my right moved forward until it came under the fire of the enemy's skirmishers near the first farm-house. It was at the same time under the fire of two of the enemy's batteries, one enfilading from the right, the other on the left, which was throwing balls and spherical-case shot. The Thirty-seventh Tennessee Regiment responded to the fire of the enemy's skirmishers and drove them beyond the creek. The Forty-fourth Regiment here suffered from these batteries and from sharpshooters behind the stone wall at the creek.

The first casualties in the brigade occurred here in the Thirty-seventh and Forty-fourth Tennessee Regiments. The Forty-fourth Regiment lost several men by shells from the enemy's batteries on our left. Under the conviction that the change of front first ordered in my brigade was for the object of moving on this battery, three of my regiments, the Fifth Confederate, Twenty-fifth and Forty-fourth Tennessee Regiments, continued to wheel rapidly to the left and speedily advanced to the height the enemy appeared to occupy, fixing their bayonets for a charge. Upon reaching that height it was found that General Adams had occupied that position. The Fifth Confederate Regiment was then promptly moved by Col. J. A. Smith upon the enemy behind the stone fences. The Twenty-fifth and Forty-fourth Regiments took a position, at the request of General Adams, in support of the battery placed in position on the height to which they advanced. Colonel Fulton, of the Forty-fourth, reports to me that when he moved with a view to unite his regiment with the brigade which had been advanced and driven the enemy from the stone fence beyond the creek, General Adams found his position so threatened by a column of the enemy that he thought it necessary to detain these regiments. He also reports that they were afterward put in position under cover of woods and in support of a battery by the major-general commanding the division. The remaining four regiments, the Thirty-seventh, Seventeenth, Twenty-third, and Fifth Confederate Regiments, advanced down the slope of the hill and under fire from artillery and infantry, driving the enemy from their strong defensive positions behind the stone walls and into the open field beyond the farm-houses on the north of the Doctor's Fork. These regiments then occupied the stone wall above the farm-house. A portion of the Thirty-seventh Regiment took position along the Mackville road, partly flanking the position of the enemy in the field and protected by the side slope of rock. The Twenty-third Regiment moved to a position to the left of the farm-house and in the open field.

The conflict continued here for about two hours, and was

maintained with remarkable vigor and stubbornness on both sides and with heavy loss on the part of the enemy, who for a long time maintained their position in the open field exposed to the deadly aim of the regiment behind the stone fence. Early in this part of the conflict the houses in advance of the upper stone fence took fire and were consumed. The fire of the Fifth Confederate Regiment was particularly destructive, plainly thinning the enemy's ranks at every volley. Three times the flag of the enemy was cut down, and finally they were beaten back, utterly whipped.

The command of the enemy opposed to my brigade was that of Colonel Lytle, of the Tenth Ohio Regiment, commanding the Seventeenth Brigade, which consisted of the Tenth Ohio, the Fifteenth Kentucky, the Thirty-second Indiana, and perhaps the Third Ohio. Two of the four regiments of my command opposed to the enemy at this point (the Twenty-third and Thirty-seventh Tennessee Regiments) were very small, averaging only about 230 effective strength. Three of these regiments now, at about 5 p.m., reported their ammunition exhausted, and not knowing what fresh troops we might encounter by advancing beyond the stone wall and seeing Brigadier-General Cleburne advancing to our support, I directed them to wait until their cartridges could be replenished and reported to General Cleburne the condition of my command, suggesting the propriety of an advance upon the enemy. I immediately sent to the rear to have some ammunition brought up.[33]

Report of Brig. Gen. Daniel W. Adams, CSA, Commanding Adams's Brigade, Anderson's Division, Left Wing, Army of the Mississippi

At about 11.30 a.m., when advancing, I received an order from Brigadier-General [Patton] Anderson, commanding the division, to halt or move slowly until the Third Brigade, commanded by Colonel [Samuel] Powel, arrived opposite my line. In obedience to this order I halted the brigade several times and moved very slowly until I came near the enemy at the foot of a hill on Beech Fork Creek [*sic*]. Before reaching this point I sent several messengers to Colonel Powel to move up as rapidly as possible. On reaching the point above designated I halted the command, had the artillery put in position so as to command that of the enemy, and again sent a messenger to Colonel Powel by my aide-de-camp, Lieut. E. M. Scott. Receiving no answer, and as it was then getting late in the day, I ordered the artillery to open fire, and after a very brisk, well-directed, and effective fire for a half or three-quarters of an hour, by direction of General Buckner I moved the infantry forward on the enemy's right at and near a very strong position on a hill. After a short but spirited contest we dislodged and drove them before us. They fled in great disorder, panic, and confusion, throwing their arms and equipments away as they fled. We followed them about a mile, the Washington Artillery coming up and halting at two positions, as directed, where they again opened fire with great accuracy and effect. Finding my brigade in the advance and entirely unsupported on the right or left except by General Cleburne's brigade, which was in our rear to the right, and inactive from being out of ammunition, as I was informed, I halted my command under a very heavy and rapid fire from this point, when I was soon opened upon from the left and rather to the rear by a well-directed battery of artillery. Using my glass, I discerned the enemy moving their forces and forming line of battle at a distance of 600 or 800 yards to my left. Deeming this position untenable I ordered the brigade to fall back, which they did in perfect order. I communicated this intention to General Cleburne, with my reasons for doing it. After passing the first hill which we drove the enemy from I met General Hardee, who ordered the command to return and take position on that hill. This was promptly executed, and the Washington Artillery again opened fire with great force and effect and continued it until 7.30 o'clock p.m. My brigade remained at this position until 2 o'clock a.m. of the 9th instant, when, the balance of the command having moved in obedience to General Buckner's orders, I moved in, bringing up the rear, and reached our position near Perryville about 3.30 o'clock a.m.

The killed, wounded, and missing from my brigade amounted to 152, of whom 6 are known to be killed, 78 wounded, and 68 missing.[34]

Walk the short distance to Position 6D, Doctor's Creek. This creek was a primary cause of the Battle of Perryville, as its pools of water were so necessary for the soldiers on both sides of the fighting. Brig. Gen. Lovell H. Rousseau ordered the Forty-Second Indiana to obtain much-needed water in

Appendix I

Doctor's Creek, and it did so in the area just north of the bridge. The Federals did not realize that the high embankment created a trap. The Rebels would soon attack here.

Report of Brig. Gen. Lovell H. Rousseau, USA, Commanding Third Division, First Corps, Army of the Ohio

Everything indicated that the enemy had retired and it was so believed. General McCook rode off to see General Buell, understood to be 2 or 3 miles to our right.

Waiting perhaps an hour, I concluded to resume the march to Chaplin Creek, then probably a mile to our front, to get water for my men, who were suffering intensely for the want of it. There was a small pool in the bed of a little stream to the right of Loomis' two pieces, to which the Forty-second Indiana was directed in order to obtain a supply, and the main column was then ordered forward; but when the head of the column was within a hundred or two yards of Loomis' pieces I halted it and went forward to see what was reported to be the enemy reappearing in the woods beyond, and in a few minutes I could see him plainly, and the discharge of shell from three batteries massed gave unmistakable evidence of his presence in force.[35]

Narrative of Kenneth W. Noe, *Perryville*

Rousseau thus made the ultimately momentous decision to march his two brigades down to Doctor's Creek without McCook's permission. The 42nd Indiana, already forward supporting [Capt. William A.] Hotchkiss's 2nd Battery, Minnesota Light Artillery], would go first, while the rest of Lytle's brigade formed into column with the 3rd Ohio in front and began advancing, snaking slowly downhill to the waterway. Harris would go after Lytle. Although ordered to fill their canteens as quickly as possible so as to make room for the next regiment, the Hoosiers seemed to be in no hurry; the Rebels, after all, were retreating [or so they thought]. Stacking their arms and crawling down into the creek bed north of the road [where you are positioned], they looked forward to boiling water, making some coffee, and eating dinner in peace. As fate would have it, the Hoosiers went into the creek where its western bank was stony, high, and indeed al-

> most perpendicular. Entering there was a simple matter. Extricating themselves would be another thing entirely.
>
> ... Adam's Battery and skirmishers coincidentally opened fire on the 42nd Indiana roughly at the same moment that Johnson's brigade was launching its attack.... Men raced down the creek bed or else climbed the precipitous bank of the ravine and then fled uphill as fast as they could run.[36]

Return to your vehicle at Position 6D. The next stop is on the Old Springfield Pike, where Col. Samuel Powel advanced his brigade west toward Sheridan's division, about two or so miles southwest. Continue across the bridge over Doctor's Creek, and follow the road as it turns southeast. In about 1.2 miles you will come to the intersection with Battlefield Road / Highway 1920. Turn right (south) and drive a couple of blocks to the intersection with US Highway 150 / Second Street. Turn right (west) and drive 1.8 miles to the intersection with the Old Springfield Road. Turn right (north) onto the Old Springfield Road, and drive about 0.4 mile to the bridge crossing Bull Run and park. Note that this is near Peters Hill, the site of the night fighting. Leave your vehicle and face west. This is approximately where Powel's Brigade began to encounter fire from the advanced regiments of Brig. Gen. Phillip Sheridan's division as it marched west.

Stop 7—Powel's Reconnaissance in Force

Critical Decision: (16) Powel Is Ordered to Conduct a Reconnaissance in Force

Per the Stop 7 map, you are standing near where Powel's Brigade, consisting of three regiments, around 4:30 p.m. advanced toward some of the fourteen Union regiments positioned in the area of the Old Springfield Pike. Needless to say, Powel was unable to sustain his momentum, and he ordered a retreat.

In an effort to assist Bragg in overwhelming McCook's First Corps, Maj. Gen. Simon B. Buckner ordered Powel's Brigade to conduct a reconnaissance in force moving west just south and along the Old Springfield Pike. Unbeknownst to Buckner and Powel, fourteen regiments commanded by Sheridan and Brig. Gen. Robert D. Mitchell were positioned to block Powel's advance. Thus this maneuver quickly stalled. However, it did keep

Appendix I

View along the Old Springfield Pike, near Perryville. Photo by Chuck Lott.

Sheridan and Mitchell occupied and concerned that more advances by other Rebel units might occur. Powel's reconnaissance in force served to keep Gilbert's Third Corps from further participating in the battle and possibly rolling up the Confederate left.

Report of Maj. Gen. William J. Hardee, CSA, Commanding Left Wing, Army of the Mississippi

The two remaining brigades of Anderson's division, under command of General (D. W.) Adams and Col. (Sam.) Powel, (Twenty-ninth Tennessee), covered the extreme left of our line.

. . . Simultaneously the brigades of Adams and Powel, on the left of Cleburne and Johnson, assailed the enemy in front, while Adams', diverging to the right, united with Buckner's left.

. . . Both brigades were gallantly conducted by General Adams and Colonel Powel, the latter having suffered severely in the unequal contest. To Brigadier-General Anderson the defense of the extreme left in the direction of Danville was intrusted. His operations were not under my immediate supervision. Two of his brigades were detached and advanced boldly, but one brigade was compelled by greatly superior numbers to resume its original ground, from which, under the cool direction of General Anderson, it subsequently with-

Driving Tour of the Critical Decisions of the Battle of Perryville

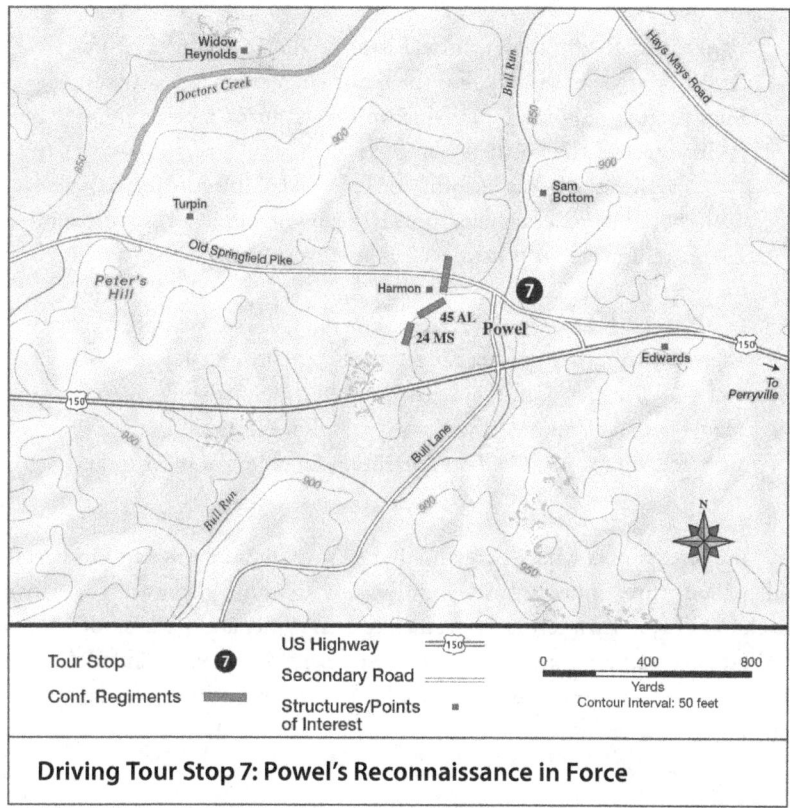

Driving Tour Stop 7: Powel's Reconnaissance in Force

drew in good order. Both brigades were gallantly conducted by General Adams and Colonel Powel, the latter having suffered severely in the unequal contest.³⁷

Narrative of Earl J. Hess, *Banners to the Breeze*

The Confederate force along the Springfield Road, which was supposed to hold the Federals in place, did its job reasonably well. Patton Anderson had no real knowledge of his opponent's numbers. Neither did he know that Crittenden's corps was positioned only a short distance to the south. He sent a single brigade, Col. Samuel Powell's [*sic*], to demonstrate westward. From their observation post on Peter's Hill, which was the target of Powell's [*sic*] advance, the Federals could see this brigade assemble a battle line south of the

> Springfield Road. They assumed it to be the vanguard of a much larger Confederate attack. For the time being, everyone on the front lines forgot the disturbing evidence that a major battle might be taking place to the north.
>
> ... The attack was heading for Peter's Hill into the teeth of an overwhelming Federal force, three Rebel regiments against fourteen Union regiments with artillery support from at least four Federal batteries.
>
> Yet the Tennessee and Alabama regiments boldly marched on to a fence within easy musket range of their enemy and gamely traded volley after volley with them. The odds in this "unequal contest," as Hardee would later put it, were too great. Powell [sic] retired, having succeeded in focusing Gilbert's attention for at least a short time.[38]

The next stop is where part of Mitchell's division advanced to in Perryville, about three miles away. Carefully turn around and retrace your drive back to US 150. Turn left (east), return to Perryville, and park off of US 150 / West Second Street next to the cemetery located between Liddell Avenue and Jackson Street on your right (south). Leave your vehicle and safely face north.

Stop 8—Mitchell's Advance

Critical Decision: (18) Gilbert Refuses to Let Mitchell Advance into Perryville

You are located at the right flank of Mitchell's division, part of which had advanced this far into Perryville when Gilbert ordered Mitchell to retreat west of the town. This location gives you an idea of how far into Perryville Mitchell and his men were. The Stop 8 map depicts the approximate location of Carlin's brigade at around 6:00 p.m. Gilbert was located a couple of miles west of this location when he made the critical decision to halt Mitchell. Had Mitchell been supported, perhaps he might have been able to partially roll up Bragg's left flank. However, Mitchell was likely unaware of Brig. Gen. Preston Smith's fresh brigade defending the east side of Perryville. Yet if Mitchell had been allowed to advance, this likely would have forced Liddell's Brigade to assist Powel and Smith, making it unavailable to assault the Mackville Road near the Dixville Crossroads.[39]

Driving Tour of the Critical Decisions of the Battle of Perryville

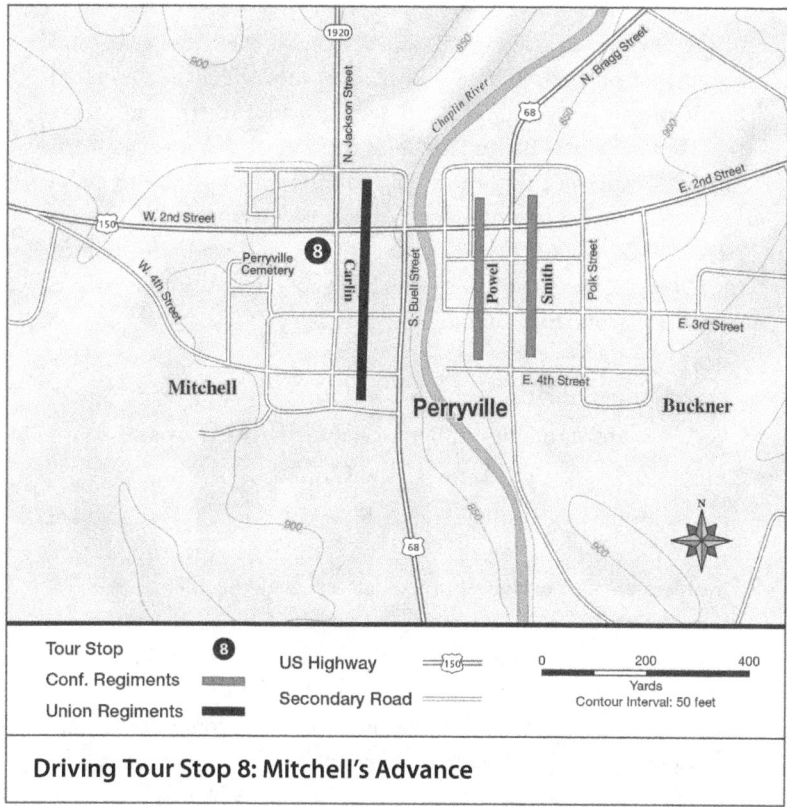

Driving Tour Stop 8: Mitchell's Advance

Note that Gilbert omitted recalling Mitchell in his report.

Report of "Acting Maj. Gen." Charles C. Gilbert, USA, Commanding Third Corps, Army of the Ohio

Shortly after Major Wright brought an order to send two brigades from Schoepf's division to support the First Corps, but as one brigade had already gone and my own lines were undergoing a dangerous assault I dispatched only one of Schoepf's brigades. That moved toward the right of the First Corps. The enemy's columns, as they followed up their success, came now to present their left flank to Sheridan's batteries, and he at once turned his guns upon them and disposed his infantry to demand their farther attention if they should presume to continue their progress. This, with the movement of the brigade from Schoepf's division, brought to a stand the left of the enemy's attack. At the same time Mitchell threw forward his right upon the repulsed and broken lines which had attacked Sheridan and himself, and, with gallant Carlin in the lead, drove them beyond Perryville and occupied the town with his skirmishers. Sheridan could not venture to join in following up the successful repulse of the enemy from his front, as his entire attention was directed to the columns then threatening to continue their progress toward my left and rear. It was about one hour before sunset that the enemy was repulsed from the front of my lines.[40]

Report of Brig. Gen. Robert D. Mitchell, USA, Commanding Ninth Division, Third Corps, Army of the Ohio

I placed my men in position about 12 o'clock on the right of the road in sight of the town of Perryville. This was on the 8th. I remained there for orders until Sheridan's line was attacked by the enemy. It was a pretty severe skirmish. An effort was made to take a battery that was in an advanced position and was repulsed by Sheridan, and a few moments after that time to Sheridan's right and my front there was a large force of the enemy, a full division, if not more, concentrated, and had commenced a movement on Sheridan's right. In the mean time Sheridan had sent a messenger saying that unless he was supported or re-enforced he would have to fall back. I directed the messenger

View of western Perryville. Photo by Chuck Lott.

to return and to say to Sheridan that I was watching the movements of the enemy and would strike them before they reached his right. In ten minutes I ordered Colonel Carlin, colonel Thirty-eighth Illinois, then in command of the Thirty-first Brigade, to advance under cover of the timber as far as possible, and directed him to break the enemy's lines there without firing a gun. He proceeded under the order until he had arrived within 150 yards of this concentration under cover of the timber and a kind of half-hedge fence. There were thorn bushes innumerable along the fence after he left the timber that covered his movements. In consequence of the timber and the brush he got to within 150 yards without being discovered, and under my direction ordered a double quick at the charge of the bayonet and drove the enemy without firing a gun. As soon as they [Powel's Brigade] were repulsed they were driven into the town of Perryville, 1 or 2 miles. That must have been about 3 o'clock or probably later, perhaps nearly 4. There is an elevation on the side of the town. On our arrival at that elevation there was a battery opened upon us, shooting across the town. I ordered up four pieces of Carlin's battery, two pieces having been detached for supporting General McCook, and two or three pieces of another battery in my division opened fire upon this battery, in the mean time throwing our skirmishers into Perryville. In twenty minutes we silenced the battery on the other side of the town and had driven the enemy out of the town of Perryville. I sent my aide-de-camp to direct the commanding officer of that regiment to change his direction to the left of the town and rather to the rear of the enemy and directed Colonel Carlin to support him. I rode back to the brigade that was following up for the purpose of supporting Carlin's brigade about 600 yards; it may have been more, but not exceeding 700 yards. This regiment that had changed their direction to the left of the town had captured thirteen wagon loads of ammunition, two ambulances, and two caissons, said to be of the Washington Battery, and brought them off the field.

Before I had changed my direction I was visited by General Gilbert's aide-de-camp and directed to hold back; that I was acting rashly and would not be sustained. I had not followed General Gilbert's aide-de-camp's directions, but preferred my own, and took possession of the hill, and I said if General Gilbert desires to give me orders I wanted them in writing; that I had received a great many orders from his staff officers that were not sustained by him, and if he

> desired me to fall back he must bring me a written order from General Gilbert. At the time of the capture of these wagons—perhaps a little before—I received an order in pencil, directing me to fall back on a line with General Sheridan, who commanded the left of our army corps, in that fight. I told him I would obey the order, and fell back with one brigade in line with General Sheridan. With the other brigade I exercised my own discretion, and so far as Carlin's brigade was concerned I directed him to remain till we got further orders. After falling back I occupied a commanding position, with artillery covering the town of Perryville and the Danville road.[41]

The next stop is Starkweather's Hill, where we will return to the action on the north end of the battlefield, about 4 miles northwest. Carefully leave your parking location, and drive east to the first intersection, which is Jackson Street. Turn left (north) onto North Jackson Street, and drive 0.6 mile to the intersection with Hayes-Mays Road on the left. Turn left (west) onto Hayes-Mays Road, and drive 3.5 miles, past the H. P. Bottom House (at 1.9 miles), to the intersection with White Road. The White Road is the modern name for what was the Benton Road during the time of the battle. This intersection was labeled the Dixville Crossroads during the Battle of Perryville and actually then was a crossroads. Turn right (northeast) onto the White Road, and drive about 0.6 mile, past a sharp curve to the left, to the small parking lot on the left (northwest) side of the road where there is an opening in the rail fence. This is the location of Starkweather's Hill. Park, walk up to the top of the small hill to the interpretive markers, and face northeast toward the Open Knob.

Stop 9—Starkweather's Hill

Critical Decision: (17) Starkweather Holds the Union Left

Note that you are standing in the midst of the twelve cannon Starkweather rounded up and several Union units supported. Augmented by Stewart's Brigade, Maney's Brigade repeatedly assaulted this position after it had forced the Union left back here. Ultimately, the Rebels drove the Yankees from this small hill.

After the Rebels of Maney's Brigade, which included the Forty-First Georgia and the First, Sixth, Ninth and Twenty-Seventh Tennessee, captured the Open Knob, the Union forces in the area retreated west through a cornfield, where the Yankees briefly held off the advancing Confederates.

Driving Tour of the Critical Decisions of the Battle of Perryville

Starkweather's Hill, Perryville Battlefield State Historic Site. Photo by Chuck Lott.

Forced to retire once again, the Federals retreated to just across the Benton Road (today's White Road) and fortified the top of a ridge there that was quickly named Starkweather's Hill. Capt. Asahel K. Bush's Fourth Battery, Indiana Light Artillery, and Capt. David C. Stone's Battery A, Kentucky Light Artillery, of six guns each, were positioned on the hill. Maney's Brigade, augmented with Stewart's Fourth and Fifth Tennessee regiments, continued driving west through a cornfield toward Starkweather's Hill. Col. John Starkweather cobbled together the disorganized Union commands at this location in order to resist the Rebel advance.[42]

After several attempts the Rebels drove the Yankees off of the hill, forcing them to abandon Stone's cannon and retreat several hundred yards farther west. There, on the Union left flank, the Yankees formed what became the final line of defense that afternoon, and they managed to repel the final assaults by Maney's and Stewart's totally exhausted men. The fighting here was finished for the day, and the Union line held.

Report of Maj. Gen. Alexander McD. McCook, USA, Commanding, First Corps, Army of the Ohio

...When General Terrill's brigade gave way, a portion of his troops fell back with him to the position occupied by Stone's and Bush's batteries, and at this point, when in the act of rallying his broken

Appendix I

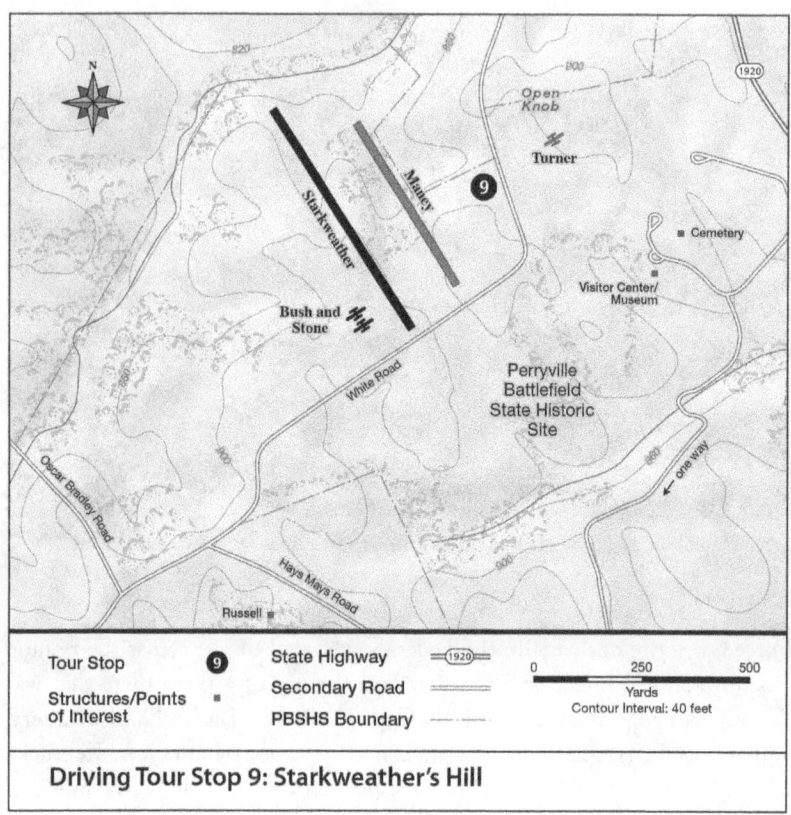

Driving Tour Stop 9: Starkweather's Hill

troops, at 4 p.m. he was struck in the side by the fragment of a shell, carrying away a portion of his left lung. He died at 11 p.m. ...

The posting of Starkweather's brigade and Stone's and Bush's batteries saved my left and secured to us the Mackville road, upon which stood our entire ammunition train and ambulances. The ground to the right of the road being rough and rugged prevented the train from being taken off the road and parked.

I have previously stated that the firing on both sides ceased at dark.[43]

Report of Col. Hume R. Feild, CSA, Commanding First Tennessee, Maney's Brigade, Cheatham's Division, Right Wing, Army of the Mississippi

My regiment went into the action of the 8th instant in rear and on the left of the brigade at the field where we captured the eight-gun battery. I lost only some 3 or 4 men killed and wounded at that place. The brigade was ordered immediately forward to take another battery about a half mile in advance, planted on a very steep hill, commanding a large corn field, through which we had to advance. This battery and its support was making terrible havoc with the right wing of the brigade, so reported by the field officers of the Forty-first Georgia to me, whereupon I sent Captain Malone to General Maney asking for my regiment to be sent to the right, which request was granted. After deploying the regiment to the extreme right it was ordered to charge, which it did in splendid style, with close, compact ranks, killing all the horses and men of the battery and driving its support away. In this charge the brigade became very much disorganized, and after taking the battery by some mistake fell back in confusion. My regiment lost in that charge its gallant lieutenant-colonel (John Patterson) and some 40 or 50 men and officers. I rallied the regiment at the foot of the hill, no other regiment forming but mine, some 30 or 40 men of the other regiments falling into the ranks. In the mean time the enemy came back to the guns behind the battery, and also marched two regiments on our left on a wooded hill which lay at right angles with the hill that we charged up.

I led the regiment up the hill alone, without any support, under a heavy fire of musketry, driving the enemy back and taking his gums again. The regiments on our left then opened their fire upon us, killing and wounding a dozen officers and men at each discharge. Just then I discovered Hardee's battle-flag coming up on our left about 500 yards in rear. Expecting that the regiment that carried the flag would engage the enemy that were cross-firing upon us I determined to hold the hill at every cost, thinking they would drive the enemy before them; they failed to do so and fell back before they had arrived in 200 yards of my position; whereupon I ordered my regiment to retire, which it did in much better order than could have been expected, leaving half their number dead and wounded on the top of the hill. My whole loss amounts to 181 killed, wounded, and missing.[44]

Appendix I

Starkweather's final position, Perryville Battlefield State Historic Site. Photo by the author.

Report of Brig. Gen. John C. Starkweather, USA, Commanding Twenty-Eighth Brigade, Third Division, First Corps, Army of the Ohio

[I] arrived on the field of battle at about 1.30 p.m., having marched 12 miles, about 3 miles thereof being through fields, woods, &c. Finding the troops already engaged well on the right, center, and left, and thinking the extreme left position most accessible, and, from appearances, one that should be held at all hazards, I placed my command at once in position facing the enemy's right (countermarching a portion of my brigade for such purpose), the Twenty-fourth Illinois and Seventy-ninth Pennsylvania forming the right wing, to be supported by the First Wisconsin and Twenty-first Wisconsin, when the last-mentioned regiment should arrive, and holding my two batteries to act as the disposition of the enemy might require. General (D. S.) Donelson's brigade at this moment engaged the Twenty-fourth Illinois and Seventy-ninth Pennsylvania on the right, but were driven from the field, after most desperate fighting. While this engagement was progressing, I placed, by your order, Bush's battery on the extreme left, Stone's battery next on its right, the First Wisconsin to the rear of Bush, to support him, and the Twenty-first Wisconsin, which had arrived (excepting two companies acting as flankers to the ammunition train), to the front of the two batteries, in a corn-field at the foot of the hill, upon which artillery was placed, forming it at once in line of battle. This disposition

> of my forces was hardly complete before General Maney's brigade attacked me in front, assisted by a battery, and General Donelson's brigade again attacked on the extreme right, the enemy at the same time placing a battery on my extreme left, upon a well-chosen position, to flank me. The flank movement on the left was prevented by Stone's battery shelling the position chosen, and Donelson's brigade was again forced to retire by the well-directed and continuous fire of the Twenty-fourth Illinois and Seventy-ninth Pennsylvania. I then ordered the Twenty-first Wisconsin to fire and charge the front, but, being a new regiment, their colonel being severely wounded and their major killed at about the time such order was given, no field officer was left to carry the command into execution, although several companies, hearing the order, attempted to obey it, but being sorely pressed by the brigade and battery in front, it retired in some disorder and confusion. I immediately advanced the First Wisconsin to the front, supported by an oblique fire from the Seventy-ninth and with canister from my artillery, and held such position until many of the artillery horses were killed and the balance became unmanageable, creating such confusion that proper discharges could not be continued. Other regiments on my right at this time were retiring, and being unable to obtain any support from them, I ordered the Seventy-ninth, Twenty-fourth, and First to hold their positions, while Stone's battery, of four guns, and Bush's battery, of two (all that was manageable), were retired to a new and safer position. The retirement was made in good order, and the fire from the artillery again opened. A part of the First Wisconsin then charged to the front, capturing the colors of the First Tennessee. The fire from the Seventy-ninth and Twenty-fourth held the enemy in check, while the balance of the First Wisconsin took by hand every remaining gun and caisson from the field. The enemy by this time was completely routed, the firing ceased on our front and flank, and the regiments were retired to the support of the batteries in their new position, which was occupied until 12 o'clock at night, when a change was made by your order.[45]

The final stop on the tour is the site of the Russell House, back on the Hayes-Mays Road just southeast of the Dixville Crossroads, just over a mile south of Starkweather's Hill. Turn around and drive southwest 0.6 mile back to the Dixville Crossroads / intersection with today's Hayes-Mays Road. Turn

Appendix I

left (southeast) onto the Hays-Mays Road, drive 0.2 mile, and park near the site of the Russell House on the right. Leave your vehicle and face northeast, looking across the road.

Stop 10—The Russell House

Critical Decisions: (14) Buell Orders Reinforcements to McCook, (19) Hardee Orders Liddell to Make a Final Assault, (20) Polk Orders all Fighting to Cease

You are located near where the final Rebel assaults were made on McCook's corps as evening closed in. The Stop 10 map depicts the final location of the Union and Confederate lines after the fighting ceased at around 7:00 p.m. Many hours after the fighting began, McCook finally requested reinforcements. Although not fully believing the combat was that severe, Buell made the critical decision to have Gilbert send two brigades to McCook. Gilbert dispatched Col. Michael Gooding's and Brig. Gen. James B. Goodman's brigades, and they arrived in this area in the nick of time, helping save the Union left from being rolled up.

> **Report of Brig. Gen. James Steedman, USA, Commanding Third Brigade, First Division, Third Corps, Army of the Ohio**
>
> Captain: I have the honor to report, pursuant to Special Orders, No. 14, from corps headquarters, that late in the afternoon of the 8th instant, having been ordered with my brigade to support Major-

Russell House, Perryville Battlefield State Historic Site, circa 1927. Photo by *Louisville Courier Journal*.

Driving Tour of the Critical Decisions of the Battle of Perryville

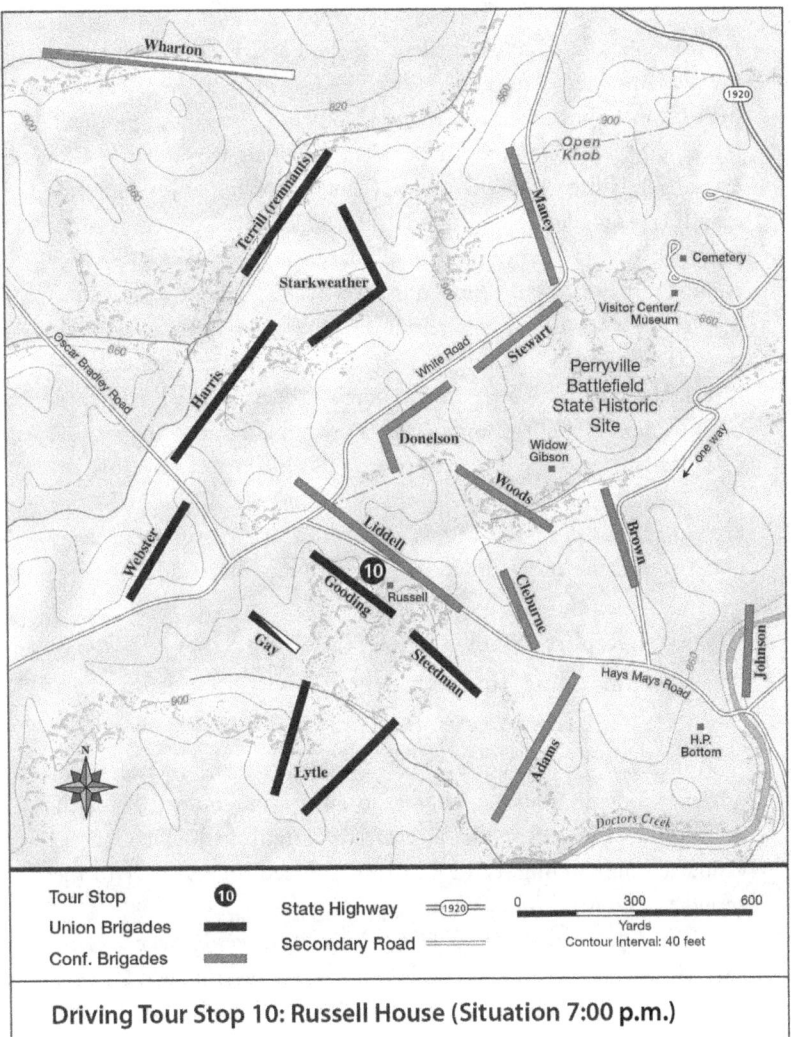

Driving Tour Stop 10: Russell House (Situation 7:00 p.m.)

General McCook, my command, in obedience to the orders of that officer, took position on the right of the division commanded by Brigadier-General Rousseau, where it was exposed to a quite severe fire of shot and shell and some musketry without being able to reply, except with the artillery attached (Company I, Fourth U.S. Artillery, commanded by Lieut. Frank G. Smith), which opened and fired with effect for about forty-five minutes, dismounting two guns, exploding one caisson, and effectually silencing the battery against which its fire was directed. The casualties of this command were: Thirty-fifth Ohio Volunteers, Col. F. Van Derveer commanding—Lieut. Joseph S. Claypoole and 3 men taken prisoners (since paroled for exchange), Ninth Ohio Volunteers, Lieut. Col. Charles Joseph, commanding—1 man severely wounded and 2 men taken prisoners (since paroled); Eighty-seventh Indiana Volunteers, Col. K. G. Shyrock commanding—2 men wounded, 1 severely; Eighteenth U.S. Infantry, Maj. F. Townsend commanding—3 men wounded, 1 severely; Second Minnesota Volunteers, Col. James George commanding—1 man taken prisoner; Company I, Fourth U.S. Artillery, Lieut. F. G. Smith commanding—1 man severely wounded and 1 man taken prisoner (since paroled); Lieut. Richard Schneider, serving on my staff, captured while conveying orders on the field (since paroled for exchange). I avail myself of this opportunity to reassure you of my entire confidence in the officers and men of my command.[46]

Report of Col. Michael Gooding, USA, Commanding Thirtieth Brigade, Ninth Division, Third Corps, Army of the Ohio

...As ordered, I had massed my brigade in the edge of a dense wood, joining General Rousseau's right, to await your orders. Precisely at 3.30 o'clock p.m. I received orders directly from Major-General Gilbert, commanding Third Corps to proceed immediately to the support of General McCook, on my left.

I then proceeded at double-quick in the direction where General McCook's forces were engaged. On reaching the field I found the forces badly cut up and retreating (they then having fallen, back nearly 1 mile) and were being hotly pressed by the enemy. After receiving instructions from General McCook I ordered my brigade forward into the fight, the Twenty-second Indiana taking position on the right, the Fifty-ninth Illinois on the left, and the Seventy-fifth Illinois in the center, and the battery took position on an eminence in our rear, which was bordered by a dense wood. I again ordered the brigade to the support of the brigade fighting on my left, which, as soon as I had become engaged, retreated and fell back in confusion.

The battle now raged furiously; one after one my men were cut down, but still, with unyielding hearts, they severely pressed the enemy, and in many instances forced them to give way. Here we fought alone and unsupported for two hours and twenty minutes, opposed to the rebel General Wood's entire division, composed of fifteen regiments and a battery of ten guns. Fiercer and fiercer grew the contest and more dreadful became the onslaught. Almost hand-to-hand they fought at least five times their own number, often charging upon them with such fearlessness and impetuosity as would force them to reel and give way, but as fast as they were cut down their ranks were filled with fresh ones. At one time the Twenty-second Indiana charged at them with fixed bayonets and succeeded in completely routing and throwing them from their position on our right, but at the same time they brought in a reserve force on our left. I now ordered the Twenty-second Indiana as quickly as possible to the aid of the Fifty-ninth Illinois on the left, which order was promptly obeyed.

The impetuosity of the firing now ceased for a moment, and I advanced to ascertain if possible the position of the enemy. As I advanced down the line we were greeted with a heavy volley of musketry, which plainly enough told me the direction of the enemy. With shouts and exclamations my men again rallied to the onset. Here it was that fell the gallant Lieutenant-Colonel Keith, [after Polk confronted him—see below] while at the head of his regiment and in the act of flourishing his sword and urging his men onward to victory. At this time my horse was shot from under me, and before I could escape through the darkness I was taken prisoner and conveyed from the field. Although my men fought desperately it was of no avail, for being overwhelmed by vastly superior numbers they were compelled to withdraw from the field.

Retreating under cover of a hill the brigade was again formed in line of battle by the senior officer of the brigade, when, after consultation and learning that we had no support within 1 mile distant, it was deemed advisable to withdraw from the field and fall back upon our lines, which they did.[47]

Hardee ordered Brig. Gen. St. John R. Liddell's brigade to make what turned out to be the final assault on McCook's reformed line, now augmented by Gooding and Steedman. It failed to break the Union line, and the Federals managed to retain control of the Dixville Crossroads.

Report of Brig. Gen. St. John R. Liddell, CSA, Commanding Liddell's Brigade, Buckner's Division, Left Wing, Army of the Mississippi

... About 5.30 p.m., Colonel (S. H.) Perkins, of General Hardee's staff, directed me to follow him with my brigade to the valley, and after reaching Doctor's Fork said to me, "General Hardee wishes you now to move upon the enemy where the firing is hottest." Some latitude being here given me, which was fully appreciated, I thought proper to continue my movement toward the enemy's extreme left, as indicated by the heavy firing apparently moving in that direction on the Nashville [sic] road. As soon as I had reached the place where I desired to form my line of battle, I moved forward at once. Here I met with Major-General Cheatham, who urged me anxiously to push on and relieve his troops from the heavy pressure upon them. In pressing on, I caused the battery to open fire from high points upon the enemy beyond our lines as chance offered. Alter passing through and overlapping the right of Major-General Cheatham's lines, I soon found myself in the immediate presence of the enemy. I commenced firing. It being twilight, however, with a bright full moon shining, and dress not clearly distinguishable, my men mistook the enemy for friends; at the same time the cry came from the enemy's lines, "You are killing your friends," which serving to strengthen the impression, I gave the signal to cease firing, intending to push up the line; but at this moment Major-General Polk, who had joined me a few moments before, ordered the ranks to be opened for him to pass, and riding hastily up to the lines in front of us, distant not more than 25 paces, quickly returned, exclaiming, "They are enemies; fire upon them." Heavy volleys were at once rapidly poured into this mass of men, and after the lapse of some ten minutes I again ordered the firing to cease, and when the smoke had cleared away nothing was visible of the enemy but their wounded, dying, and dead. It was at this place that the brave young Captain (W. H.) Grissom, of the Second Arkansas, fell, regretted by all the command. I now forthwith ordered my battery to the top of the hill, in advance of our forces, and placed it in position to fire upon the woods, some 200 yards distant and directly opposite. When I felt satisfied that the enemy had hastily retired in confusion, I was about to recommence firing, fully intending to follow up without delay our success, when General

> Polk ordered me to desist, and to keep my command nearby to await further instructions. Meanwhile some skirmishers, pushing forward to the edge of these woods, reported a battery of the enemy there, under protection of some cavalry; but my orders to remain stationary being imperative, I could do nothing toward its capture, and in a short time it was heard rapidly moving away. My time was now taken up in receiving and disposing of the prisoners who were being constantly brought in. Two fine ambulances, now in possession of General Bragg, were captured by the Second Arkansas Regiment and by the battery, one of which contained the personal baggage of General McCook; the other was supposed to belong to General Rosecrans, both of which officers were reported by the prisoners to have been nearby at the close of the action. Two flags are now in my possession, taken by the Second Arkansas Regiment. Two others were taken by this regiment and one by the Sixth, but, not being valued by the captors, were torn to pieces, and the fragments retained as trophies of the day's work. The fields and woods in front and around us on every side were strewn with the enemy's dead and wounded; their loss could hardly have been less than 500 killed and wounded in the space of four to five acres.[48]

Lieut. Gen. Leonidas Polk, having mistakenly ridden into the Union line and miraculously escaped, ordered the fighting to cease as it was simply too dark to differentiate friend from foe. Liddell briefly described Polk's move to the Union line:

> ### Narrative of Brig. Gen. St. John R. Liddell, CSA, *Liddell's Record*
>
> The full moon was high up, and the twilight of a clear October evening had rapidly merged into a bright moonlight. Suddenly we confronted a dark line hardly more than twenty-five paces off on the crest of the elevation we were ascending. Immediately, without orders, a desultory fire issued from my line. It so happened that at this moment a sudden and, to me then, unaccountable cessation of firing took place on both sides. In this momentary silent interval a distressing cry came from the dark line before us. "You are firing upon friends; for God's sake stop!"

In an instant everything was still. Uncertain who was before me and not having found another line, I was just about to give the order to forward with bayonets fixed when General Leonidas Polk rode up. I don't know whence he came, but he quickly expressed his delight at seeing me in that place. I interrupted him by informing him of my men having fired by mistake into Cheatham's Division. General Polk seemed shocked at the accident and said, "What a pity, I hope not. I don't think so. Let me go and see. Open your ranks."

It was done. The brave old man spurred his horse with a jump through the opening. My suspense was but for a few seconds when he hastily returned, exclaiming, "General, every mother's son of them are Yankees. I saw the colonel commanding the brigade and looked closely at the dark clothing of the men and am sure of not being mistaken."

I waited no longer. The news was circulated loudly, "Yankees!" The trumpet sounded to "fire." A tremendous flash of musketry for the whole extent of the line for nearly one quarter of a mile in length followed. It continued for some fifteen minutes. I discovered that the return fire had ceased and therefore directed the trumpeter to signal cessation on our part . . .

I now directed my battery forward and had the bodies removed from its path for that purpose. General Polk asked my object. I answered that I designed taking the heavy battery, which I knew to have been withdrawn from its first position and was then in the edge of the woods in advance of the skirmish line. General Polk objected, "I want no more night fighting. It will be a waste of ammunition. Await orders just as you are."[49]

Polk made the final critical decision of the Battle of Perryville when he ordered the Confederates to cease fire, ending the fighting for the day.

Report of Maj. Gen. Leonidas Polk, CSA, Commanding Right Wing, Army of the Mississippi

As the enemy was yielding toward the close of the day the brigade of Brigadier-General Liddell approached from my left and rear and halted on the crest of a hill to determine the point at which to offer its support. It was directed to the place where it was most wanted and moved upon it with deafening cheers. Here, owing to the fading twilight, it was for a few moments difficult to determine whether the firing in our front was from our own or the enemy's troops. This difficulty, however, was speedily removed; it was the enemy, and in obedience to orders that veteran brigade, Liddell, its gallant commander, closed the operations of the day in that part of the field with a succession of the most deadly volleys I have witnessed. The enemy's command in their immediate front was well-nigh annihilated.

At this point a number of prisoners were taken, and among them several corps, division, and brigade staff officers; and, darkness closing in, I ordered the troops to cease firing and to bivouac for the night.[50]

This concludes the driving tour. You may return to the visitor center by driving southeast on Hayes-Mays Road back to the intersection with Battlefield Road. Turn left (north) and proceed to the battlefield's main entrance, or depart to another location of your choice.

APPENDIX II

UNION ORDER OF BATTLE[1]

ARMY OF THE OHIO
   Maj. Gen. Don Carlos Buell
   Second in Command, Maj. Gen. George H. Thomas

ESCORT
   Anderson's Troop, Pennsylvania Cavalry, Lieut. Thomas S. Maple
   4th US Cavalry (6 Companies), Lieut. Col. James Oakes

FIRST CORPS
   Maj. Gen. Alexander McDowell McCook

THIRD DIVISION
   Brig. Gen. Lovell H. Rousseau

NINTH BRIGADE
   Col. Leonard A. Harris
   38th Indiana, Col. Benjamin F. Scribner
   2nd Ohio, Lieut. Col. John Kell
   33rd Ohio, Lieut. Col. Oscar F. Moore
   94th Ohio, Col. John W. Frizell
   10th Wisconsin, Col. Alfred R. Chapin
   5th Indiana Light Artillery, Capt. Peter Simonson

SEVENTEENTH BRIGADE
  Col. William H. Lytle
  42nd Indiana, Col. James G. Jones
  88th Indiana, Col. George Humphrey
  15th Kentucky, Col. Curran Pope
  3rd Ohio, Col. John Beatty
  10th Ohio, Lieut. Col. Joseph Burke
  1st Battery, Michigan Light Artillery, Capt. Cyrus O. Loomis

TWENTY-EIGHTH BRIGADE
  Col. John C. Starkweather
  24th Illinois, Capt. August Mauff
  79th Pennsylvania, Col. Henry A. Hambright
  1st Wisconsin, Lieut. Col. George B. Bingham
  21st Wisconsin, Col. Benjamin Sweet
  4th Battery, Indiana Light Artillery, Capt. Asahel K. Bush
  Battery A, Kentucky Light Artillery, Capt. David C. Stone

UNATTACHED
  2nd Kentucky Cavalry (6 Companies), Col. Buckner Board
  1st Michigan Engineers and Mechanics (3 Companies),
    Maj. Enos Hopkins

TENTH DIVISION
  Brig. Gen. James S. Jackson

THIRTY-THIRD BRIGADE
  Brig. Gen. William R. Terrill
  Garrard's Detachment (3 Companies), Col. Theophilius T. Garrard
  80th Illinois, Col. Thomas G. Allen
  123rd Illinois, Col. James Monroe
  105th Ohio, Col. Albert S. Hall
  Parson's (Improvised) Battery, Lieut. Charles C. Parson

THIRTY-FOURTH BRIGADE
  Col. George Webster
  80th Indiana, Col. Jonah R. Taylor
  50th Ohio, Lieut. Col. Silas Strickland
  98th Ohio, Lieut. Col. Christian Poorman
  121st Ohio, Col. William P. Reid
  19th Battery, Indiana Light Artillery, Capt. Samuel J. Harris

SECOND CORPS
Maj. Gen. Thomas L. Crittenden

FOURTH DIVISION
Brig. Gen. William Sooy Smith

Tenth Brigade
Col. William Grose
84th Illinois, Col. Louis H. Waters
36th Indiana, Lieut. Col. Oliver H. P. Cary
23rd Kentucky, Lieut. Col. J. P. Jackson
6th Ohio, Col. N. L. Anderson
24th Ohio, Lieut. Col. Frederick C. Jones
Battery H, 4th US Artillery, Lieut. S. Canby
Battery M, 4th US Artillery (2 Sections), Capt. John Mendenhall

Nineteenth Brigade
Col. William B. Hazen
110th Illinois, Col. Thomas S. Casey
9th Indiana, Col. William H. Blake
6th Kentucky, Col. Walter C. Whitaker
27th Kentucky, Col. C. D. Pennebaker
41st Ohio, Lieut. Col. George S. Mygatt
Battery F, 1st Ohio Light Artillery, Capt. Daniel T. Cockerill

Twenty-second Brigade
Brig. Gen. Charles Cruft
31st Indiana, Lieut. Col. John Osborn
1st Kentucky, Lieut. Col. David A. Enyart
2nd Kentucky, Col. Thomas D. Sedgewick
20th Kentucky, Lieut. Col. Charles S. Hanson
90th Ohio, Col. Isaac N. Rose
Battery B, 1st Ohio Light Artillery, Capt. William E. Standart

Cavalry
2nd Kentucky Cavalry (4 Companies), Lieut. Col. Thomas Cochran

FIFTH DIVISION
Brig. Gen. Horatio P. Van Cleve

Eleventh Brigade
Col. Samuel Beatty

79th Indiana, Col. Frederick Knefler
9th Kentucky, Lieut. Col. George Cram
13th Kentucky, Lieut. Col. J. B. Carlile
19th Ohio, Lieut. Col. E. W. Hollingsworth
59th Ohio, Col. James P. Fyffe
7th Battery, Indiana Light Artillery, Capt. George Swallow

FOURTEENTH BRIGADE
Col. Pierce B. Hawkins
44th Indiana, Col. Hugh B. Reed
86th Indiana, Col. Orville S. Hamilton
11th Kentucky, Lieut. Col. S. P. Love
26th Kentucky, Col. Cicero Maxwell
13th Ohio, Col. Joseph C. Hawkins
Battery B, 26th Pennsylvania Light Artillery, Lieut. Alanson Stevens

TWENTY-THIRD BRIGADE
Col. Stanley Matthews
35th Indiana, Col. Bernard Mullen
8th Kentucky, Col. Sidney Barnes
21st Kentucky, Col. Samuel W. Price
51st Ohio, Lieut. Col. Richard McClain
99th Ohio, Lieut. Col. John E. Cummins
3rd Battery, Wisconsin Light Artillery, Capt. Lucius Drury

FOURTH DIVISION
Brig. Gen. Thomas J. Wood

FIFTEENTH BRIGADE
Brig. Gen. Milo S. Hascall
100th Illinois, Col. Frederick Bartleson
17th Indiana, Lieut. Col. George W. Gorman
58th Indiana, Col. George P. Buell
3rd Kentucky, Lieut. Col. William Scott
26th Ohio, Maj. Chris Degenfeld
8th Battery, Indiana Light Artillery, Lieut. George Estep

TWENTIETH BRIGADE
Col. Charles Harker
51st Indiana, Col. Abel D. Streight
73rd Indiana, Col. Gilbert Hathaway
13th Michigan, Lieut. Col. F. W. Gordon

64th Ohio, Col. John Ferguson
65th Ohio, Lieut. Col. William Young
6th Battery, Ohio Light Artillery, Capt. Cullen Bradley

Twenty-first Brigade
Col. George D. Wagner
15th Indiana, Lieut. Col. Gustavus Wood
40th Indiana, Col. John Blake
57th Indiana, Col. Cyrus Hines
24th Kentucky, Col. Lewis B. Grigsby
97th Ohio, Col. John Lane
10th Battery, Indiana Light Artillery, Capt. Jerome B. Cox

First Cavalry Brigade
Col. Edward D. McCook
2nd Indiana Cavalry, Lieut. Col. Robert Stewart
1st Kentucky Cavalry, Col. Frank Wolford
3rd Kentucky Cavalry, Col. Eli Murray
7th Pennsylvania Cavalry (1st Battalion), Maj. John E. Wynkoop
Battery M, 4th US Light Artillery (1 Section),
  Lieut. Henry A. Huntington

Unattached
1st Michigan Engineers and Mechanics (4 Companies),
  Col. William Innes
1st Ohio Cavalry (4 Companies), Maj. James Laughlin
3rd Ohio Cavalry (4 Companies), Maj. John H. Foster

THIRD CORPS
(Acting Maj. Gen.) Charles C. Gilbert

FIRST DIVISION
Brig. Gen. Albin Schoepf

First Brigade
Col. Moses B. Walker
82nd Indiana, Col. Morton Hunter
12th Kentucky, Col. William Hoskins
17th Ohio, Col. John Connell
31st Ohio, Lieut. Col. Frederick Lister
38th Ohio, Lieut. Col. William Choate
Battery D, 1st Michigan Light Artillery, Capt. J. W. Church

SECOND BRIGADE
  Brig. Gen. Speed S. Fry
  10th Indiana, Col. William Kise
  74th Indiana, Col. Charles W. Chapman
  4th Kentucky, Col. John Croxton
  10th Kentucky, Lieut. Col. William Hayes
  14th Ohio, Lieut. Col. George Este
  Battery C, 1st Ohio Light Artillery, Capt. D. K. Southwick

THIRD BRIGADE
  Brig. Gen. James B. Steedman
  87th Indiana, Col. Kline G. Shyrock
  2nd Minnesota, Col. James George
  9th Ohio, Lieut. Col. Charles Joseph
  35th Ohio, Col. Ferdinand Van Derveer
  18th US, Maj. Frederick Townsend
  Battery I, 4th US Light Artillery, Lieut. Frank G. Smith

UNATTACHED
  1st Ohio Cavalry (6 Companies), Col. Minor Milliken

NINTH DIVISION
  Brig. Gen. Robert D. Mitchell

THIRTEENTH BRIGADE
  Col. Michael Gooding
  59th Illinois, Maj. Joshua C. Winters
  74th Illinois, Col. James B. Kerr
  75th Illinois, Lieut. Col. John E. Bennett
  22nd Indiana, Lieut. Col. Squire I. Keith
  5th Battery, Wisconsin Light Artillery, Capt. Oscar F. Pinney

THIRTY-FIRST BRIGADE
  Col. William P. Carlin
  21st Illinois, Col. John Alexander
  38th Illinois, Maj. Daniel Gilmer
  101st Ohio, Col. Leander Stem
  15th Wisconsin, Col. Hans C. Heg
  2nd Minnesota Battery (2 Sections), Lieut. Richard L. Dawley

THIRTY-SECOND BRIGADE
  Col. William W. Caldwell
  25th Illinois, Lieut. Col. James McClelland

35th Illinois, Lieut. Col. William Chandler
81st Indiana, Lieut. Col. John Timberlake
8th Kansas Battalion, Lieut. Col. John Martin
8th Battery, Wisconsin Light Artillery, Capt. Stephen J. Carpenter

CAVALRY
36th Illinois (1 Company), Capt. Samuel B. Sherer

ELEVENTH DIVISION
Brig. Gen. Philip H. Sheridan

THIRTY-FIFTH BRIGADE
Lieut. Col. Bernard Laiboldt
44th Illinois, Capt. Wallace W. Barrett
73rd Illinois, Col. James F. Jaques
2nd Missouri, Capt. Walter Hoppe
15th Missouri, Maj. John Weber

THIRTY-SIXTH BRIGADE
Col. Daniel McCook
85th Illinois, Col. Robert S. Moore
86th Illinois, Col. David D. Irons
125th Illinois, Col. Oscar Harmon
52nd Ohio, Lieut. Col. Daniel D. T. Cowen

THIRTY-SEVENTH BRIGADE
Col. Nicholas Greusel
36th Illinois, Capt. Silas Miller
88th Illinois, Col. Francis T. Sherman
21st Michigan, Col. Ambrose Stevens
24th Wisconsin, Col. Charles H. Larrabee

ARTILLERY
Battery I, Illinois Light Artillery, Capt. Charles M. Barnett
Battery G, 1st Missouri Light Artillery, Capt. Henry Hescock

THIRD CAVALRY BRIGADE
(Acting Brig. Gen.) Ebenezer Gay
9th Kentucky Cavalry (8 Companies), Lieut. Col. John Boyle
2nd Michigan Cavalry, Lieut. Col. Archibald Campbell
9th Pennsylvania Cavalry, Lieut. Col. Thomas James
2nd Battery, Minnesota Light Artillery (1 Section), Capt. William A. Hotchkiss

APPENDIX III

CONFEDERATE ORDER OF BATTLE[1]

ARMY OF THE MISSISSIPPI
    Gen. Braxton Bragg

ESCORT
    3rd Tennessee Cavalry (4 Companies), Capt. W. C. Bacot
    13th Tennessee Cavalry Battalion (Company I),
        Capt. William W. Lillard

RIGHT WING
    Maj. Gen. Leonidas Polk

CHEATHAM'S DIVISION
    Maj. Gen. Benjamin F. Cheatham

DONELSON'S BRIGADE
    Brig. Gen. Daniel S. Donelson
    8th Tennessee, Col. William L. Moore
    15th Tennessee, Col. Robert C. Tyler
    16th Tennessee, Col. John H. Savage
    18th Tennessee, Col. John C. Carter

51st Tennessee, Col. John Chester
Carnes's Tennessee Battery, Capt. William W. Carnes

STEWART'S BRIGADE
Brig. Gen. Alexander P. Stewart
4th Tennessee, Col. Otho F. Strahl
5th Tennessee, Col. Calvin D. Venable
24th Tennessee, Lieut. Col. Hugh L. W. Bratton
31st Tennessee, Col. Egbert E. Tansil
33rd Tennessee, Col. Warner P. Jones
Stanford's Mississippi Battery, Capt. Thomas J. Stanford

MANEY'S BRIGADE
Brig. Gen. George Maney
41st Georgia, Col. Charles A. McDaniel
1st Tennessee, Col. Hume R. Feild
6th Tennessee, Col. George C. Porter
9th Tennessee, Lieut. Col. John W. Buford
27th Tennessee, Lieut. Col. William Frierson
Smith's Mississippi Battery, Lieut. William B. Turner

SMITH'S BRIGADE
Brig. Gen. Preston Smith
12th Tennessee, Col. Tyree H. Bell
13th Tennessee, Col. Alfred J. Vaughan Jr.
47th Tennessee, Col. Munson R. Hill
154th Senior Tennessee, Col. Michael Magevney Jr.
9th Texas, Col. William H. Young
Scott's Tennessee Battery, Capt. William L. Scott

WHARTON'S CAVALRY BRIGADE
Col. John A. Wharton
2nd Georgia Cavalry (5 Companies), Lieut. Col. Arthur Hood
1st Kentucky Cavalry, (4 Companies), Capt. Thomas A. Ireland
4th Tennessee Cavalry, (5 Companies), Maj. Baxter Smith
Davis's Tennessee Cavalry Battalion (4 Companies), Maj. John Davis
8th Texas Cavalry, Lieut. Col. Thomas Harrison

LEFT WING
Maj. Gen. William J. Hardee

ANDERSON'S DIVISION
Brig. Gen. J. Patton Anderson

Brown's Brigade
Brig. Gen. John C. Brown
1st Florida, Col. William Miller
3rd Florida, Col. Daniel B. Bird
41st Mississippi, Col. William F. Tucker
Battery A, 14th Battalion, Georgia Light Artillery,
    Capt. Joseph E. Palmer

Adams's Brigade
Brig. Daniel W. Adams
13th Louisiana, Col. Randall L. Gibson
14th Battalion, Louisiana Sharpshooters, Maj. John Austin
16th Louisiana, Col. Daniel C. Gober
20th Louisiana, Col. August Reichard
25th Louisiana, Col. Stewart W. Fisk
5th Company, Washington Artillery, Capt. Cuthbert H. Slocomb

Powel's Brigade
Col. Samuel Powel
45th Alabama, Col. James G. Gilchrist
1st Arkansas, Col. John W. Colquitt
24th Mississippi, Col. William F. Dowd
29th Tennessee, Lieut. Col. Horace Rice
Barret's Missouri Battery, Capt. Overton W. Barret

Jones's Brigade
Col. Thomas M. Jones
27th Mississippi, Lieut. Col. James L. Autry
30th Mississippi, Col. George G. F. Neill
34th Mississippi, Col. Samuel Benton
Battery F, 2nd Alabama Light Artillery, Capt. Charles L. Lumsden

BUCKNER'S DIVISION
Maj. Gen. Simon B. Buckner

Liddell's Brigade
Brig. Gen. St. John R. Liddell
2nd Arkansas, Col. John Gratiot

5th Arkansas, Col. Lucius P. Featherstone
6th Arkansas, Col. Alexander T. Hawthorn
7th Arkansas, Col. D. A. Gillespie
8th Arkansas, Col. John H. Kelly
Swett's Mississippi Battery, Lieut. Thomas Havern

Cleburne's Brigade
Brig. Gen. Patrick R. Cleburne
13th/15th Arkansas, Col. Lucius E. Polk
2nd Tennessee, Capt. C. P. Moore
35th Tennessee, Col. Benjamin J. Hill
48th Tennessee, Col. George H. Nixon
Key's Section, Calvert's Arkansas Battery, Lieut. Thomas J. Key

Johnson's Brigade
Brig. Gen. Bushrod R. Johnson
5th Confederate, Col. James A. Smith
17th Tennessee, Col. Albert S. Marks
23rd Tennessee, Lieut. Col. Richard H. Keeble
25th Tennessee, Col. John M. Hughes
37th Tennessee, Col. Moses White
44th Tennessee, Col. John S. Fulton
Darden's Mississippi Battery, Capt. Putnam Darden

Wood's Brigade
Brig. Gen. Sterling A. M. Wood
16th Alabama, Col. William B. Wood
33rd Alabama, Col. Samuel Adams
3rd Confederate, Lieut. Col. Henry V. Keep
3rd Georgia Cavalry, (2 Companies), Capt. Reuben L. Hill
15th Battalion Mississippi Sharpshooters, Maj. A. T. Hawkins
32nd Mississippi, Col. Mark P. Lowrey
45th Mississippi, Col. Aaron B. Hardcastle
Semple's Alabama Battery, Capt. Henry C. Semple

Wheeler's Cavalry Brigade
Col. Joseph Wheeler
1st Alabama Cavalry, Col. William W. Allen
3rd Alabama Cavalry, Col. James Hagan
6th Confederate Cavalry, Lieut. Col. James Pell
8th Confederate Cavalry, Col. W. B. Wade
2nd Georgia Cavalry Battalion, Maj. C. A. Whaley
Smith's Georgia Cavalry Battalion, Col. John R. Hart

1st Kentucky Cavalry (5 Companies), Maj. John W. Caldwell
6th Kentucky Cavalry (3 Companies), Col. J. Warren Grigsby
9th Tennessee Cavalry, Lieut. James D. Bennett
12th Tennessee Cavalry Battalion (4 Companies),
    Lieut. Col. T. W. Adrian
Hanley's Section, Calvert's Arkansas Battery, Lieut. S. G. Hanley

NOTES

Preface

1. Larry Peterson, *Decisions at Chattanooga: The Nineteen Critical Decisions That Defined the Battle* (Knoxville: University of Tennessee Press, 2018).
2. Larry Peterson, *Decisions of the 1862 Kentucky Campaign: The Twenty-Seven Critical Decisions That Defined the Outcome* (Knoxville: University of Tennessee Press, 2019).
3. Kurt Holman, *Battle of Perryville: Movement Maps Showing the Fighting Ground of the Union Left and Centre, 12:00 PM to 8:00 PM* (Perryville, KY: Friends of Perryville Battlefield, 2016).

Introduction

1. James M. McPherson, *Battle Cry of Freedom: The Civil War Era* (New York: Ballantine Books, 1988), 264–75.
2. McPherson, *Battle Cry of Freedom*, 423–27.
3. McPherson, *Battle Cry of Freedom*, 524–45.
4. Roy P. Basler, ed., *The Collected Works of Abraham Lincoln* (New Brunswick, NJ: Rutgers University Press, 1953), 4:532.

5. Huston Horn, *Leonidas Polk: Warrior Bishop of the Confederacy* (Lawrence: University Press of Kansas, 2019), 177–80.
6. Larry J. Daniel, *Conquered: Why the Army of Tennessee Failed* (Chapel Hill: University of North Carolina Press, 2019), 15.
7. Kenneth A. Hafendorfer, *Mill Springs: Campaign and Battle of Mill Springs, Kentucky* (Louisville: KH Press, 2001), 17, 438–46; Stuart W. Sanders, *The Battle of Mill Springs, Kentucky* (Charleston, SC: History Press, 2013), 121–28.
8. McPherson, *Battle Cry of Freedom*, 396–414; James L. McDonough, *War in Kentucky: From Shiloh to Perryville* (Knoxville: University of Tennessee Press, 1994), 36–37, 63.
9. McPherson, *Battle Cry of Freedom*, 396–414; McDonough, *War in Kentucky*, 36–37, 63.
10. McDonough, *War in Kentucky*, 69–76; Peterson, *Decisions of the 1862 Kentucky Campaign*, 23.
11. McPherson, Battle Cry of Freedom, 516–17.
12. US War Department, *The War of the Rebellion: A Compilation of the Official Records of the Union and Confederate Armies* (Washington, DC: US Government Printing Office, 1880–1901), vol. 16, pt. 2, pp. 733–34 (hereafter referred to as *OR*); McDonough, *War in Kentucky*, 75–81.
13. McDonough, *War in Kentucky*, 81, 116–45; Earl J. Hess, *Banners to the Breeze: The Kentucky Campaign, Corinth, and Stones River* (Lincoln: University of Nebraska Press, 2000), 30–43.
14. Hess, *Banners to the Breeze*, 57, 63–70; Thomas L. Connelly, *Army of the Heartland: The Army of Tennessee, 1861–1862* (Baton Rouge: Louisiana State University Press, 1967), 221–34; Daniel, *Conquered*, 39.

Chapter 1

1. The author posits (borrowed from Dr. Richard McMurry) that the turning point of the Civil War was Grant's capture of Paducah in September 1861.
2. Philip Leigh, *The Confederacy at Flood Tide* (Yardley, PA: Westholme, 2016), x. For a great deal more information and an in-depth review of the Confederate High Tide, Leigh is a good source.
3. Archer Jones, *Civil War Command & Strategy: The Process of Victory and Defeat* (New York: Free Press, 1992), 300.

4. Joseph L. Harsh, *Confederate Tide Rising: Robert E. Lee and the Making of Southern Strategy, 1861–1862* (Kent, OH: Kent State University Press, 1998), 11.

5. Joseph L. Harsh, *Taken at the Flood: Robert E. Lee and Confederate Strategy in the Maryland Campaign of 1862* (Kent, OH: Kent State University Press, 1999), viii, xi, 2.

6. Harsh, *Taken at the Flood*, 2.

7. Harsh, *Taken at the Flood*, viii; Leigh, *Confederacy at Flood Tide*, 192–93.

8. Thomas L. Livermore, *Number and Losses in the Civil War in America* (1901; repr., Dayton, OH: Morningside, 1986), 63; Harsh, *Confederate Tide Rising*, 12.

9. Harsh, *Confederate Tide Rising*, 13.

10. Harsh, *Confederate Tide Rising*, 13.

11. *OR*, vol. 24, pt. 3, pp.156–57; *OR*, series 3, vol. 3, pp. 101–6; Gabor S. Boritt, ed., *Why the Confederacy Lost* (New York: Oxford University Press, 1992), 159. Boritt maintains ten thousand blacks served in the US Navy, while other sources indicate that twenty thousand did so. Edward H. Bonekemper III, *The 10 Biggest Civil War Blunders* (Washington, DC: Regnery History, 2018), 70.

12. Harsh, *Confederate Tide Rising*, 17; Leigh, *Confederacy at Flood Tide*, vii–viii.

13. Harsh, *Confederate Tide Rising*, 17, 21; William C. Davis, *Jefferson Davis: The Man and His Hour* (Baton Rouge: Louisiana State University Press, 1991), 469.

14. For an in-depth review of the Seven Days Battles, the Battle of Second Manassas, and the Battle of Antietam, see Leigh, *Confederacy at Flood Tide*, 29–142.

15. Ezra J. Warner, *Generals in Gray: Lives of the Confederate Commanders* (Baton Rouge: Louisiana State University Press, 1959), 154. For a review of this campaign, see Terry Lowry, *The Battle of Charleston and the 1862 Kanawha Valley Campaign* (Charleston, WV: Star, 2016), 45–75.

16. For a brief review of the Battle of Fredericksburg, see McPherson, *Battle Cry of Freedom*, 570–74.

17. Warner, *Generals in Gray*, 212–13; Peterson, *Decisions of the 1862 Kentucky Campaign*, 67; Hess, *Banners to the Breeze*, 45.

18. Peterson, *Decisions of the 1862 Kentucky Campaign*, 90; Hess, *Banners to the Breeze*, 20–24; McDonough, *War in Kentucky*, 74–82.

19. McPherson, *Battle Cry of Freedom*, 523; Harsh, *Taken at the Flood*, 106.
20. Kenneth W. Noe, *Perryville: This Grand Havoc of Battle* (Lexington: University Press of Kentucky, 2001), 334.
21. McPherson, *Battle Cry of Freedom*, 578; Warner, *Generals in Gray*, 314–15.
22. Wikipedia, *Battle of Prairie Grove*; McPherson, *Battle Cry of Freedom*, 668.
23. Leigh, *Confederacy at Flood Tide*, 200–204; Harsh, *Taken at the Flood*, 495; McPherson, *Battle Cry of Freedom*, 855, 858.

Chapter 2

1. Kenneth A. Hafendorfer, *Perryville: Battle for Kentucky* (Louisville: KH Press, 1991), 66–67; Ezra J. Warner, *Generals in Blue: Lives of the Union Commanders* (Baton Rouge: Louisiana State University Press, 1964), 51.
2. Noe, *Perryville*, 10–11, 94–95; Stephen D. Engle, *Don Carlos Buell: Most Promising of All* (Chapel Hill: University of North Carolina Press, 1999), 23–28, 92, 117; Gerald J. Prokopowicz, *All for the Regiment: The Army of the Ohio, 1861–1862* (Chapel Hill: University of North Carolina Press, 2001), 125.
3. Larry J. Daniel, *Days of Glory: The Army of the Cumberland, 1861–1865* (Baton Rouge: Louisiana State University Press, 2004), 123–27; Hafendorfer, *Perryville*, 66, 84; Noe, *Perryville*, 113.
4. *OR*, vol. 16, pt. 2, pp. 360, 421, 538–39, 554–55, 557–58; Noe, *Perryville*, 94; McDonough, *War in Kentucky*, 196–97; Hafendorfer, *Perryville*, 70; Hess, *Banners to the Breeze*, 79; Engle, *Don Carlos Buell*, 298–302.
5. *OR*, vol. 16, pt. 2, p. 558; Warner, *Generals in Blue*, 116, 173–74; Noe, *Perryville*, 93–94; Peterson, *Decisions of the 1862 Kentucky Campaign*, 63–64; McDonough, *War in Kentucky*, 195–96; Hess, *Banners to the Breeze*, 78; Hafendorfer, *Perryville*, 67–68; Engle, *Don Carlos Buell*, 297; Prokopowicz, *All for the Regiment*, 153.
6. Noe, *Perryville*, 84, 97; Daniel, *Days of Glory*, 137; Prokopowicz, *All for the Regiment*, 155; Engle, *Don Carlos Buell*, 303.
7. Noe, *Perryville*, 84, 97; Daniel, *Days of Glory*, 137; Prokopowicz, *All for the Regiment*, 155; Engle, *Don Carlos Buell*, 303; Warner, *Generals in Blue*, 424–25.
8. *OR*, vol. 16, pt. 1, pp. 375–76; *OR*, vol. 16, pt. 2, p. 493; Warner, *Generals in Blue*, 173–74; Noe, *Perryville*, 97; Christopher L. Kolakowski, *The Civil War*

Notes to Pages 19–24

at Perryville: Battling for the Bluegrass (Charleston, SC: History Press, 2009), 74; Prokopowicz, *All for the Regiment*, 155; Engle, *Don Carlos Buell*, 303.

9. *OR*, vol. 16, pt. 2, p. 558; Noe, *Perryville*, 97; Warner, *Generals in Blue*, 174; Hess, *Banners to the Breeze*, 78; Hafendorfer, *Perryville*, 68; Engle, *Don Carlos Buell*, 303; Prokopowicz, *All for the Regiment*, 155.

10. *OR*, vol. 16, pt. 2, p. 560; author's in-depth conversations with Perryville Battlefield State Historic Site manager Kurt Holman, July 22, 2015 and July 25, 2016; Peterson, *Decisions of the 1862 Kentucky Campaign*, 66; Hafendorfer, *Perryville*, 296; Hess, *Banners to the Breeze*, 79; Noe, *Perryville*, 231.

11. Conversations with Kurt Holman, July 22, 2015 and July 25, 2016; Hafendorfer, *Perryville*, 296; Noe, *Perryville*, 231; Peterson, *Decisions of the 1862 Kentucky Campaign*, 66–67.

12. *OR*, vol. 16, pt. 2, p. 555; Noe, *Perryville*, 98; McDonough, *War in Kentucky*, 196–97; Stanley F. Horn, *The Army of Tennessee* (1941; repr., Norman: University of Oklahoma Press, 1993), 176; Prokopowicz, *All for the Regiment*, 155–56; Engle, *Don Carlos Buell*, 300–302.

13. *OR*, vol. 16, pt. 1, pp. 1033–36; Noe, *Perryville*, 373–80; Hafendorfer, *Perryville*, 444–52; Kolakowski, *Civil War at Perryville*, 74; Engle, *Don Carlos Buell*, 295–96; Prokopowicz, *All for the Regiment*, 157.

14. Kolakowski, *Civil War at Perryville*, 77–80; Noe, *Perryville*, 98; Engle, *Don Carlos Buell*, 303–4; Prokopowicz, *All for the Regiment*, 160.

15. Noe, *Perryville*, 112–14; Hafendorfer, *Perryville*, 94; Prokopowicz, *All for the Regiment*, 160.

16. Noe, *Perryville*, 112–14; Hafendorfer, *Perryville*, 94; Prokopowicz, *All for the Regiment*, 160.

17. Hafendorfer, *Perryville*, 71; Kolakowski, *Civil War at Perryville*, 76; Engle, *Don Carlos Buell*, 303–4.

18. *OR*, vol. 16, pt. 1, p. 184; Noe, *Perryville*, 98; Hess, *Banners to the Breeze*, 80; Kolakowski, *Civil War at Perryville*, 76; Engle, *Don Carlos Buell*, 303–4; Prokopowicz, *All for the Regiment*, 160.

19. *OR*, vol. 16, pt. 2, pp. 560–61; Noe, *Perryville*, 112; Hafendorfer, *Perryville*, 77, 82; Kolakowski, *Civil War at Perryville*, 77; Prokopowicz, *All for the Regiment*, 160.

20. Hess, *Banners to the Breeze*, 80; Noe, *Perryville*, 124, 139; Kolakowski, *Civil War at Perryville*, 76; Hafendorfer, *Perryville*, 84–85; Daniel, *Conquered*, 40–42.

21. Hess, *Banners to the Breeze*, 80; Noe, *Perryville*, 124, 139; Kolakowski, *Civil War at Perryville*, 76; Hafendorfer, *Perryville*, 84–85; Daniel, *Conquered*, 40–42.
22. Author's conjecture based on interpreting the above references.
23. Daniel, *Days of Glory*, 123–25; Daniel, *Conquered*, 39–41; Noe, *Perryville*, 76–77; Kolakowski, *Civil War at Perryville*, 69, Horn, *Army of Tennessee*, 170–72.
24. Warner, *Generals in Gray*, 30; Earl J. Hess, *Braxton Bragg: The Most Hated Man of the Confederacy* (Chapel Hill: University of North Carolina Press, 2016), 50–51.
25. Daniel, *Conquered*, 34–35; Grady McWhiney, *Braxton Bragg and Confederate Defeat* (Tuscaloosa: University of Alabama Press, 1969), 1:101–19, 136–37; Daniel, *Conquered*, 35; Noe, *Perryville*, 15–16.
26. *OR*, vol. 16, pt. 1, pp. 1091, 1109; *OR*, vol. 16, pt. 2, pp. 896–97, 901; Kolakowski, *Civil War at Perryville*, 76, 78–79; Hafendorfer, *Perryville*, 85; Hess, *Banners to the Breeze*, 81–82; Noe, *Perryville*, 104, 124; Daniel, *Conquered*, 40–41.
27. Warner, *Generals in Gray*, 242–43; Wikipedia, *Reverend McIlvaine*, June 2, 2020; Joseph H. Parks, *General Leonidas Polk, C.S.A: The Fighting Bishop* (1962; repr. Baton Rouge: Louisiana State University Press, 1992), 41, 43, 45, 54.
28. William Glenn Robertson, *River of Death: The Chickamauga Campaign*, vol. 1, *The Fall of Chattanooga* (Chapel Hill: University of North Carolina Press, 2018), 66–67; Warner, *Generals in Gray*, 242–43; Wikipedia, *Reverend McIlvaine*, June 2, 2020; Parks, *General Leonidas Polk, C.S.A*, 41, 43, 45, 54.
29. Warner, *Generals in Gray*, 243; Robertson, *River of Death*, 1:67; Parks, *General Leonidas Polk*, 170; Horn, *Leonidas Polk*, 163.
30. Horn, *Leonidas Polk*, 134–45, 148, 307; Charles T. Quintard, *Doctor Quintard, Chaplain C.S.A. and Second Bishop of Tennessee: The Memoir and Civil War Diary of Charles Todd Quintard*, ed. Sam D. Elliott (Baton Rouge: Louisiana State University Press, 2003), 69–70; Wikipedia, *Episcopal Church (United States*, September 11, 2020*)*; author's conversation with clergyman Everett Brailey, November 1, 2019.
31. Robertson, *River of Death*, 1:68–69; Hess, *Braxton Bragg*, 68; Grady McWhiney, *Braxton Bragg and Confederate Defeat* (Tuscaloosa: University of Alabama Press, 1969), 1:307; Braxton Bragg Papers, Rubenstein

Rare Book and Manuscript Library, Duke University, Durham, NC; Horn, *Leonidas Polk*, 263.

32. Bryan S. Bush, "My Whole Life Must Speak for Me: Southern Honor and Confederate General Leonidas Polk" (master's thesis, University of Louisville, 2015), 15–16, 168. As of the date of this book's publication, Bush is the site manager at Perryville Battlefield State Historic Site.

33. *OR*, vol. 16, pt. 1, p. 1092; Noe, *Perryville*, 139; Parks, *General Leonidas Polk*, 264; Hess, *Banners to the Breeze*, 81.

34. *OR*, vol. 16, pt. 1, pp. 1094–95, 1109; Hess, *Banners to the Breeze*, 82; Hafendorfer, *Perryville*, 85; Kolakowski, *Civil War at Perryville*, 78–79; Daniel, *Conquered*, 41.

35. *OR*, vol. 16, pt. 1, pp. 1094–95, 1109; Hess, *Banners to the Breeze*, 82; Hafendorfer, *Perryville*, 85; Kolakowski, *Civil War at Perryville*, 78–79; Daniel, *Conquered*, 41.

36. *OR*, vol. 16, pt. 1, pp. 1094–95, 1109; Hess, *Banners to the Breeze*, 82; Hafendorfer, *Perryville*, 85; Kolakowski, *Civil War at Perryville*, 78–79; Daniel, *Conquered*, 41.

37. *OR*, vol. 16, pt. 1, pp. 1094–95, 1109; Hess, *Banners to the Breeze*, 82; Hafendorfer, *Perryville*, 85; Kolakowski, *Civil War at Perryville*, 78–79; Daniel, *Conquered*, 41.

38. *OR*, vol. 16, pt. 1, pp. 1094–95, 1109; Kolakowski, *Civil War at Perryville*, 82; Horn, *Leonidas Polk*, 256. The wing level of command would be replaced by the corps level when the Army of the Mississippi was reorganized into the Army of Tennessee in December 1862, after the 1862 Kentucky Campaign. Hess, *Banners to the Breeze*, 185.

39. Noe, *Perryville*, 127–28.

40. This, of course, was Bragg's plan all along. He did not correctly determine where Buell's main force was, but by attacking only a part of this force, Bragg's chance of success was much greater.

41. *OR*, vol. 16, pt. 2, p. 905; Kolakowski, *Civil War at Perryville*, 78, 82–83; Joseph H. Parks, *General Edmund Kirby Smith, C.S.A.* (1954; repr., Baton Rouge: Louisiana State University Press, 1992), 232–33; Hess, *Banners to the Breeze*, 81–83; Connelly, *Army of the Heartland*, 246–47; Hafendorfer, *Perryville*, 76–77.

42. Kolakowski, *Civil War at Perryville*, 82–83; Hess, *Banners to the Breeze*, 81–83; McDonough, *War in Kentucky*, 200; Daniel, *Conquered*, 38, 40.

43. *OR*, vol. 16, pt. 2, p. 905; Parks, *General Edmund Kirby Smith*, 233.
44. *OR*, vol. 16, pt. 2, p. 905; Parks, *General Edmund Kirby Smith*, 233.
45. McDonough, *War in Kentucky*, 199–200; Hess, *Banners to the Breeze*, 82–83; Kolakowski, *Civil War at Perryville*, 83.
46. Parks, *General Edmund Kirby Smith*, 233; Connelly, *Army of the Heartland*, 245, 250–51.
47. Hafendorfer, *Perryville*, 89–90; Connelly, *Army of the Heartland*, 250–51.
48. *OR*, vol. 16, pt. 1, p. 1087; *OR*, vol. 16, pt. 2, p. 903; Parks, *General Edmund Kirby Smith*, 233; Connelly, *Army of the Heartland*, 251; Hafendorfer, *Perryville*, 89; Kolakowski, *Civil War at Perryville*, 82–83; Hess, *Banners to the Breeze*, 81–83; McDonough, *War in Kentucky*, 200; Hess, *Braxton Bragg*, 67.
49. *OR*, vol. 16, pt. 1, p. 1087; *OR*, vol. 16, pt. 2, p. 903; *Hawes Installation*, Braxton Bragg Papers, Western Reserve Historical Society, Cleveland, OH; J. Stoddard Johnston Diary, October 4, 1862, and Brent Diary, October 4, 1862; J. Stoddard Johnston, *Memoranda of Facts Bearing on General Bragg's Kentucky Campaign, January 8, 1863*, J. Stoddard Johnston Military Papers, Filson Club Historical Society, Louisville, KY; Connelly, *Army of the Heartland*, 251–52; Hafendorfer, *Perryville*, 89; Hess, *Braxton Bragg*, 67.
50. Connelly, *Army of the Heartland*, 253; Hess, *Banners to the Breeze*, 83.
51. Hardee said to Wheeler, "This is a most execrable road—hilly, rocky, and slippery"; this quote is in *OR*, vol. 16, pt. 2, p. 905. Kolakowski, *Civil War at Perryville*, 82; Noe, *Perryville*, 127, 130, 133; Hess, *Banners to the Breeze*, 84; Nathaniel C. Hughes Jr., *General William J. Hardee: Old Reliable* (Baton Rouge: Louisiana State University Press, 1965), 125.
52. *OR*, vol. 16, pt. 1, p. 1120; Kolakowski, *Civil War at Perryville*, 87–88; Noe, *Perryville*, 133; Hafendorfer, *Perryville*, 117.
53. Warner, *Generals in Gray*, 124–25; Hughes, *General William J. Hardee*, 50, 67, 125; St. John Richardson Liddell, *Liddell's Record*, ed. Nathaniel C. Hughes Jr. (Baton Rouge: Louisiana State University Press, 1985), 170; Daniel, *Conquered*, 54; Steven E. Woodworth, *No Band of Brothers: Problems of the Rebel High Command* (Columbia: University of Missouri Press, 1999), 85; McWhiney, *Braxton Bragg*, 1:262.
54. Warner, *Generals in Gray*, 124–25; Hughes, *General William J. Hardee*, 50, 67, 125; St. John Richardson Liddell, *Liddell's Record*, ed. Nathaniel C. Hughes Jr. (Baton Rouge: Louisiana State University Press, 1985),

170; Daniel, *Conquered*, 54; Steven E. Woodworth, *No Band of Brothers: Problems of the Rebel High Command* (Columbia: University of Missouri Press, 1999), 85; McWhiney, *Braxton Bragg*, 1:262.

55. *OR*, vol. 16, pt. 1, p. 1120; Kolakowski, *Civil War at Perryville*, 87–88; Noe, *Perryville*, 133; Hafendorfer, *Perryville*, 117.

56. *OR*, vol. 16, pt 1, p. 1120; Kolakowski, *Civil War at Perryville*, 87–88; Noe, *Perryville*, 133; Hafendorfer, *Perryville*, 117.

57. *OR*, vol. 16, pt. 1, p. 1120; Kolakowski, *Civil War at Perryville*, 87–88; Noe, *Perryville*, 133; Hafendorfer, *Perryville*, 117.

58. *OR*, vol. 16, pt. 1, p. 1120; Kolakowski, *Civil War at Perryville*, 87–88; Noe, *Perryville*, 133; Hafendorfer, *Perryville*, 117.

59. *OR*, vol. 16, pt. 1, p. 1109; Hughes, *General William J. Hardee*, 125.

60. Kolakowski, *Civil War at Perryville*, 87–88; Noe, *Perryville*, 133; McDonough, *War in Kentucky*, 203–4.

61. *OR*, vol. 16, pt. 1, p. 1095; Noe, *Perryville*, 133.

62. *OR*, vol. 16, pt. 1, p. 1091; Noe, *Perryville*, 124–25.

63. *OR*, vol. 16, pt. 1, pp. 1092, 1109; Noe, *Perryville*, 132.

64. *OR*, vol. 16, pt. 1, p. 1091; Noe, *Perryville*, 133.

65. Noe, *Perryville*, 132–33.

66. *OR*, vol. 16, pt. 1, p. 1092; McDonough, *War in Kentucky*, 206; Kolakowski, *Civil War at Perryville*, 78.

67. *OR*, vol. 16, pt. 1, p. 1091; Noe, *Perryville*, 124.

68. *OR*, vol. 16, pt. 1, p. 1091; Kolakowski, *Civil War at Perryville*, 78; Hafendorfer, *Perryville*, 84–85.

69. *OR*, vol. 16, pt. 1, p. 1091; Kolakowski, *Civil War at Perryville*, 78; Hafendorfer, *Perryville*, 84–85.

70. *OR*, vol. 16, pt. 1, p. 1091; Kolakowski, *Civil War at Perryville*, 78; Hafendorfer, *Perryville*, 84–85.

71. *OR*, vol. 16, pt. 1, pp. 1087, 1091; Hess, *Banners to the Breeze*, 82; Horn, *Army of Tennessee*, 179–82.

72. *OR*, vol. 16, pt. 1, pp. 1092, 1096; Noe, *Perryville*, 140.

73. Noe, *Perryville*, 128–29.

Chapter 3

1. *OR*, vol. 16, Pt. 1, p. 1081; Noe, *Perryville*, 145; Kolakowski, *Civil War at Perryville*, 90, 94; Daniel, *Days of Glory*, 144.
2. *OR*, vol. 16, pt. 1, pp. 525–26, 1072; *OR*, vol. 16, pt. 2, p. 580; Noe, *Perryville*, 135–38; Hafendorfer, *Perryville*, 122; Daniel, *Days of Glory*, 144.
3. Noe, *Perryville*, 139; Kolakowski, *Civil War at Perryville*, 84; Hafendorfer, *Perryville*, 119; Engle, *Don Carlos Buell*, 304–5; Daniel, *Days of Glory*, 145.
4. *OR*, vol. 16, pt. 2, pp. 580–81; Noe, *Perryville*, 143; Daniel, *Days of Glory*, 146; *Don Carlos Buell*, 305.
5. *OR*, vol. 16, pt. 1, pp.1157–58; Liddell, *Liddell's Record*, 87–88; Noe, *Perryville*, 134–35; Hafendorfer, *Perryville*, 110–11; Horn, *Army of Tennessee*, 180.
6. *OR*, vol. 16, pt. 1, pp. 1157–58; Liddell, *Liddell's Record*, 87–88; McDonough, *War in Kentucky*, 217, 219; Engle, *Don Carlos Buell*, 305.
7. McDonough, *War in Kentucky*, 216–17, 219; Hess, *Banners to the Breeze*, 85; Engle, *Don Carlos Buell*, 305.
8. McDonough, *War in Kentucky*, 216–17, 219; Hess, *Banners to the Breeze*, 85; Engle, *Don Carlos Buell*, 305.
9. *OR*, vol. 16, pt. 1, pp. 1024, 1081, 1083–84; Kolakowski, *Civil War in Perryville*, 88–94; McDonough, *War in Kentucky*, 220–23; Engle, *Don Carlos Buell*, 305.
10. *OR*, vol. 16, pt. 1, pp. 1024, 1072, 1081, 1083–84; Liddell, *Liddell's Record*, 87–88; Hafendorfer, *Perryville*, 129–36; Engle, *Don Carlos Buell*, 305; Daniel, *Days of Glory*, 146.
11. *OR*, vol. 16, pt. 1, p. 1037; Hafendorfer, *Perryville*, 129; Kolakowski, *Civil War at Perryville*, 90–91; Prokopowicz, *All for the Regiment*, 164.
12. *OR*, vol. 16, pt. 1, p. 1092; Noe, *Perryville*, 139; Daniel, *Conquered*, 42.
13. *OR*, vol. 16, pt. 1, pp. 1092, 1096, 1109; Noe, *Perryville*, 156–57; Horn, *Leonidas Polk*, 265.
14. *OR*, vol. 16, pt. 1, pp. 1092, 1110; Noe, *Perryville*, 157; McDonough, *War in Kentucky*, 228; Parks, *General Leonidas Polk*, 268; Horn, *Leonidas Polk*, 265; Bush, "My Whole Life Must Speak for Me," 15–16, 114–15.
15. *OR*, vol. 16, pt. 1, pp. 1092, 1095; Hafendorfer, *Perryville*, 136; Noe, *Perryville*, 132, 157; Daniel, *Conquered*, 42; Horn, *Leonidas Polk*, 265–66.

16. *OR*, vol. 16, pt. 1, pp. 1092, 1102; Parks, *General Leonidas Polk*, 268; Connelly, *Army of the Heartland*, 257–58; Horn, *Leonidas Polk*, 265; Noe, *Perryville*, 158.
17. *OR*, vol. 16, pt. 1, pp. 1099–100, 1102; Noe, *Perryville*, 157; Parks, *General Leonidas Polk*, 269; Horn, *Leonidas Polk*, 265.
18. *OR*, vol. 16, pt. 1, pp. 1092, 1098, 1110; Parks, *General Leonidas Polk*, 270; Hafendorfer, *Perryville*, 136; Connelly, *Army of the Heartland*, 259–60; Kolakowski, *Civil War at Perryville*, 94; McDonough, *War in Kentucky*, 228–29; Daniel, *Conquered*, 43.
19. *OR*, vol. 16, pt. 1, pp. 1092, 1098, 1110; Parks, *General Leonidas Polk*, 270; Hafendorfer, *Perryville*, 136; Connelly, *Army of the Heartland*, 259–60; Kolakowski, *Civil War at Perryville*, 94; McDonough, *War in Kentucky*, 228–29; Daniel, *Conquered*, 43.
20. *OR*, vol. 16, pt. 1, p. 1092; Noe, *Perryville*, 158; McDonough, *War in Kentucky*, 226–28; Connelly, *Army of the Heartland*, 262; Daniel, *Conquered*, 42.
21. Historian Kenneth Noe provides a good discussion of this issue in *Perryville*, 158. Horn, *Army of Tennessee*, 183, 186; Parks, *General Leonidas Polk*, 269–70, 273; Kolakowski, *Civil War at Perryville*, 94; Connelly, *Army of the Heartland*, 260–61; McDonough, *War in Kentucky*, 228–32; McWhiney, *Braxton Bragg*, 1:305–7; Steven E. Woodworth, *Jefferson Davis and His Generals: The Failure of Confederate Command in the West* (Lawrence: University Press of Kansas, 1990), 156–58; Hess, *Braxton Bragg*, 70–71.
22. Noe, *Perryville*, 158. Horn, *Army of Tennessee*, 183, 186; Parks, *General Leonidas Polk*, 269–70, 273; Kolakowski, *Civil War at Perryville*, 94; Connelly, *Army of the Heartland*, 260–61; McDonough, *War in Kentucky*, 228–32; McWhiney, *Braxton Bragg*, 1:305–7; Steven E. Woodworth, *Jefferson Davis and His Generals: The Failure of Confederate Command in the West* (Lawrence: University Press of Kansas, 1990), 156–58; Hess, *Braxton Bragg*, 70–71.
23. *OR*, vol. 16, pt. 1, pp. 1087, 1092, 1110; Noe, *Perryville*, 170; Hafendorfer, *Perryville*, 162–64; Kolakowski, *Civil War at Perryville*, 97–98; McWhiney, *Braxton Bragg*, 1:312; Hess, *Braxton Bragg*, 69; Daniel, *Conquered*, 43; McPherson, *Battle Cry of Freedom*, 718.
24. *OR*, vol. 16, pt. 1, pp. 1087, 1110; Connelly, *Army of the Heartland*, 262; McWhiney *Braxton Bragg*, 1:312–14; Noe, *Perryville*, 171–72; Daniel, *Conquered*, 43.

25. *OR*, vol. 16, pt. 1, pp. 1087, 1110; Connelly, *Army of the Heartland*, 262; McWhiney *Braxton Bragg*, 1:312–14; Noe, *Perryville*, 171–72; Daniel, *Conquered*, 43.

26. *OR*, vol. 16, pt. 1, pp. 1087, 1110; Connelly, *Army of the Heartland*, 262; McWhiney *Braxton Bragg*, 1:312–14; Noe, *Perryville*, 171–72; Daniel, *Conquered*, 43.

27. *OR*, vol. 16, pt. 1, pp. 1087, 1110; Connelly, *Army of the Heartland*, 262; McWhiney *Braxton Bragg*, 1:312–14; Noe, *Perryville*, 171–72; Daniel, *Conquered*, 43.

28. *OR*, vol. 16, pt. 1, pp. 1087, 1110; Connelly, *Army of the Heartland*, 262; McWhiney *Braxton Bragg*, 1:312–14; Noe, *Perryville*, 171–72; Daniel, *Conquered*, 43.

29. *OR*, vol. 16, pt. 1, pp. 1087, 1110; Connelly, *Army of the Heartland*, 262; McWhiney *Braxton Bragg*, 1:312–14; Noe, *Perryville*, 171–72; Daniel, *Conquered*, 43.

30. *OR*, vol. 16, pt. 1, pp. 1087, 1092; Noe, *Perryville*, 171; Hess, *Banners to the Breeze*, 87–91.

31. *OR*, vol. 16, pt. 1, pp. 1092, 1110; Hess, *Banners to the Breeze*, 87–91; Noe, *Perryville*, 181–83; McWhiney, *Braxton Bragg*, 1:314–15; Kolakowski, *Civil War at Perryville*, 100.

32. Author's conjecture based on the situation.

33. *OR*, vol. 16, pt. 1, p. 526; Noe, *Perryville*, 168–69; Hafendorfer, *Perryville*, 160; McDonough, *War in Kentucky*, 234; Engle, *Don Carlos Buell*, 305; Prokopowicz, *All for the Regiment*, 162–63.

34. *OR*, vol. 16, pt. 1, pp. 1025, 1038, 1044–45; *OR*, vol. 16, pt. 2, pp. 580–81, 587; McDonough, *War in Kentucky*, 234; Hess, *Banners to the Breeze*, 91; Daniel, *Days of Glory*, 146; Engle, *Don Carlos Buell*, 305–6.

35. McDonough, *War in Kentucky*, 234–35; Hafendorfer, *Perryville*, 160; Noe, *Perryville*, 168; Engle, *Don Carlos Buell*, 305–6.

36. McDonough, *War in Kentucky*, 234–35; Hafendorfer, *Perryville*, 160; Noe, *Perryville*, 168; Engle, *Don Carlos Buell*, 305–6.

37. *OR*, vol. 16, pt. 1, p. 1025; Hess, *Banners to the Breeze*, 91; McDonough, *War in Kentucky*, 234–35; Engle, *Don Carlos Buell*, 305–7; Prokopowicz, *All for the Regiment*, 163; Daniel, *Days of Glory*, 148.

38. *OR*, vol. 16, pt. 1, pp. 49–51; McDonough, *War in Kentucky*, 234–35; Hafendorfer, *Perryville*, 160; Engle, *Don Carlos Buell*, 307.

39. *OR*, vol. 16, pt. 1, pp. 49–51; McDonough, *War in Kentucky*, 234; author's lengthy conversation with Kurt Holman regarding Nelson's likely participation had he been in command of the Third Corps, July 22, 2016.

40. *OR*, vol. 16, pt. 1, pp. 50, 1024; Don Carlos Buell, *East Tennessee and the Campaign of Perryville*, in *Battles and Leaders of the Civil War*, ed. Robert U. Johnson and Clarence C. Buel (1881; repr., New York: Thomas Yoseloff, 1956), 3:47; Kolakowski, *Civil War at Perryville*, 94; McDonough, *War in Kentucky*, 234.

41. Noe, *Perryville*, 166–69, 171; Hafendorfer, *Perryville*, 161–62; Hess, *Braxton Bragg*, 69.

Chapter 4

1. *OR*, vol. 16, pt. 1, pp. 1022–23; Hafendorfer, *Perryville*, 161–62; McDonough, *War in Kentucky*, 234; Daniel, *Days of Glory*, 146–48; Prokopowicz, *All for the Regiment*, 163–64.

2. Noe, *Perryville*, 43–44; Warner, *Generals in Blue*, 294; Hafendorfer, *Perryville*, 70, 72.

3. *OR*, vol. 16, pt. 1, pp. 1038–39; Noe, *Perryville*, 183–84; Hafendorfer, *Perryville*, 153–54, 172; Holman, *Battle of Perryville: Movement Maps*, 12:00 p.m.–1:00 p.m. Note that Holman depicts a movement map in fifteen-minute intervals from 12:00 p.m. to 8:00 p.m. The range listed includes those maps portraying troops' location every fifteen minutes between the beginning and ending times shown.

4. *OR*, vol. 16, pt. 1, p. 90; Holman, *Battle of Perryville: Movement Maps*, 1:00 p.m.–1:30 p.m.; Noe, *Perryville*, 186; Prokopowicz, *All for the Regiment*, 166–67; Daniel, *Days of Glory*, 148–49.

5. *OR*, vol. 16, pt. 1, pp. 1087, 1110; Connelly, *Army of the Heartland*, 262; McWhiney *Braxton Bragg*, 1:312–14; Noe, *Perryville*, 171–72; Daniel, *Conquered*, 43; US Department of Defense, *Dictionary of Military and Associated Terms*, World Wide Web, June, 2020.

6. Noe, *Perryville*, 186; Hafendorfer, *Perryville*, 189; Holman, *Battle of Perryville: Movement Maps*, 1:00 p.m.–1:30 p.m.

7. *OR*, vol. 16, pt. 1, p. 90; Noe, *Perryville*, 186; Hafendorfer, *Perryville*, 189; Holman, *Battle of Perryville: Movement Maps*, 1:00 p.m.–2:00 p.m.

8. *OR*, vol. 16, pt. 1, p. 90; Noe, *Perryville*, 186; Hafendorfer, *Perryville*, 189; Holman, *Battle of Perryville: Movement Maps*, 1:00 p.m.–2:00 p.m.

9. Holman, *Battle of Perryville: Movement Maps*, 2:15 p.m.–3:15 p.m.; Christopher Losson, *Tennessee's Forgotten Warriors: Frank Cheatham and His Confederate Division* (Knoxville: University of Tennessee Press, 1989), 66–67.
10. *OR*, vol. 16, pt. 1, p. 1087; Noe, *Perryville*, 172; author's conjecture.
11. Holman, *Battle of Perryville: Movement Maps*, 1:45 p.m.–2:00 p.m.; Noe, *Perryville*, 182; Hafendorfer, *Perryville*, 164, 173, 204–5; Stuart W. Sanders, *Maney's Confederate Brigade at the Battle of Perryville* (Charleston, SC: History Press, 2014), 25.
12. *OR*, vol. 16, pt. 1, p. 1110; Holman, *Battle of Perryville: Movement Maps*, 1:15 p.m.–1:30 p.m.; Warner, *Generals in Gray*, 331–32; Hafendorfer, *Perryville*, 75, 180–81; Noe, *Perryville*, 182–83; Sanders, *Maney's Confederate Brigade*, 26.
13. *OR*, vol. 16, pt. 1, p. 1110; Holman, *Battle of Perryville: Movement Maps*, 1:15 p.m.–1:30 p.m.; Warner, *Generals in Gray*, 331–32; Hafendorfer, *Perryville*, 75, 180–81; Noe, *Perryville*, 182–83; Sanders, *Maney's Confederate Brigade*, 26.
14. *OR*, vol. 16, pt. 1, p.1110; Holman, *Battle of Perryville: Movement Maps*, 1:15 p.m.–1:30 p.m.; Warner, *Generals in Gray*, 331–32; Hafendorfer, *Perryville*, 75, 180–81; Noe, *Perryville*, 182–83; Sanders, *Maney's Confederate Brigade*, 26.
15. *OR*, vol. 16, pt. 1, p. 1110; Holman, *Battle of Perryville: Movement Maps*, 1:15 p.m.–1:30 p.m.; Warner, *Generals in Gray*, 331–32; Hafendorfer, *Perryville*, 75, 180–81; Noe, *Perryville*, 182–83; Sanders, *Maney's Confederate Brigade*, 26.
16. *OR*, vol. 16, pt. 1, p. 1110; Holman, *Battle of Perryville: Movement Maps*, 1:15 p.m.–1:30 p.m.; Warner, *Generals in Gray*, 331–32; Hafendorfer, *Perryville*, 75, 180–81; Noe, *Perryville*, 182–83; Sanders, *Maney's Confederate Brigade*, 26.
17. *OR*, vol. 16, pt. 1, p. 1040; Kolakowski, *Civil War at Perryville*, 99–100; Holman, *Battle of Perryville: Movement Maps*, 1:45 p.m.–2:00 p.m.; Sanders, *Maney's Confederate Brigade*, 37.
18. *OR*, vol. 16, pt. 1, p. 1040; Kolakowski, *Civil War at Perryville*, 99–100; Holman, *Battle of Perryville: Movement Maps*, 1:45 p.m.–2:00 p.m.; Sanders, *Maney's Confederate Brigade*, 37.
19. Holman, *Battle of Perryville: Movement Maps*, 1:45 p.m.–2:00 p.m.; Noe, *Perryville*, 193; Hafendorfer, *Perryville*, 191–92.

20. Holman, *Battle of Perryville: Movement Maps*, 1:45 p.m.–2:00 p.m.; Noe, *Perryville*, 193; Hafendorfer, *Perryville*, 191–92.
21. *OR*, vol. 16, pt. 1, pp. 1087, 1109–10; Holman, *Battle of Perryville: Movement Maps*, 2:00 p.m.–2:30 p.m.; Noe, *Perryville*, 172.
22. US Department of Defense, *Dictionary of Military and Associated Terms*; Warner, *Generals in Gray*, 47; Losson, *Tennessee's Forgotten Warriors*, 23.
23. *OR*, vol. 16, pt. 1, pp. 1038–40; Holman, *Battle of Perryville: Movement Maps*, 2:00 p.m.–2:30 p.m.; Kolakowski, *Civil War at Perryville*, 96–97, 101–4; Losson, *Tennessee's Forgotten Warriors*, 66.
24. *OR*, vol. 16, pt. 1, pp. 1060, 1062–65, 1110–11; Holman, *Battle of Perryville: Movement Maps*, 2:15 p.m.–2:30 p.m.; Losson, *Tennessee's Forgotten Warriors* 66; Hafendorfer, *Perryville*, 204–5; Hess, *Braxton Bragg*, 69. Fort Donelson, located on the Cumberland River just south of the Kentucky border and captured by then Brig. Gen. Ulysses S. Grant, was named in Donelson's honor per Timothy B. Smith, *Grant Invades Tennessee: The 1862 Battles for Forts Henry and Donelson* (Lawrence: University Press of Kansas, 2016), 14.
25. *OR*, vol. 16, pt. 1, pp. 1111–12; Holman, *Battle of Perryville: Movement Maps*, 2:30 p.m.–2:45 p.m.; Hafendorfer, *Perryville*, 207; Losson, *Tennessee's Forgotten Warriors*, 66–67; Kolakowski, *Civil War at Perryville*, 100–104; Noe, *Perryville*, 195–204.
26. *OR*, vol. 16, pt. 1, pp. 1111–12; Holman, *Battle of Perryville: Movement Maps*, 2:30 p.m.–2:45 p.m.; Hafendorfer, *Perryville*, 207; Losson, *Tennessee's Forgotten Warriors*, 66–67; Kolakowski, *Civil War at Perryville*, 100–104; Noe, *Perryville*, 195–204.
27. *OR*, vol. 16, pt. 1, pp. 1111–12; Holman, *Battle of Perryville: Movement Maps*, 2:30 p.m.–2:45 p.m.; Hafendorfer, *Perryville*, 207; Losson, *Tennessee's Forgotten Warriors*, 66–67; Kolakowski, *Civil War at Perryville*, 100–104; Noe, *Perryville*, 195–204.
28. *OR*, vol. 16, pt. 1, pp. 1111–12; Holman, *Battle of Perryville: Movement Maps*, 2:30 p.m.–2:45 p.m.; Hafendorfer, *Perryville*, 207; Losson, *Tennessee's Forgotten Warriors*, 66–67; Kolakowski, *Civil War at Perryville*, 100–104; Noe, *Perryville*, 195–204.
29. *OR*, vol. 16, pt. 1, pp. 1111–12; Holman, *Battle of Perryville: Movement Maps*, 2:30 p.m.–2:45 p.m.; Hafendorfer, *Perryville*, 207; Losson, *Tennessee's Forgotten Warriors*, 66–67; Kolakowski, *Civil War at Perryville*, 100–104; Noe, *Perryville*, 195–204.

30. *OR*, vol. 16, pt. 1, pp. 1111–12; Holman, *Battle of Perryville: Movement Maps*, 2:30 p.m.–2:45 p.m.; Hafendorfer, *Perryville*, 207; Losson, *Tennessee's Forgotten Warriors*, 66–67; Kolakowski, *Civil War at Perryville*, 100–104; Noe, *Perryville*, 195–204; Sanders, *Maney's Confederate Brigade*, 36–39; Sam D. Elliott, *Soldier of Tennessee: General Alexander P. Stewart and the Civil War in the West* (Baton Rouge: Louisiana State University Press, 1999), 54–55.

31. *OR*, vol. 16, pt. 1, p. 1111; Holman, *Battle of Perryville: Movement Maps*, 2:45 p.m.–6:00 p.m.; Elliott, *Soldier of Tennessee*, 55–59; Sanders, *Maney's Confederate Brigade*, 38–39; Prokopowicz, *All for the Regiment*, 166–68.

32. *OR*, vol. 16, pt. 1, pp. 1111–19; Holman, *Battle of Perryville: Movement Maps*, 2:45 p.m.–3:45 p.m.; Kolakowski, *Civil War at Perryville*, 104–7; Losson, *Tennessee's Forgotten Warriors*, 67–71; Sanders, *Maney's Confederate Brigade*, 40–68; Prokopowicz, *All for the Regiment*, 173–77.

33. *OR*, vol. 16, pt. 1, pp. 1111–19; Holman, *Battle of Perryville: Movement Maps*, 2:45 p.m.–3:45 p.m.; Kolakowski, *Civil War at Perryville*, 104–7; Losson, *Tennessee's Forgotten Warriors*, 67–71; Sanders, *Maney's Confederate Brigade*, 40–68; Prokopowicz, *All for the Regiment*, 173–77.

34. *OR*, vol. 16, pt. 1, p. 91, Noe, *Perryville*, 233–34. Wikipedia, August 22, 2020, defines long-distance acoustic shadow as follows: "An acoustic shadow is to sound what a mirage is to light." For example, at the Battle of Iuka, a northerly wind prevented Gen. Ulysses S. Grant from hearing the sounds of battle and sending more troops. Acoustic shadowing was prevalent during the American Civil War, occurring in the Battles of Seven Pines, Gaines' Mill, Perryville, and Five Forks. Indeed, this phenomenon is addressed in Ken Burns's documentary *The Civil War*, produced by Florentine Films and aired on PBS in September 1990. Observers of nearby battles would sometimes see the smoke and flashes of light from cannon but not hear the corresponding roar of battle, while those in more distant locations would hear the sounds distinctly. Hafendorfer, *Perryville*, 287–88; Daniel, *Days of Glory*, 155.

35. *OR*, vol. 16, pt. 1, pp. 50–51, 91; Noe, *Perryville*, 290; Hafendorfer, *Perryville*, 288–89; Prokopowicz, *All for the Regiment*, 180–82.

36. *OR*, vol. 16, pt. 1, pp. 50–51, 91; Buell, *East Tennessee and the Campaign of Perryville*, 3:48; Hafendorfer, *Perryville*, 289; Kolakowski, *Civil War at Perryville*, 123; Prokopowicz, *All for the Regiment*, 182–83.

37. *OR*, vol. 16, pt. 1, pp. 50–51, 91; Buell, *East Tennessee and the Campaign of Perryville*, 3:48; Hafendorfer, *Perryville*, 289; Kolakowski, *Civil War at Perryville*, 123; Prokopowicz, *All for the Regiment*, 182–83.

38. *OR*, vol. 16, pt. 1, pp. 50–51, 91; Buell, *East Tennessee and the Campaign of Perryville*, 3:48; Hafendorfer, *Perryville*, 289; Kolakowski, *Civil War at Perryville*, 123; Prokopowicz, *All for the Regiment*, 182–83.

39. *OR*, vol. 16, pt. 1, pp. 50–51, 91; Buell, *East Tennessee and the Campaign of Perryville*, 3:48; Hafendorfer, *Perryville*, 289; Kolakowski, *Civil War at Perryville*, 123; Prokopowicz, *All for the Regiment*, 182–83.

40. *OR*, vol. 16, pt. 1, pp. 50–51, 91; Buell, *East Tennessee and the Campaign of Perryville*, 3:48; Hafendorfer, *Perryville*, 289; Kolakowski, *Civil War at Perryville*, 123; Prokopowicz, *All for the Regiment*, 182–83; Engle, *Don Carlos Buell*, 309.

41. *OR*, vol. 16, pt. 1, p. 91; Buell, *East Tennessee and the Campaign of Perryville*, 3:48; Holman, *Battle of Perryville: Movement Maps*, 4:45 p.m.–8:00 p.m.; Kolakowski, *Civil War at Perryville*, 123–25; Hess, *Banners to the Breeze*, 100–101; Prokopowicz, *All for the Regiment*, 183; Daniel, *Days of Glory*, 154–55.

42. Holman, *Battle of Perryville: Movement Maps*, 8:00 p.m.; Daniel, *Days of Glory*, 155–56; Prokopowicz, *All for the Regiment*, 177–78.

43. Author's conjecture based on the above sources.

44. *OR*, vol. 16, pt. 1, p. 1121; Holman, *Battle of Perryville: Movement Maps*, 2:45 p.m.–3:45 p.m.; Kolakowski, *Civil War at Perryville*, 114–16; Noe, *Perryville*, 216; Hafendorfer, *Perryville*, 208–9, 215, 217–18, 233, 238, 247–48; 250–51, 256.

45. *OR*, vol. 16, pt. 1 pp. 1121, 1057–58, 1124–27; Holman, *Battle of Perryville: Movement Maps*, 3:00 p.m.–4:15 p.m.; Hafendorfer, *Perryville*, 232; Kolakowski, *Civil War at Perryville*, 121; Hughes, *General William J. Hardee*, 129.

46. Holman, *Battle of Perryville: Movement Maps*, 3:30 p.m.–3:45 p.m.; Warner, *General in Gray*, 38; Noe, *Perryville*, 56–57, 68, 228; Kolakowski, *Civil War at Perryville*, 121; Hafendorfer, *Perryville*, 333.

47. Holman, *Battle of Perryville: Movement Maps*, 3:30 p.m.–3:45 p.m.; Warner, *General in Gray*, 38; Noe, *Perryville*, 56–57, 68, 228; Kolakowski, *Civil War at Perryville*, 121; Hafendorfer, *Perryville*, 333.

48. Holman, *Battle of Perryville: Movement Maps*, 3:30 p.m.–3:45 p.m.; Warner, *General in Gray*, 38; Noe, *Perryville*, 56–57, 68, 228; Kolakowski, *Civil War at Perryville*, 121; Hafendorfer, *Perryville*, 333.

49. Holman, *Battle of Perryville: Movement Maps*, 3:30 p.m.–3:45 p.m.; Warner, *General in Gray*, 38; Noe, *Perryville*, 56–57, 68, 228; Kolakowski, *Civil War at Perryville*, 121; Hafendorfer, *Perryville*, 333.

50. *OR*, vol. 16, pt. 1, pp. 1121, 1123; Noe, *Perryville*, 228, 264.
51. *OR*, vol. 16, pt. 1, pp. 1121, 1123; Noe, *Perryville*, 228, 264.
52. *OR*, vol. 16, pt. 1, p. 1123; Holman, *Battle of Perryville: Movement Maps*, 4:00 p.m.–5:00 p.m.; Noe, *Perryville*, 271; Kolakowski, *Civil War at Perryville*, 121–22.
53. *OR*, vol. 16, pt. 1, p. 1120; Holman, *Battle of Perryville: Movement Maps*, 12:00 p.m.–3:45 p.m.; Connelly, *Army of the Heartland*, 262; Kolakowski, *Civil War at Perryville*, 133; Noe, *Perryville*, 277.
54. *OR*, vol. 16, pt. 1, p. 897; Connelly, *Army of the Heartland*, 266; Hess, *Banners to the Breeze*, 100; Hafendorfer, *Perryville*, 258–59, 286.
55. *OR*, vol. 16, pt. 1, p. 1120; Hess, *Banners to the Breeze*, 100; Noe, *Perryville*, 233, 277.
56. Holman, *Battle of Perryville: Movement Maps*, 12:00 p.m.–3:45 p.m.; Hafendorfer, *Perryville*, 286; Connelly, *Army of the Heartland*, 266; Noe, *Perryville*, 233, 277.
57. Holman, *Battle of Perryville: Movement Maps*, 12:00 p.m.–3:45 p.m.; Hafendorfer, *Perryville*, 286; Connelly, *Army of the Heartland*, 266; Noe, *Perryville*, 233, 277.
58. *OR*, vol. 16, pt. 1, p. 1121; Holman, *Battle of Perryville: Movement Maps*, 3:45 p.m.–4:00 p.m.; Noe, *Perryville*, 277; Hafendorfer, *Perryville*, 290; Hess, *Banners to the Breeze*, 100; Kolakowski, *Civil War at Perryville*, 133–34.
59. *OR*, vol. 16, pt. 1, pp. 1081–82, 1121; Holman, *Battle of Perryville: Movement Maps*, 3:45 p.m.–5:00 p.m.; Hafendorfer, *Perryville*, 287, 290–91; Kolakowski, *Civil War at Perryville*, 133–34; Noe, *Perryville*, 277–84.
60. *OR*, vol. 16, pt. 1, p. 1121; Holman, *Battle of Perryville: Movement Maps*, 4:15 p.m.–4:45 p.m.; Hafendorfer, *Perryville*, 290–91; Hess, *Banners to the Breeze*, 100–101; Noe, *Perryville*, 282–83; Prokopowicz, *All for the Regiment*, 181–83; Kolakowski, *Civil War at Perryville*, 134.
61. *OR*, vol. 16, pt. 1, p. 1122; Holman, *Battle of Perryville: Movement Maps*, 4:30 p.m.–5:00 p.m.; Hess, *Banners to the Breeze*, 100–101; Hafendorfer, *Perryville*, 291–96; Kolakowski, *Civil War at Perryville*, 134; Prokopowicz, *All for the Regiment*, 181–83.
62. Hafendorfer, *Perryville*, 296–97; Hess, *Banners to the Breeze*, 101. See the following critical decision for information about Mitchell's frustration over not being allowed to remain in a forward position.
63. Holman, *Battle of Perryville: Movement Maps*, 2:45 p.m.–3:30 p.m.;

Warner, *Generals in Blue*, 472; Hafendorfer, *Perryville*, 142, 147, 162; Noe, *Perryville*, 165, 188–89, 250–51, 374; Kolakowski, *Civil War at Perryville*, 108–9; Sanders, *Maney's Confederate Brigade*, 82–84; Prokopowicz, *All for the Regiment*, 176.

64. *OR*, vol. 16, pt. 1, p. 1046; Holman, *Battle of Perryville: Movement Maps*, 3:00 p.m.–4:00 p.m.; Noe, *Perryville*, 256–58; Kolakowski, *Civil War at Perryville*, 109–11; Sanders, *Maney's Confederate Brigade*, 70–103.

65. *OR*, vol. 16, pt. 1, p. 1045; Holman, *Battle of Perryville: Movement Maps*, 4:00 p.m.–4:30 p.m.; Kolakowski, *Civil War at Perryville*, 125–26; Hafendorfer, *Perryville*, 311–12, 319–20; Noe, *Perryville*, 258–60; Sanders, *Maney's Confederate Brigade*, 106.

66. *OR*, vol. 16, pt. 1, p. 1045; Holman, *Battle of Perryville: Movement Maps*, 4:00 p.m.–4:30 p.m.; Kolakowski, *Civil War at Perryville*, 125–26; Hafendorfer, *Perryville*, 311–12, 319–20; Noe, *Perryville*, 258–60; Sanders, *Maney's Confederate Brigade*, 106.

67. *OR*, vol. 16, pt. 1, p. 1045; Holman, *Battle of Perryville: Movement Maps*, 4:00 p.m.–4:30 p.m.; Kolakowski, *Civil War at Perryville*, 125–26; Hafendorfer, *Perryville*, 311–12, 319–20; Noe, *Perryville*, 258–60; Sanders, *Maney's Confederate Brigade*, 106.

68. Holman, *Battle of Perryville: Movement Maps*, 4:15 p.m.–4:30 p.m.; Noe, *Perryville*, 259–60; Kolakowski, *Civil War at Perryville*, 126; Hafendorfer, *Perryville*, 319; Sanders, *Maney's Confederate Brigade*, 106–8.

69. *OR*, vol. 16, pt. 1, pp. 1042, 1046; Holman, *Battle of Perryville: Movement Maps*, 4:30 p.m.–5:00 p.m.; Kolakowski, *Civil War at Perryville*, 126; Hafendorfer, *Perryville*, 320; Sanders, *Maney's Confederate Brigade*, 106–8.

70. Noe, *Perryville*, 261; Kolakowski, *Civil War at Perryville*, 126; Sanders, *Maney's Confederate Brigade*, 109–11.

71. Noe, *Perryville*, 261; Kolakowski, *Civil War at Perryville*, 126; Sanders, *Maney's Confederate Brigade*, 109–11.

72. *OR*, vol. 16, pt. 1, pp. 1073, 1077, 1082; Kolakowski, *Civil War at Perryville*, 134–36; Hafendorfer, *Perryville*, 340–41; Engle, *Don Carlos Buell*, 307.

73. *OR*, vol. 16, pt. 1, p. 1077; Holman, *Battle of Perryville: Movement Maps*, 5:30 p.m.–8:00 p.m.; Kolakowski, *Civil War at Perryville*, 134; Warner, *Generals in Blue*, 329; Noe, *Perryville*, 286–87, 291–92; Hafendorfer, *Perryville*, 357.

74. *OR*, vol. 16, pt. 1, pp. 1077–78; Noe, *Perryville*, 287; Hafendorfer, *Perryville*, 340–41, 356–58.

75. *OR*, vol. 16, pt. 1, pp. 1077–78; Noe, *Perryville*, 287; Hafendorfer, *Perryville*, 340–41, 356–58.

76. *OR*, vol. 16, pt. 1, pp. 1077–78; Noe, *Perryville*, 287; Hafendorfer, *Perryville*, 340–41, 356–58.

77. *OR*, vol. 16, pt. 1, pp. 1077–78; Noe, *Perryville*, 287; Hafendorfer, *Perryville*, 340–41, 356–58.

78. *OR*, vol.16, pt. 1, p. 94; Noe, *Perryville*, 291–92; Hafendorfer, *Perryville*, 357–58; Prokopowicz, *All for the Regiment*, 183.

79. *OR*, vol.16, pt. 1, p. 94; Noe, *Perryville*, 291–92; Hafendorfer, *Perryville*, 357–58; Prokopowicz, *All for the Regiment*, 183.

80. Noe, *Perryville*, 291–92; Hafendorfer, *Perryville*, 357–58; Prokopowicz, *All for the Regiment*, 183.

81. Author's conjecture. Sunset on October 8, 1862 was a 5:32 p.m. per Charles L. Flint, ed. *The Old Franklin Almanac for 1862* (Philadelphia: A. Winch, 1862), 24. This was many years before time zones were established by the railroads on November 18, 1883. See Wikipedia, *Standard Time in the United States*, October 2, 2020.

82. *OR*, vol. 16, pt. 1, p. 1121; Holman, *Battle of Perryville: Movement Maps*, 4:45 p.m.–6:00 p.m.; Kolakowski, *Civil War at Perryville*, 129; Noe, *Perryville*, 295; Sanders, *Maney's Confederate Brigade*, 117–18; Kolakowski, *Battle of Perryville*, 131.

83. *OR*, vol. 16, pt. 1, pp. 1073, 1075–76, 1079–80; Holman, *Battle of Perryville: Movement Maps*, 6:15 p.m.–7:00 p.m.; Kolakowski, *Civil War at Perryville*, 130–31; Noe, *Perryville*, 295–96; Hafendorfer, *Perryville*, 346–50; Sanders, *Maney's Confederate Brigade*, 117–18. See note 81 regarding sunset.

84. Holman, *Battle of Perryville: Movement Maps*, 6:15 p.m.–7:00 p.m.; Hafendorfer, *Perryville*, 350; Noe, *Perryville*, 298.

85. Holman, *Battle of Perryville: Movement Maps*, 6:15 p.m.–7:00 p.m.; Hafendorfer, *Perryville*, 350; Noe, *Perryville*, 298.

86. Holman, *Battle of Perryville: Movement Maps*, 6:15 p.m.–7:00 p.m.; Hafendorfer, *Perryville*, 350; Noe, *Perryville*, 298.

87. *OR*, vol. 16, pt. 1, pp. 1121, 1159; Liddell, *Liddell's Record*, 91–92; Noe, *Perryville*, 298–300; Hafendorfer, *Perryville*, 350.

88. *OR*, vol. 16, pt. 1, p. 1159; Liddell, *Liddell's Record*, 92; Holman, *Battle of Perryville: Movement Maps*, 5:30 p.m.–6:45 p.m.; Hafendorfer, *Perryville*, 362. Noe, *Perryville*, 300.

89. *OR*, vol. 16, pt. 1, p. 1159; Liddell, *Liddell's Record*, 93; Holman, *Battle of Perryville: Movement Maps*, 6:45 p.m.–7:15 p.m.; Noe, *Perryville*, 305.

90. *OR*, vol. 16, pt. 1, p. 1159; Liddell, *Liddell's Record*, 93; Kolakowski, *Civil War at Perryville*, 131; Hafendorfer, *Perryville*, 362.

91. *OR*, vol. 16, pt. 1, p. 1159; Liddell, *Liddell's Record*, 93; Holman, *Battle of Perryville: Movement Maps*, 6:45 p.m.–7:15 p.m.; Kolakowski, *Civil War at Perryville*, 133; Hafendorfer, *Perryville*, 368; Noe, *Perryville*, 301–2; Horn, *Leonidas Polk*, 269–70.

92. *OR*, vol. 16, pt. 1, pp. 1059–60, 1111; Liddell, *Liddell's Record*, 93; Noe, *Perryville*, 302.

93. *OR*, vol. 16, pt. 1, pp. 1059–60, 1111; Liddell, *Liddell's Record*, 93; Noe, *Perryville*, 302.

94. *OR*, vol. 16, pt. 1, pp. 1059–60, 1111; Liddell, *Liddell's Record*, 93; Noe, *Perryville*, 302.

95. *OR*, vol. 16, pt. 1, pp. 1111, 1159–60; Liddell, *Liddell's Record*, 94; Holman, *Battle of Perryville: Movement Maps*, 7:15 p.m.–8:00 p.m.; Kolakowski, *Civil War at Perryville*, 133; Noe, *Perryville*, 305; Hafendorfer, *Perryville*, 375.

96. Holman, *Battle of Perryville: Movement Maps*, 8:00 p.m.; Noe, *Perryville*, 305.

97. Liddell, *Liddell's Record*, 94; Noe, *Perryville*, 312.

98. *OR*, vol. 16, pt. 1, p. 1023; Noe, *Perryville*, 315–18.

Chapter 5

1. *OR*, vol. 16, pt. 1, pp. 1088, 1093; Noe, *Perryville*, 313; Hess, *Banners to the Breeze*, 105; Kolakowski, *Civil War at Perryville*, 137.

2. *OR*, vol. 16, pt. 1, pp. 1088, 1093; *OR*, vol. 16, pt. 2, pp. 733–34; Noe, *Perryville*, 66, 313; Kolakowski, *Civil War at Perryville*, 137; Hafendorfer, *Perryville*, 389.

3. *OR*, vol. 16, pt. 1, p. 1093; Hafendorfer, *Perryville*, 389; Hess, *Banners to the Breeze*, 107; Connelly, *Army of the Heartland*, 266–67.

4. *OR*, vol. 16, pt. 1, p. 1093; Hafendorfer, *Perryville*, 389; Hess, *Banners to the Breeze*, 107; Connelly, *Army of the Heartland*, 266–67.

5. *OR*, vol. 16, pt. 1, p. 1093; Hafendorfer, *Perryville*, 389; Hess, *Banners to the Breeze*, 107; Connelly, *Army of the Heartland*, 266–67.

6. *OR*, vol. 16, pt. 1, p. 1093; Hafendorfer, *Perryville*, 389; Hess, *Banners to the Breeze*, 107; Connelly, *Army of the Heartland*, 266–67.

7. *OR*, vol. 16, pt. 1, p. 1093; Noe, *Perryville*, 314; McDonough, *War in Kentucky*, 305; Hess, *Banners to the Breeze*, 107; Connelly, *Army of the Heartland*, 266–67.

8. *OR*, vol. 16, pt. 1, p. 1093; Kolakowski, *Civil War at Perryville*, 138; McDonough, *War in Kentucky*, 305–7; Connelly, *Army of the Heartland*, 267.

9. *OR*, vol. 16, pt. 1, p. 1093; Hess, *Banners to the Breeze*, 110; McDonough, *War in Kentucky*, 307; Kolakowski, *Civil War at Perryville*, 140; Connelly, *Army of the Heartland*, 267; Engle, *Don Carlos Buell*, 312.

10. *OR*, vol. 16, pt. 1, p. 1093; McDonough, *War in Kentucky*, 30. See Peterson, *Decisions of the 1862 Kentucky Campaign*, 89–93 for more details.

11. *OR*, vol. 16, pt. 1, pp. 1023, 1027; Hess, *Banners to the Breeze*, 106–7; Kolakowski, *Civil War at Perryville*, 138; Stuart W. Sanders, *Perryville Under Fire: The Aftermath of Kentucky's Largest Civil War Battle* (Charleston, SC: History Press, 2012), 35.

12. *OR*, vol. 16, pt. 1, p. 1027; Kolakowski, *Civil War at Perryville*, 138; Noe, *Perryville*, 321–23; Engle, *Don Carlos Buell*, 312.

13. *OR*, vol. 16, pt. 1, p. 1027; Kolakowski, *Civil War at Perryville*, 138; Noe, *Perryville*, 321–23; Engle, *Don Carlos Buell*, 312.

14. *OR*, vol. 16, pt. 1, p. 1027; Kolakowski, *Civil War at Perryville*, 138; Noe, *Perryville*, 321–23; Engle, *Don Carlos Buell*, 312; Sanders, *Perryville Under Fire*, 35–36.

15. *OR*, vol. 16, pt. 1, p. 1027; Kolakowski, *Civil War at Perryville*, 138; Noe, *Perryville*, 321–23; Engle, *Don Carlos Buell*, 312; Sanders, *Maney's Confederate Brigade*, 131; Sanders, *Perryville Under Fire*, 35–36, 39.

16. *OR*, vol. 16, pt. 1, p. 510; Noe, *Perryville*, 321; Hafendorfer, *Perryville*, 405–9; Engle, *Don Carlos Buell*, 312.

17. Noe, *Perryville*, 323; Sanders, *Perryville Under Fire*, 33–39.

18. *OR*, vol. 16, pt. 1, p. 1027; Noe, *Perryville*, 339–41. See Peterson, *Decisions of the 1862 Kentucky Campaign*, 93–94 for more details.

19. Author's conjecture.

Chapter 6

1. *OR*, vol. 16, pt. 1, pp. 1028, 1092; Sanders, *Perryville Under Fire*, 7, 27.

2. *OR*, vol. 16, pt. 1, pp. 1028, 1092; Kolakowski, *Civil War at Perryville*. 137–38, 140; Hafendorfer, *Perryville*, 72. See Kenneth A. Hafendorfer, *They Died by Twos and Tens: The Confederate Cavalry in the Kentucky Campaign of 1862* (Louisville: KH Press, 1995) for details.

3. *OR*, vol. 16, pt. 1, pp. 1033–36, 1087, 1108, 1112; Sam Watkins, *Company Aytch, or A Side Show of the Big Show and Other Sketches*, ed. M. Thomas Inge (1882; repr., New York: Penguin Books, 1999), 44; Noe, *Perryville*, 344, 369, 373; Hafendorfer, *Perryville*, 444–59; Wikipedia, *Civil War, Highest Casualty Battles, March 11, 2020*. Per the American Battlefield Trust (formerly the Civil War Trust), the top ten bloodiest battles in terms of casualties were as follows: Gettysburg, 51,000; Chickamauga, 34,624; Spotsylvania, 30,000; The Wilderness, 29,800; Chancellorsville, 24,000; Shiloh, 23,746; Stones River, 23,515; Antietam, 22,717; Second Manassas, 22,180; and Vicksburg, 19,233.

4. *OR*, vol. 16, pt. 1, pp. 1033–36, 1087, 1108, 1112; Noe, *Perryville*, 344, 369, 373; Hafendorfer, *Perryville*, 444–59.

5. Noe, *Perryville*, 346–47; Hafendorfer, *Perryville*, 413–14; Sanders, *Perryville Under Fire*, 38–39.

6. Hafendorfer, *Perryville*, 423; Noe, *Perryville*, 359; Buell, *East Tennessee*, 3:23; Sanders, *Perryville Under Fire*, 51. In 2018 Camp Nelson was proclaimed a national monument with much else of interest to see there.

7. Per chapters 2–5.

8. Hafendorfer, *Perryville*, 356–58; McDonough, *War in Kentucky*, 270; several of author's conversations with Kurt Holman, July 22, 2015 and July 25, 2016.

9. *OR*, vol. 16, pt. 1, p. 1088; McDonough, *War in Kentucky*, 307; Hafendorfer, *Perryville*, 425–26; Daniel, *Conquered*, 43.

10. Noe, *Perryville*, 334; Hafendorfer, *Perryville*, 425, 441; Connelly, *Army of the Heartland*, 279. See Peterson, *Decisions of the 1862 Kentucky Campaign*, 89–93 for more information on Bragg's retreat.

11. McDonough, *War in Kentucky*, 314, 319; Noe, *Perryville*, 339; Daniel, *Conquered*, 44–45.

12. Hafendorfer, *Perryville*, 436–38; Noe, *Perryville*, 340–42; McDonough, *War in Kentucky*, 317; Engle, *Don Carlos Buell*, 312–18.

13. *OR*, vol. 16, pt. 2, pp. 652, 654; Hafendorfer, *Perryville*, 436–38; Noe, *Perryville*, 340–42; McDonough, *War in Kentucky*, 317; Engle, *Don Carlos Buell*, 312–18.

14. McDonough, *War in Kentucky*, 310. See chapter 1 for a review of the Confederate High Tide.
15. See Peter Cozzens, *No Better Place to Die: The Battle of Stones River* (Urbana: University of Illinois Press, 1991) and Matt Spruill and Lee Spruill, *Decisions at Stones River: The Sixteen Critical Decisions That Defined the Battle* (Knoxville: University of Tennessee Press, 2018) for details. Lincoln utilized the power of this victory to formally invoke the Emancipation Proclamation on January 1, 1863.
16. McPherson, *Battle Cry of Freedom*, 663–64.
17. McPherson, *Battle Cry of Freedom*, 669. See Peter Cozzens, *This Terrible Sound: The Battle of Chickamauga* (Urbana: University of Illinois Press, 1992) and Dave Powell, *Decisions at Chickamauga: The Twenty-Four Critical Decisions That Defined the Battle* (Knoxville: University of Tennessee Press, 2018) for more information on the battle.
18. See Peterson, *Decisions at Chattanooga*, and Larry Peterson, *Decisions of the Atlanta Campaign: The Twenty-One Critical Decisions That Defined the Operation* (Knoxville: University of Tennessee Press, 2019) for details.

Appendix I

1. Hess, *Banners to the Breeze*, 78–79.
2. *OR*, vol. 16, pt. 1, p. 1024.
3. *OR*, vol. 16, pt. 1, p. 1091. Exhibit 1 refers to Bragg following up with Polk as to his disobedience of orders. See *OR*, vol. 16, pt. 1, p. 1094.
4. *OR*, vol. 16, pt. 1, p. 1109.
5. *OR*, vol. 16, pt. 1, p. 1091.
6. *OR*, vol. 16, pt. 1, p. 1120.
7. *OR*, vol. 16, pt. 1, p. 1109.
8. *OR*, vol. 16, pt. 1, p. 1092. On the reference to Exhibit 4, see note 2 above.
9. *OR*, vol. 16, pt. 1, pp. 1109–10.
10. *OR*, vol. 16, pt. 1, pp. 1109, 1022, 1072; Noe, *Perryville*, 143, 146, Buell, *East Tennessee*, 3:47.
11. *OR*, vol. 16, pt. 1, p. 1024.
12. *OR*, vol. 16, pt. 1, p. 1081.
13. *OR*, vol. 16, pt. 1, p. 1083.

14. *OR*, vol. 16, pt. 1, p.1025.
15. *OR*, vol. 16, pt. 1, p. 1025.
16. *OR*, vol. 16, pt. 1, p. 1027.
17. Noe, *Perryville*, 236; Hafendorfer, *Perryville*, 219–20, 259; Buell, *East Tennessee*, 3:16; McDonough, *War in Kentucky*, 287.
18. *OR*, vol. 16, pt. 1, pp. 897–98.
19. *OR*, vol. 16, pt. 1, pp. 1109–10.
20. *OR*, vol. 16, pt. 1, p. 1087.
21. Losson, *Tennessee's Forgotten Warriors*, 65.
22. *OR*, vol. 16, pt. 1, p. 1087.
23. Noe, *Perryville*, 186.
24. *OR*, vol. 16, pt. 1, p. 1038.
25. Hess, *Banners to the Breeze*, 88–89.
26. Noe, *Perryville*, 193.
27. *OR*, vol. 16, pt. 1, pp. 1110–11.
28. *OR*, vol. 16, pt. 1, p. 1113.
29. *OR*, vol. 16, pt. 1, p. 1121.
30. *OR*, vol. 16, pt. 1, pp. 1057–58.
31. Hafendorfer, *Perryville*, 232.
32. Kolakowski, *Civil War at Perryville*, 121.
33. *OR*, vol. 16, pt. 1, pp. 1124–27.
34. *OR*, vol. 16, pt. 1, pp. 1122–23.
35. *OR*, vol. 16, pt. 1, pp. 1044–45.
36. Noe, *Perryville*, 165, 221–22.
37. *OR*, vol. 16, pt. 1, pp. 1121–22.
38. Hess, *Banners to the Breeze*, 100–101.
39. Noe, *Perryville*, 292.
40. *OR*, vol. 16, pt. 1, p. 1073.
41. *OR*, vol. 16, pt. 1, p. 94.
42. Noe, *Perryville*, 383.
43. *OR*, vol. 16, pt. 1, pp. 1041–42.
44. *OR*, vol. 16, pt. 1, pp. 1041–42; 1113–14. "Feild" is the correct spelling.
45. *OR*, vol. 16, pt. 1, pp. 1155–56.

46. *OR*, vol. 16, pt. 1, pp. 1075–76.
47. *OR*, vol. 16, pt. 1, pp. 1079–80.
48. *OR*, vol. 16, pt. 1, pp. 1159–60.
49. Liddell, *Liddell's Record*, 93–94.
50. *OR*, vol. 16, pt. 1, p. 1111.

Appendix II

1. Compiled from *OR*, vol. 16, pt. 1, pp. 1033–36; *Battles and Leaders*, 3:29–30; Hafendorfer, *Perryville*, 444–52; Noe, *Perryville*, 373–80.

Appendix III

1. Compiled from *OR*, vol. 16, pt. 1, pp. 1108, 1112; *Battles and Leaders*, 3:30; Hafendorfer, *Perryville*, 454–58; Noe, *Perryville*, 369–73.

BIBLIOGRAPHY

Primary Sources

Basler, Roy P., ed. *The Collected Works of Abraham Lincoln*. 9 vols. New Brunswick, NJ: Rutgers University Press, 1953–55.

Bragg, Braxton. Papers. Western Reserve Historical Society, Cleveland, OH.

Buell, Don Carlos. *East Tennessee and the Campaign of Perryville*. In *Battles and Leaders of the Civil War*, edited by Robert U. Johnson and Clarence C. Buel. 1881. Reprint. New York: Thomas Yoseloff, 1956.

Confederate Veteran: Published Monthly In the Interest of Confederate Veterans And Kindred Topics 1–40 (1893–1922). Edited by S. A. Cunningham, 1893–1913. Reprint. Wilmington, NC: Broadfoot Pub. Co., 1987–1988. https://catalog.hathitrust.org/Record/100813931.

Flint, Charles L. ed. *The Old Franklin Almanac for 1862*. Philadelphia: A. Winch, 1862.

Johnson, Robert Underwood, and Clarence Clough Buel, eds. *Battles and Leaders of the Civil War*. Vol. 3. 1887. Reprint. New York: Thomas Yoseloff, 1956.

Johnston, J. Stoddard. *Memoranda of Facts Bearing on General Bragg's Kentucky Campaign, January 8, 1863*. J. Stoddard Johnston Military Papers. Filson Club Historical Society, Louisville, KY.

Liddell, St. John Richardson. *Liddell's Record: St. John Richardson Liddell: Brigadier General, CSA, Staff Officer and Brigade Commander, Army of Tennessee.* Edited by Nathaniel C. Hughes Jr. Baton Rouge: Louisiana State University Press, 1985.

Lowe, Richard, ed. *A Texas Cavalry Officer's Civil War: The Diary and Letters of James C. Bates.* Baton Rouge: Louisiana State University Press, 1999.

Polk, Leonidas. Papers. Repository/library, Duke University, Durham, NC.

Quintard, Charles T. *Doctor Quintard, Chaplain C.S.A. and Second Bishop of Tennessee: The Memoir and Civil War Diary of Charles Todd Quintard.* Edited by Sam D. Elliott. Baton Rouge: Louisiana State University Press, 2003.

Schofield, John M. *Forty-Six Years in the Army.* 1887. Reprint. Harrisburg, PA: Archive Society, 1997.

US War Department. *The War of the Rebellion: A Compilation of the Official Records of the Union and Confederate Armies.* 128 vols. Washington, DC: US Government Printing Office, 1880–1901.

Watkins, Sam. *Company Aytch, or A Side Show of the Big Show and Other Sketches.* Edited by M. Thomas Inge. 1882. Reprint. New York: Penguin Books, 1999.

Secondary Sources

Black, Robert C., III. *The Railroads of the Confederacy.* Chapel Hill: University of North Carolina Press, 1998.

Bonekemper, Edward H., III. *The 10 Biggest Civil War Blunders.* Washington, DC: Regnery History, 2018.

Boritt, Gabor S., ed. *Why the Confederacy Lost.* New York: Oxford University Press, 1992.

Bush, Bryan S. "My Whole Life Must Speak for Me: Southern Honor and Confederate General Leonidas Polk." Master's thesis, University of Louisville, 2015.

Connelly, Thomas Lawrence. *Army of the Heartland: The Army of Tennessee, 1861–1862.* Baton Rouge: Louisiana State University Press, 1967.

Connelly, Thomas Lawrence, and Archer Jones. *The Politics of Command: Factions and Ideas in Confederate Strategy.* Baton Rouge: Louisiana State University Press, 1973.

Cozzens, Peter. *No Better Place to Die: The Battle of Stones River.* Urbana: University of Illinois Press, 1991.

Cummings, Charles M. *Yankee Quaker, Confederate General: The Curious Career of Bushrod Rust Johnson.* Columbus, OH: General's Books, 1993.

Daniel, Larry J. *Conquered: Why the Army of Tennessee Failed.* Chapel Hill: University of North Carolina Press, 2019.

———. *Days of Glory: The Army of the Cumberland, 1861–1865.* Baton Rouge: Louisiana State University Press, 2004.

Davis, William C. *Jefferson Davis: The Man and His Hour.* Baton Rouge: Louisiana State University Press, 1991.

Elliott, Sam D. *Soldier of Tennessee: General Alexander P. Stewart and the Civil War in the West.* Baton Rouge: Louisiana State University Press, 1999.

Engerud, Hal. *The Battle of Munfordville: September 14th–17th, 1862.* Munfordville, KY: Hart County Historical Society, 1994.

Engle, Stephen D. *Don Carlos Buell: Most Promising of All.* Chapel Hill: University of North Carolina Press, 1999.

Foote, Shelby. *The Civil War: A Narrative; Fort Sumter to Perryville.* New York: Vintage Books, 1958.

Hafendorfer, Kenneth A. *The Battle of Richmond, Kentucky, August 30, 1862.* Louisville: KH Press, 2006.

———. *Mill Springs: Campaign and Battle of Mill Springs, Kentucky.* Louisville: KH Press, 2001.

———. *Perryville: Battle for Kentucky.* Louisville: KH Press, 1991.

———. *They Died by Twos and Tens: The Confederate Cavalry in the Kentucky Campaign of 1862.* Louisville: KH Press, 1995.

Harsh, Joseph L. *Confederate Tide Rising: Robert E. Lee and the Making of Southern Strategy, 1861–1862.* Kent, OH: Kent State University Press, 1998.

———. *Taken at the Flood: Robert E. Lee and Confederate Strategy in the Maryland Campaign of 1862.* Kent, OH: Kent State University Press, 1999.

Hess, Earl J. *Banners to the Breeze: The Kentucky Campaign, Corinth, and Stones River.* Lincoln: University of Nebraska Press, 2000.

———. *Braxton Bragg: The Most Hated Man of the Confederacy.* Chapel Hill: University of North Carolina Press, 2016.

———. *The Civil War in the West: Victory and Defeat from the Appalachians to the Mississippi.* Chapel Hill: University of North Carolina Press, 2012.

Hewitt, Lawrence L., and Arthur W. Bergeron Jr., eds. *Confederate Generals in the Western Theater: Classic Essays on America's Civil War.* Vol. 1. Knoxville: University of Tennessee Press, 2010.

———. *Confederate Generals in the Western Theater: Essays on America's Civil War.* Vol. 2. Knoxville: University of Tennessee Press, 2010.

———. *Confederate Generals in the Western Theater: Essays on America's Civil War.* Vol. 3. Knoxville: University of Tennessee Press, 2011.

Hewitt, Lawrence L., Arthur W. Bergeron Jr., and Thomas E. Schott, eds. *Confederate Generals in the Trans-Mississippi.* Vol. 1. Knoxville: University of Tennessee Press, 2013.

Holman, Kurt. *Battle of Perryville Movement Maps: Showing the Fighting Ground of the Union Left and Centre, 12:00 PM to 8:00 PM.* Perryville, KY: Friends of Perryville Battlefield, 2016.

Horn, Huston. *Leonidas Polk: Warrior Bishop of the Confederacy.* Lawrence: University Press of Kansas, 2019.

Horn, Stanley F. *The Army of Tennessee.* Norman: University of Oklahoma Press, 1941. Reprint 1993.

Hughes, Nathaniel C., Jr. *General William J. Hardee: Old Reliable.* Baton Rouge: Louisiana State University Press, 1965.

Jones, Archer. *Civil War Command & Strategy: The Process of Victory and Defeat.* New York: Free Press, 1992.

Lambert, D. Warren. *When the Ripe Pears Fell: The Battle of Richmond, Kentucky.* Richmond, KY: Madison County Historical Society, 1995.

Leigh, Philip. *The Confederacy at Flood Tide: The Political and Military Ascension, June to December 1862.* Yardley, PA: Westholme, 2016.

Livermore, Thomas L. *Number and Losses in the Civil War in America.* 1901. Reprint. Dayton, OH: Morningside, 1986.

Losson, Christopher. *Tennessee's Forgotten Warriors: Frank Cheatham and His Confederate Division.* Knoxville: University of Tennessee Press, 1989.

Lowry, Terry. *The Battle of Charleston and the 1862 Kanawha Valley Campaign.* Charleston, WV: Star, 2016.

McDonough, James L. *War in Kentucky: From Shiloh to Perryville.* Knoxville: University of Tennessee Press, 1994.

McMurry, Richard M. *Two Great Rebel Armies: An Essay in Confederate Military History.* Chapel Hill: University of North Carolina Press, 1989.

McWhiney, Grady. *Braxton Bragg and Confederate Defeat.* Vol. 1. Tuscaloosa: University of Alabama Press, 1969.

Noe, Kenneth W. *Perryville: This Grand Havoc of Battle.* Lexington: University Press of Kentucky, 2001.

Parks, Joseph H. *General Edmund Kirby Smith, C.S.A.* 1954. Reprint. Baton Rouge: Louisiana State University Press, 1992.

———. *General Leonidas Polk, C.S.A.: The Fighting Bishop.* Baton Rouge: 1962. Reprint. Louisiana State University Press, 1992.

Perello, Christopher. *The Quest for Annihilation: The Role & Mechanics of Battle in the American Civil War.* Bakersfield, CA: Strategy and Tactics, 2009.

Peterson, Lawrence K. *Confederate Combat Commander: The Remarkable Life of Brigadier General Alfred Jefferson Vaughan Jr.* Knoxville: University of Tennessee Press, 2013.

———. *Decisions of the 1862 Kentucky Campaign: The Twenty-Seven Critical Decisions That Defined the Operation.* Knoxville: University of Tennessee Press, 2019.

———. *Decisions of the Atlanta Campaign: The Twenty-One Critical Decisions That Defined the Operation.* Knoxville: University of Tennessee Press, 2019.

Prokopowicz, Gerald J. *All for the Regiment: The Army of the Ohio, 1861–1862.* Chapel Hill: University of North Carolina Press, 2001.

Robertson, William Glenn. *River of Death: The Chickamauga Campaign.* Vol. 1, *The Fall of Chattanooga.* Chapel Hill: University of North Carolina Press, 2018.

Sanders, Stuart W. *The Battle of Mill Springs, Kentucky.* Charleston SC: History Press, 2013.

———. *Maney's Confederate Brigade at the Battle of Perryville.* Charleston, SC: History Press, 2014.

———. *Perryville Under Fire: The Aftermath of Kentucky's Largest Civil War Battle.* Charleston, SC: History Press, 2012.

Smith, Timothy B. *Grant Invades Tennessee: The 1862 Battles for Forts Henry and Donelson.* Lawrence: University Press of Kansas, 2016.

Spruill, Matt, and Lee Spruill. *Decisions at Stones River: The Sixteen Critical Decisions That Defined the Battle.* Knoxville: University of Tennessee Press, 2018.

Warner, Ezra J. *Generals in Blue: Lives of the Union Commanders.* Baton Rouge: Louisiana State University Press, 1964.

———. *Generals in Gray: Lives of the Confederate Commanders.* Baton Rouge: Louisiana State University Press, 1959.

Weber, Thomas. *The Northern Railroads in the Civil War: 1861–1865*. Bloomington: Indiana University Press, 1952.

Woodworth, Steven E. *Decision in the Heartland: The Civil War in the West*. Westport, CT: Praeger, 2008.

———. *Jefferson Davis and His Generals: The Failure of Confederate Command in the West*. Lawrence: University Press of Kansas, 1990.

———. *No Band of Brothers: Problems of the Rebel High Command*. Columbia: University of Missouri Press, 1999.

INDEX

Page numbers in **boldface** refer to illustrations. Ranks reflect officers' attainment at the time of the Battle of Perryville.

acoustic shadow, 68
Adams, Daniel W., Brig. Gen., CSA, brigade of, 39, 71–75, 82, 85
Alabama, 27
Alabama regiments, CSA: 45th, 76
Anderson, J. Patton, Maj. Gen., CSA, 76; division of, 36, 58, 71, 73, 75
Antietam (or Sharpsburg), MD, Battle of, 1, 10–12
Appomattox Court House, 102
Arkansas, 13
Arkansas regiments, CSA: 2nd, 87; 5th, 42, 44; 7th, 42, 44
Army of Kentucky (Provisional), USA, 7, 18–19, 99
Army of Kentucky, CSA, 93, 97
Army of Tennessee, CSA, 17, 101
Army of the Cumberland, USA, 101

Army of the Mississippi, CSA, 4, 7, 17, 25, 27, 30, 72, 93, 96
Army of the Ohio, USA, 4, 16–17, 19–20, 32, 97
Army of the Potomac, USA, 1, 16, 48
Atlanta Campaign, 102

Bardstown, KY, 8, 20, 22–26, 29, 33, 38, 48
Bardstown Junction, KY, 23
Barnett, Charles, Capt., USA, battery of, 44
Barrett, Overton, Capt., CSA, battery of, 76, 82
Bates, Caleb, Maj., USA, 68
Beauregard, P. G. T., Gen., CSA, 4, 25
Belmont, MO, Battle of, 4
Benton Road, 61, 79, 87

Bloomfield, KY, 23, 25, 30
Bottom, Henry P. "Squire," House of, **71**–75, 85
Bottom, Samuel, 42
Bottom Hill, 42–43, 45
Bowling Green, KY, 3
Bragg, Braxton, Gen., CSA: pre-battle, 4, 7, 8, 13, 17, 19–20, 22–**26**, 28–33, 36–39, 73; during battle, 42, 45–51, 53, 57, 59–63, 72, 75–77, 81–86; post-battle, 91–97, 99–101
Breckinridge, John C., Maj. Gen., CSA, 13, 100
Britain, 10–11
Brown, John C., Brig. Gen., CSA, brigade of, 71–72, 74
Bryantsville, KY, 92–93, 97
Buckner, Simon B., Maj. Gen., CSA, 35, **72**–75, 99; division of, 58, 71–72, 74
Buell, Don Carlos, Maj. Gen., USA: pre-battle, 3, 4, 7–8, 13, 15–**16**, 18–19, 21–24, 29–33, 35, 37–39; during battle, 42–43, 48, 51–52, 56, 68–70, 76–77, 81, 84, 90, 99; post-battle, 91–93, 95–97, 100; army of, 39, 45, 51, 53, 55, 84
Buena Vista, Mexico, Battle of, 25
Bull Run, 34, 42, 44, 82
Bull Run (or First Manassas), VA: Battle of, 1; Second Battle of, 12
Burnside, Ambrose, Maj. Gen., USA, 3, 12–13
Bush, Asahel K., Capt., USA, battery of, 79
Bush, Bryan, Site Manager, PBSHS, 28

Caldwell, William W., Col., USA, brigade of, 83–84

Camp Breckinridge (formerly Camp Dick Robinson), KY, 29, 33, 35, 53, 77, 84, 92–93, 96–7, 99
Camp Nelson, Nicholasville, KY, USA, 98
Campbell, J. A., Capt., USA, 56
Carlin, William P., Col., USA, brigade of, 82–84
Carnes, William, Capt., CSA, battery of, 59, 63, 79
casualties, 95–98
Chaplin River, 34, 46–47, 50, 57, 61, 93
Charleston, SC, 1
Charleston, WV, 13
Chatham House, 86
Chattanooga, TN, 4, 7, 100–102
Cheatham, Benjamin F., Maj. Gen., CSA, 58–**62**, 66, 87, 99; division of, 39, 50–51, 58, 60–62, 68, 71, 74–75, 78, 87, 98
Chickamauga, GA, Battle of, 101
Cleburne, Patrick R., Brig. Gen., CSA, brigade of, 36, 72
Columbus, KY, 3, 4
Confederacy, 10–13, 27–28, 31–32, 38, 100–102
Confederate Congress, 11
Confederate high tide, 8–13, 45, 100
Conscription Act, CSA, 11
Corinth, MS, 4, 25, 100; Battle of, 100
Crawford, John, house of, 48–**49**, 92
Crawford Springs, 96
critical decisions: definition xv; categories of, xv; format of, xvii
Crittenden, George, Maj. Gen., USA, 3
Crittenden, Thomas L., Maj. Gen., USA: pre-battle, 17, 20; Second Corps of, 21, 23, 42, 51–53, 55, 81
Cruft, Charles, Brig. Gen., USA, 18

Cumberland Gap, KY, TN, VA, 3, 4, 7, 34, 93

Cumberland River, 3, 4

Danville, KY, 30, 33–35, 84, 96

Davis, Jefferson, President, CSA, 3, 4, 7, 25–28, 100

Davis, Jefferson C., Brig. Gen., USA, 18

Department of East Tennessee, CSA, 4

Department of the Ohio, USA, 19

District 2, CSA, 27

Dixville Crossroads, 61, 70, 73, 79, 81, 85, 87–88

Doctor's Creek, KY, 35, 87

Donelson, Daniel, Brig. Gen., CSA, 62–63; brigade of, 58–59, 62, 64, 66

Dorsey House, 43, 51, 56, 68, 76

drought, 41

Dumont, Ebenezer, Brig. Gen., USA, 23–24, 30; division of, 36, 53

East Tennessee, 3, 100

Eastern Theater, 1, 12, 102

echelon, definition of, 62

Eleventh Division, USA, 21

Emancipation Proclamation, Preliminary, 11

Episcopal Church, 26–27

Feild, Hume R., Col., CSA, 68

Fifth Division, USA, 21

First Division, USA, 21

Fisher, Horace, Capt., USA, 69

Floyd, John, Brig. Gen., CSA, 72

Fort Donelson, TN, 3, 4, 72

Fort Henry, TN, 3, 4

Fort Monroe, VA, 1

Fort Sumpter, SC, 1, 10

Fourth Division, USA, 21

France, 10

Frankfort, KY, 7, 22–25, 29–31, 33, 36–39, 46, 53, 92

Fredericksburg, VA, 13

Fry, Speed S., Brig. Gen., USA, brigade of, 45

Gay, Ebenezer, Acting Brig. Gen., USA, 45; cavalry of, 70, 85

Georgia regiments, CSA: 41st, 67

Gettysburg, PA, Battle of, 9, 101

Gilbert, Charles C., Acting Maj. Gen., USA, **18**–21, 42–43, 53, 70, 77, 81, 83–85, 99; Third Corps of, 17, 19–23, 42, 48, 51–53, 55–57, 69–70, 76, 85, 96–97, 99

Gooding, Michael, Col., USA, brigade of, 70, 81, 85, 88

Goodknight House, 58

Granger, Gordon, Brig. Gen., USA, 99

Grant, Ulysses S., Maj. Gen., USA, 3, 4, 46, 48, 100–102

Green River, KY, 7, 24

Greusel, Nicholas, Col., USA, brigade of, 76

Halleck, Henry, Maj. Gen., USA, 4, 17

Hardee, William J. "Old Reliable," Maj. Gen., CSA: pre-battle, 3, 23–24, 33–**34**, 35–39; battle, 42, 45–46, 72–74, 86; post-battle, 99; Left Wing of, 39, 42, 48–50, 62, 66

Harris, Leonard, Col., USA, 57; brigade of, 71

Harris, Samuel J., USA, battery of, 66

Harrodsburg, KY, 30, 33, 36, 39, 47, 92–93, 95–96

Hawes, Richard, Governor of KY, CSA, 31, 33, 92

Index

Haysville, KY, 42, 52
Hescock, Henry, Capt., USA, battery of, 45
high-water mark, CSA, 81
Hindman, Thomas C., Maj. Gen., CSA, 13
Hoblitzell, W. T., Capt., USA, 69
Holly Springs, MS, 13
Holman, Kurt, former Site Manager, PBSHS, 20, 99
Horn, Stanley, 25
Hotchkiss, William, Capt., USA, battery of, 82

Illinois regiments, USA: 21st, 82; 24th, 66, 78, 81; 38th, 82; 123rd, 68
Indiana, 18
Indiana regiments, USA: 22nd, 88
Island Number 10, 4

Jackson, James S., Brig. Gen., USA, 18, 21, 60, 68; division of, 56–57
Jenkins, Albert G., Brig. Gen., CSA, 13
Johnson, Bushrod R., Brig. Gen., CSA, brigade of, 42, 72
Johnston, Albert S., Gen., CSA, 3, 4, 25, 27
Johnston, Joseph E., Gen., CSA, 1, 34
Jones, Thomas M., Col., CSA, brigade of, 71, 74

Keith, Squire, Lieut. Col., USA, 88
Kentucky, Commonwealth of, 3, 7, 13, 20–21, 24, 30–32, 34, 36, 38, 43, 53, 58, 81, 93, 95–96, 99–100, 102
Kentucky Campaign of 1862, 7–8, 25, 34, 45, 59, 94, 100
Kentucky River, 33
Knoxville, TN, 7

Laiboldt, Bernard, Lieut. Col., USA, brigade of, 45, 76
Lebanon Pike, 55, 75, 91
Lee, Robert E., Gen., CSA, 1–2, 10, 12–13, 102
Lexington, KY, 7–8, 25, 36, 38
Liddell, St. John R., Brig. Gen., CSA, 45, **86**–87; brigade of, 34, 42, 44, 47, 55, 72–73, 85, 87–90
Lincoln, Abraham, President, USA, 1, 3, 11, 17, 96, 100–102
Lincoln Administration, USA, 20, 100
Loomis's Heights, 71
Loring, William W., Maj. Gen., CSA, 12
Louisville, KY, 8, 16, 20–21, 23–24
Lumsden, Charles L., Capt., CSA, battery of, 71
Lytle, William, Col., USA, brigade of, 72–73, 85

Mackville, KY, 23, 30, 33, 42, 55
Mackville Road, 55–56, 60, 70, 72–73, 85–86
Maney, George, Brig. Gen., CSA, 67; brigade of, 59, 61–62, 64, 66, 68, 78–81
Manson, Mahlon, Brig. Gen., USA, 7, 18
March to the Sea, 18, 102
Marshall, Humphrey, Brig. Gen., CSA, 13, 36, 100
Maryland, 3, 12
McClellan, George B., Maj. Gen., USA, 1, 10, 12, 16, 19
McCook, Alexander McD., Maj. Gen., USA: pre-battle, 17, 20–21, 23; during battle, 41, 47, **56**–57, 61–63, 69–70, 73–74, 81, 85; First Corps of, pre-battle, 20, 22–23; First Corps of, during battle, 41, 47–48,

51–53, 55–56, 58, 61, 64, 68–70, 73, 75–76, 79, 83–84, 86; First Corps of, post-battle, 91, 95, 97–99
McCook, Daniel, Col., USA, brigade of, 43–44, 76
McDowell, Irvin, Maj. Gen., USA, 1
McIlvaine, Charles, Reverend, 26
McWhiney, Grady, PhD, 28
Meade, George G., Maj. Gen., USA, 48
Mexican-American War, 15, 19, 25, 34, 62, 72
Mill Springs, KY, Battle of, 3, 19
Missionary Ridge (Chattanooga, TN), 101
Mississippi, 13, 27
Mississippi regiments, CSA: 24th, 76
Mississippi River, 3, 4, 101
Mitchell, Robert D., Brig. Gen., USA, 21, 76–77, **82**–83; division of, 78, 81, 84–85
Mobile Bay, AL, 4
Morgan, John H., Col., CSA, 7, 92
Munfordville, KY, 7, 20, 72; Battle and Siege of, 24, 37, 73
Murfreesboro, TN, 101

Nashville, TN, 4, 7, 100–101
Nelson, William "Bull," Maj. Gen., USA, 7, **17**–20, 53, 77, 99
New Madrid, MO, 4
Ninth Division, USA, 21
Noe, Kenneth, PhD, 30, 47, 61

"Offensive-defensive," 47
Ohio, 13
Ohio regiments, USA: 33rd, 61; 105th, 68
Ohio River, 3
Old Kentucky Capitol Building, **31**

Open Knob, 57–58, 62–**63**, 64, 66–68, 71, 78–79

Paducah, KY, 3
Parson, Charles, Lieut., USA, battery of, 58, 64, 66, 68
Pennsylvania regiments, USA: 79th, 78, 81
Pensacola, FL, 25
Perkins, Hardin, Col., CSA, 86
Perryville, Battle of, 8–9, 12–13, 15, 18–21, 24, 30, 35, 39, 41, 43, 45, 53, 55, 58, 91–95, 97–102
Perryville, KY: pre-battle, 13, 24, 28, 30, 33–36, 38–39; during battle, 41–43, 46–48, 50–51, 53, 55–56, 62, 68, 70, 75–76, 81–86; post-battle, 91–93
Perryville Battlefield State Historic Site (PBSHS), 20, 28, 99
Perryville-Harrodsburg Road, 48
Peters Hill, 42–43, 51–52, 76, 82, 98
Pickett, George E., Maj. Gen., CSA, 19
Pillow, Gideon, Brig. Gen., CSA, 72
Pittsburg Landing, TN, 4
Polk, Leonidas, Maj. Gen., CSA: pre-battle, 3, 23–26, **27**–30, 33, 35–38; during battle, 45–48, 58–63, 88–90; post-battle, 99; Right Wing of, 33, 39
Port Hudson, LA, 13
Powel, Samuel, Col., CSA, 76; brigade of, 39, 71, 75–78, 81–83, 85, 91, 97
Prairie Grove, AK, Battle of, 13
Price, Sterling, Maj. Gen., CSA, 13, 100

reserve, definition of, 57
Richmond, KY, 7, Battle of, 7, 18–19

Index

Richmond, VA, 1, 10, 12, 27
Robertson, William Glenn, PhD, 28
Rosecrans, William S., Maj. Gen., USA, 13, 100–101
Rousseau, Lovell H., Brig. Gen., USA, 21, 57; division of, 56–57

Salt River, KY, 42
Savage, John, Col., CSA, 59
Savanah, GA, 102
Savannah, TN, 4
Schoepf, Albin, Brig. Gen., USA, 18, 21; First Division of, 69–70
Scott, John, Col., CSA, 23; cavalry of, 36
Second Division, USA, 21
Seminole Indian War, 25
Semple, Henry C., Capt., CSA, battery of, 82
Senate, USA, 19
Seven Days, Battle of, 1, 12
Sewanee, TN, 27
Shelbyville, KY, 23, 36
Shelbyville, TN, 28
Shepherdsville, KY, 23
Sheridan, Philip H., Brig. Gen., USA, 21, 43–**45**, 76–77, 81; batteries of, 74; division of, 78
Sherman, William T., Maj. Gen., USA, 18, 102
Shiloh, TN, Battle of (also Battle of Pittsburg Landing), 4, 19, 25, 56, 59
Shiloh Church, 4
Sill, Joshua, Brig. Gen., USA, 21–**22**; division(s) of, 23–25, 29–31, 35–36, 45, 52–53, 93, 95, 97
Simonson, Peter, Capt., USA, battery of, 71
Slocomb, Cuthbert H., Capt., CSA, battery of, 82, 91

Smith, Edmund Kirby, Maj. Gen., CSA, 4, 7–8, 13, 18, 23–25, 31–33, 35–**37**; army of, 38, 46, 92–93, 97, 100
Smith, Melancthon, Capt., CSA, battery of, 67
Smith, Preston, Acting Brig. Gen., CSA, brigade of 73, 75, 82, 84–86
Smith, William S., Brig. Gen., USA, 21
Somerset, KY, 3
South, 10–12
Springfield, KY, 33, 42
Springfield Pike (Old), KY, 33, 42, 51, 56, 68, 75–76
Stanford, Thomas J., Capt., CSA, battery of, 59
Stanton, Edward M., Secretary of War, USA, 17
Starkweather, John C., Col., USA, 68, **78**–81, 99; brigade of, 68, 78, 81
Starkweather's Hill, 61, 68, 79
Steedman, James, Brig. Gen., USA, brigade of, 70, 81, 85, 88
Stewart, Alexander P., Brig. Gen., CSA, **66**; brigade of, 59, 62, 64, 66, 79–81
Stone, David C., Capt., USA, battery of, 79
Stones River (Murfreesboro, TN), Battle of, 101

Taylorsville, KY, 23
Tennessee, 3–4, 7, 13, 16, 31, 100
Tennessee regiments, CSA: 1st/27th, 67, 98; 4th, 66, 79; 5th, 66, 79; 6th, 67; 8th, 59, 63; 9th, 67; 16th, 59; 24th, 66; 29th, 76; 31st, 66; 33rd, 66; 51st, 59, 63
Tennessee River, 3, 4
Tennessee State Militia, 62
Tenth Division, USA, 21

Index

Terrill, William R., Brig. Gen., USA, 68; brigade of, 57, 79–80
Terry's Texas Rangers, 59
Texas, 59
Third Corps, USA, 17, 19–23, 42, 48, 51–52, 77
Third Division, USA, 21
Thomas, George H., Maj. Gen., USA, 3, 17–20, 42, 52, 55
Trans-Mississippi West, 12–13
Tullahoma Campaign, 101
Tupelo, MS, 4
Turner, William B., Lieut., CSA, 67

United States Military Academy (West Point, NY), 3, 15, 19, 25–27, 34, 56, 72
University of the South, TN, 27

Van Cleve, Horatio, Brig. Gen., USA, 21
Van Dorn, Earl, Maj. Gen., CSA, 13, 100
Versailles, KY, 24, 29, 36, 39, 46,
Vicksburg, MS, Battle and Siege of, 101
Virginia, 1, 3, 12–13

Walker's Bend, 50–51, 58, 62
Washington, D.C., 1, 16, 95, 100–101
Watkins, Samuel, Pvt., CSA, 98
Webster, George, Col., USA, brigade of, 57, 60, 66
West Tennessee, 27
Western Theater, 3, 12–13, 102
Wharton, John H., Col., CSA, 23, **59**, 61, 63, 99; cavalry of, 36, 59–61
Wheeler, Joseph, Col., CSA, 23, 75, 91; cavalry of, 42, 52–53, 61, 75
Wildcat Mountain, KY, Battle of, 19
Wilder, John, Col., USA, 72
Williams, Beverly D., Capt., USA, 57

Wilson's Creek, 60
Wilson's Creek, MO, Battle of, 19, 82
Wisconsin regiments, USA: 1st, 78, 81; 21st, 68, 78–79, 81
Wood, Sterling A. M., Brig. Gen., CSA, brigade of, 42, 66, 72, 85
Wood, Thomas J., Brig. Gen., USA, 21
Woodworth, Steven, PhD, 34
Wright, Horatio G., Maj. Gen., USA, 19